ROGUE
ECONOMICS
CAPITALISM'S NEW REALITY

LORETTA
NAPOLEONI

SEVEN STORIES PRESS

New York • London • Melbourne • Toronto

Seven Stories Press
140 Watts Street
New York, NY 10013
www.sevenstories.com

In Canada: Publishers Group Canada, 559 College Street, Suite 402, Toronto, ON M6G 1A9

In the UK: Turnaround Publisher Services Ltd., Unit 3, Olympia Trading Estate, Coburg Road, Wood Green, London N22 6TZ

In Australia: Palgrave Macmillan, 15–19 Claremont Street, South Yarra, VIC 3141

College professors may order examination copies of Seven Stories Press titles for a free six-month trial period. To order, visit www.sevenstories.com/textbook or send a fax on school letterhead to (212) 226-1411.

Book design by Jon Gilbert

Library of Congress Cataloging-in-Publication Data

Napoleoni, Loretta.
  Rogue economics / Loretta Napoleoni.
    p. cm.
  ISBN 978-1-58322-824-1 (hardcover)
  1. Commercial crimes. 2. Corporations--Corrupt practices. I. Title.

HV6768.N36 2008
364.16'8--DC22
                2007038868
Printed in the USA.

9 8 7 6 5 4 3 2 1

CONTENTS

To Silvia
friend, sister and at times also mother

ACKNOWLEDGMENTS

Researching and writing this book coincided with a very difficult period of my life. I lost my father to pancreatic cancer soon after my grandmother left me gracefully at the age of ninety-seven, and then I had to have surgery. All these events forced me to confront aspects of rogue economics in my personal life. At times I felt I was not the author of this book, but one of the characters, part of the statistics and the stories. During those long and painful months, a group of very special people held my hand. They helped me remain focused on my work, and that is why this book is also dedicated to them: Giovanna Amato, Melinda Levitt, Simona Marazza, Valerio Nobili, Bart Stevens, and Monica Maggioni, who also brilliantly edited the Italian manuscript and with whom I share a passion for politics. Special thanks go to Mario Barbieri, an old and dear friend; Mario lent me his magical Venetian house where more than once I took refuge and where I wrote many pages of this book.

I believe that this is the best book I have yet written, because it came from my heart. I began writing it as an attempt to denounce and stop the changes which have altered and are still reshaping our world. In the end I realized that this is not only an impossible task, but an unnatural one, because rogue economics is endemic to society; it is the price of progress. So I ended up writing to empower all of us, the victims and at the same time the unaware perpetrators of this peculiar phenomenon. If circumstances had been different, I would not have been able to do such a good job. I suffered and battled with globalization's outlaws, some of whom were my acquaintances, who, by hurting and taking advantage of me, made me see through the web of illusions which entrap us. In a very unusual fashion, I want to thank those who during the last two years have not been compassionate, who have made my life much harder. Without them this book would not have had the right pathos.

As always I must thank my publishers, who believe in my work. They include Dan Simon and Ria Julien of Seven Stories Press, who initially commissioned the book and, while I was researching and writing it, became dear friends; Luca Formenton and Adolfo Frediani of Saggiatore, who fell in love with the book and gave me the honor of being part of the fiftieth anniversary of Saggiatore, the imprint I admired most while growing up in Italy; Per Alexon of Leopard, who read the first draft and made many useful suggestions; my Italian agent Roberta Oliva; and my wonderful new American agent, Diana Finch, who shares my vision of the world and has worked hard at polishing the original manuscript.

My most sincere thanks go to my research assistants: Steve Abood, Ann Berg, Jonathan Knight, Eleonor Ereira, Diego Hidalgo, Tara Morrison, Cecile Landman, Leo Pollak, Rob Petit, Ganesh Sathathevan, and Valentina Soria. This book would not have been so poignant without the research of Pablo Trincia who conducted many interviews on my behalf across the world and spent two weeks in Montana, when the temperature was twenty-five below zero, traveling in cyberspace through *Second Life*. Thanks also to Cristina Massazza, my husband's personal assistant, a brilliant, cultured and modern mind who read the chapters as I wrote them and made important comments and suggestions. Thanks also to my son Alexander Trigle, for all the information on gangs, hip-hop, and rappers he provided; to my stepson Andrew Gerson, who unveiled some of the mysteries of organic food, raw food, and dieting; and to the other two children, my stepdaughter Leigh and my son Julian Gerson, for talking to me openly about their young lives and helping me understanding the power of the Internet.

Without my sources, hundreds of people whose names I cannot mention and who, through decades of research, have pointed me in the right direction, *Rogue Economics* would not exist. My gratitude goes also to those friends who have contributed their professional knowledge to the making of this book: Ron Bee, who edited the first draft of the book, Rico Carish, Anna Chen, Vic Comras, Edith Champagne, Michael Chandler, George Magnus, Chris Petit, Charlie Smith, Vincenzo Spagnolo, Marina Valerio, Olivia Ward, Grant Woods, Pietro Biancardi, Theresa Noll, Anna Lui. Thanks to Edi Cohen and Jan Cherim, who read the chapters on China last Christmas and encouraged me to continue shaping my interpretation of Maoism. And thanks to all my readers who have provided information via the Web, people who read my work and feel compelled to help me.

A special mention goes to my dear friends Lesley Wakefield, who proofread the English version, and Luciana and Romano Deidda, who proofread the Italian edition. As always they have done a superb job.

I wrote several chapters of the book in the US while a group of friends took care of me: my neighbors, Barbra and Bruce MacEvoy; my Whitefish friends, Mary Jo and Greg Hennen; my other North American friends, Kostantine and Debby Georgiadis; Salvatore and Patricia Rondinelli, who read the first two chapters while visiting me in Whitefish; Elisabeth Peters, who shares my love for skiing and was my host in Canada; and Elisabeth's two beautiful boys, Jonathan and James, who love me and even named one of their teddy bears Loretta. Thanks to my friends from Chapter One bookstore in Hamilton, Montana, who read and comment on everything I write. Super thanks to all the Gerson family scattered throughout North America, who always welcome me in their homes, and to Claudia Gerson for reading the entire book and making important comments.

To my English friends who listen to my stories and are

always there for me—Clare and Rex Chalmers; Eleonora and Stephen Creaturo; Vivian and David Ereira; Nick and Deb Follows; Amanda and Jimmy Hochmann; Venetia and David Morrison; and Angelica and Vittorio Pignatti, who also look after my husband when I am not in London, a very special thank you. Thanks also to Isabella Annessi and Libero Maesano, my Parisian friends with whom I have endless political discussions.

I cannot avoid mentioning my three very special cousins Joelle, Marina and Patrizia, who love me as sisters, and my mother and aunt who shared with me two big losses.

Thank you to my Italian friends Mauro Amadio, Vittorio Cielo, Raffaele and Francesca Dessi, Isabella Gramegna, Marco Mariani, Cecilia Guastadisegni, Martina Giuffre, Johannes Keizer, Roberto Giuliani, Antonio Guadalupi, Sabina de Luca, Anna Maria Marinuzzi, and Cristina Ricotti, and also to my school friends from VB and those from CONI, people I met again after forty years while writing this book.

Thanks to my trainers and healers: Jen, Delia, Jodie and Sola; to Georgina Hayden, with whom I spent hours discussing the concept of the Matrix; and to Kirsty Roberts, who strengthened my body while all my energies were absorbed by my mind. Thank you to the promoters: Newman Communications; Jason Fidler, my webmaster; Domenico Moretti, the director of the book's trailer; the press office of Saggiatore; Ruth Weiner of Seven Stories Press; and many others.

Finally a special thanks to my husband Ron Gerson for loving me and for being truly unique.

INTRODUCTION

The 1990s saw the spread of a global virus: democracy. The dismantling of the Soviet Union unleashed the "freedom bug," and in the space of a decade, the number of democratic countries in the world grew from 69 to 118. Millions of people, inoculated against democracy for decades, celebrated while these countries' defenses failed and fell. All those who had never experienced Western-style democracy were finally infected. As the Berlin Wall came down, young Eastern Europeans rushed to cross the Iron Curtain, the imaginary divide between the free world and totalitarianism. People peered and cheered, mesmerized as endless caravans of Trabants, Ladas, and other Socialist-manufactured automobiles rolled westward. From the former Soviet Bloc, the freedom bug stretched across the globe, to South East Asia, Latin America, even to China,[1] leaving everywhere its indelible mark.

As democracy spread, so did slavery. By the end of the decade, an estimated 27 million people had been enslaved in a number of countries, including some in Western Europe. As early as 1990, Slavic sex slaves from the former Soviet Bloc began flooding Western markets. These women proved beautiful, cheap, and most importantly, desperate. Yet the new sex trade was only the tip of the iceberg. Globalization allowed the exploitation of slave labor at an industrial level, reaching an intensity never seen before, not even during the transatlantic slave trade. From the cocoa plantations of West Africa to the orchards of California, from the booming illegal fishing industry to counterfeit-producing factories, as I found again and again during my research, slaves have become an integral part of global capitalism.

1

Shockingly, in modern times, democracy and slavery coexist in what economists see as a strong direct correlation. In other words, the two phenomena show identical trends and one conditions the other. The 1990s confirmed a surreal trend that had already become apparent in the 1950s, during the process of decolonization. As former colonies gained independence from foreign powers and embraced freedom, the number of slaves soared and their cost plummeted. Today, the average price of a slave is less than one-tenth of its value during the Roman Empire, a time in history when democracy may well have been at its lowest ebb. To the Romans, slaves represented scarce, valuable commodities that commanded high prices; today, they are plentiful, disposable merchandise, merely another "cost of doing international business."

Democracy and slavery are seldom connected in our minds because we remain under the false impression that the advent of the former is somehow a guarantee against the return of the latter. The often-cited example of the American Civil War is used to add an overlay to this thin veneer. But as any student of American history will tell you, right after the war ended, white violence against blacks erupted in the American South with such groups as the Ku Klux Klan coming to the fore, and the period that followed was a low point for black people in America. Today slavery is commonly believed to be the product of foreign powers' exploitation of poor countries; in fact, the opposite turns out to be true: most victims are enslaved and traded by their own compatriots.

The correlation between democracy and slavery is one of the consequences of rogue economics, a recurrent phenomenon in history, often linked to rapid and unexpected great transformations. In the midst of profound changes, politics can lose control of economics, which becomes a rogue force in the hands of new entrepreneurs. We refer to the American West as the Wild West because of the anarchy and violence that marked its conquest; yet great economic fortunes grew in its shadow. The California Gold Rush led to chaos, violence, and wide-scale theft, often enriching casino owners and gamblers who built splendid cities like San Francisco. Rogue economics has marked most major historical transitions; its spread has contaminated ancient economies, destroyed old empires, and built new ones. While the discovery of America enriched Europe beyond imagination, the spoils came at the hands of ruthless conquistadores. Today, rogue economics has resurfaced because the world is experiencing an equally profound transformation, perhaps the biggest in history.

When I began researching this book, more than two years ago, I wanted to show how the transition from Communism to globalization had unleashed dark economic forces. I was convinced that this was a unique phenomenon linked to exceptional circumstances. As my research progressed and I continued to collect data, conduct interviews, and analyze information, I discovered that rogue economics is not unique but is part of the yin and yang of history. It is a real force, constantly lurking in the background of progress. So far, each time it has reemerged, politics has succeeded in taming it by striking strategic compromises with new, powerful elites. There is no reason to believe that this time the outcome will be different.

Corruption exists in any society, both Communist and capitalist, but rogue economics makes it spread on a global scale. Unlike the kind of corruption that is present in every society, a corruption that coexists with sets of values that exert a counterweight against it, rogue economics imposes a sleazy lifestyle that harms everybody, winners and losers, rich and poor. No matter where we live, in the developed or the developing world, rogue economics reshapes our personal lives; it not only dictates the way we live but how we die.

In the United States, a new killer is on the loose: obesity. About 400,000 fatalities per year, equivalent to 16 percent of all deaths in the US, are linked to obesity. Ironically, with roots in the late 1970s, this epidemic came into full bloom in the late 1980s, when America became weight conscious. The moment people decided to become skinny, they actually put on weight.

The battle of the bulge brought the advent of low-fat diets. Fat was removed from food items and substituted with carbohydrates, which are high in calories and also produce fat. Farmers have always known that grain fattens animals. The same principle applies to humans. Most of the low-fat food found in supermarkets is saturated with carbohydrates, to the extent that often the caloric intake of the low-fat version is identical to the original. Next time you shop, compare the number of calories of the non-fat and normal versions of the same product; you will be amazed at the negligible difference, if any, between the numbers.

From the United States, the new illness has moved through the Western world and beyond. Today, obesity is spreading faster in Asia than in North America and Europe, and it is on the rise even in Africa, among the wealthy who have acquired a taste for Western low-fat foods and diets. Consumers are unaware that the products promoted as "slimming" don't help them and, in some cases, may even kill them. People buy them under the illusion that they are the elixir of eternal youth.

The low-fat promotion is, more often than not, a pure lie perpetrated by food corporations, retailers, and even government agencies. It is also a multibillion-dollar business. Almost every product we consume has a hidden, dark history, from slave labor to piracy, from fakes to fraud, from theft to money laundering. The most dangerous breeding ground for rogue economics is the global market. Rogue products penetrate and corrupt traditional economies. When we buy a wedding ring produced with gold mined by Congolese children working for ruthless warlords, smuggled to Uganda, and sold with forged documents of origin by crooked trading companies, we establish a commercial link with the sinister underworld of Africa's illegal and criminal economy. Yet, we, the consumers, know very little about these interdependencies, let alone about the dark economic secrets of what we consume, because we are trapped inside the market matrix, a dense web of commercial illusions.

As in the cult film *The Matrix*, consumers live in a fantasy world. We believe that life has never been better. Why not? We can afford what our parents and grandparents could not even dream about. Thanks to modern medicine, life expectancy has risen; poverty has been marginalized; and consumption is the global pastime. Shopping is therapy for when we are depressed or bored. These are the messages we get daily. But if we try to look behind the veneer of our daily lives and attempt to verify these beliefs, tracking the origins of most products we consume, the picture that emerges is similar to the real world of *The Matrix*: a planet in deep commercial turmoil.

This is not a book about the unknown origins of the products we consume or about the marketing lies we are told by the advertisers of eternal youth. Neither is it an antiglobalization manual nor the manifesto of a consumer revolution. Rather, it has been conceived to empower consumers with knowledge of the world we inhabit. Through various examples, I will try to show that rogue economics is not exceptional but endemic, a dark force encrypted in our social DNA, constantly lurking in the background of the societies in which we live.

Stripping one or two layers from the surface of modern life is not sufficient to unveil the true nature of a phenomenon that, though always part of human history, has never before been recognized. To understand the nature of rogue economics, we have to start at its foundation: the eternal battle between politics and economics, a vicious warfare fought throughout history.

This is a book about the reshaping of the modern world at the hands of profiteering economic forces; about the web of economic and political illusions that traps consumers in a fantasy world built by emerging rogue actors; finally, this is a book about the latest battle of an eternal war, which serves to remind us that now as in the past, humanity always pays a high price for its conquests.

CHAPTER ONE

IN BED WITH THE ENEMY

"We have thankfully watched the fall
of the Berlin Wall, but unfortunately
the Wall fell on women's heads."

Comment by a participant of the
Russian State Duma

Economics is the unpredictable science of interdependency. Its hidden engine is the market. Since the Stone Age, the birth of new outlets for exchange has triggered economic progress. Human discoveries and innovations gain new meaning when they are shared with others and this happens only when they are traded.

The main beneficiaries of these business transactions are not those who create or consume new products but those who commercialize them. Throughout the ages, marketeers have accumulated immense fortunes, and politicians have been well aware of their power. Both have forged alliances to regulate, contain, and manipulate the market to their own advantage and for the benefit of entire nations.

All major civilizations rested on solid commercial structures that politicians defended with large armies; Rome crushed Carthage when Hannibal blocked its flourishing trade with the northern regions of the Italian peninsula. Endless wars have been waged to gain control of key markets. Venice, for example, bankrolled the fourth Crusade to loot Constantinople and clear the silk route of the presence of Arab merchants, thus securing a monopoly. In modern times, the Marshall Plan provides one of the best examples of how politics enslaves economics to redefine the rules of the market.[1]

7

ECONOMICS VERSUS POLITICS

The Marshall Plan, the United States aid program to rebuild Western Europe out of the ashes of World War II, laid the groundwork for America's economic supremacy. Unlike Europe and Japan, the United States' wartime economy and industry remained undamaged; after the war, they needed markets. Though the US was the donor and not the recipient, one could easily argue that America, not Europe, was the primary beneficiary of the Plan. The reconstruction created new outlets for US companies and shaped a novel market according to the specific needs of America's economy. In the aftermath of the war, fleets of cargo ships sailed the Atlantic to bring raw materials and goods to war-torn Europe. Caravans of oil tankers formed a bridge across the ocean, transporting the precious energy required to clear the debris and rebuild bombed-out cities.

By the time Western European countries got back on their feet, American consumerism was ready to mold the buying habits of Europeans. Durable goods, ranging from TVs to vacuum cleaners, appeared in shops. Images of blond, smiling American housewives, Doris Day look-alikes, playing with their "household" toys bombarded Western European families. Everybody wanted a car, a TV set, and a washing machine. America even exported novel, imaginative ways to purchase such products: payment by installments. Personal borrowing immediately soared.

The United States wanted to build a solid market for its own export economy, and to do so, it understood that it needed to sell a way of life. Consumer and durable goods made in America had to be part of a desirable lifestyle. They were essential accessories to what was known as the American Dream: products skillfully publicized by feel-good Hollywood movies. In the collective imagination of Western Europeans who flocked to the cinemas to escape the painful memories of war, America became the land of milk and honey, a continent populated by movie stars, where dreams come true. But the United States was more than a dream, it was just a cargo-ship or plane ride across the Atlantic. This idyllic world not only existed, it could be bought. The reconstruction of Western Europe through the Marshall Plan provided Western European consumers with the financial means to purchase their share of the dream. By jump-starting the postwar economy, the Plan put money in consumers' pockets so that they could buy its accessories: made-in-the-USA products.

Today, we know that the American Dream was merely a piece of clever marketing. In the 1950s, while the United States was under the grip of McCarthyism, such advertisements disguised the reality of a repressed society plagued by racial prejudice and tensions. Yet the most appealing commercial items are often constructed around illusions. Some bring about economic growth, as was the case of the American Dream; others, as we shall see with the fall of the Berlin Wall, can be crippling for society.

The Marshall Plan helped to spawn a new political order that blossomed during the Cold War, a system that sealed off the West from the Soviet Bloc. To a certain extent, this new order was the opposite of globalization; it boxed the West inside a highly regulated economic system. Engineered by remarkable economists, including John Maynard Keynes,[2] the Plan was the manifestation of a new doctrine that stressed the paramount role of the state in economics and the supremacy of the strongest country. Throughout the Cold War, its success rested on the ability of Washington to control and manipulate the economic forces that created and sustained the new European market, and several others after it, to the advantage of the United States of America and of its trading partners.[3]

During the Cold War, America's economic supremacy remained unchallenged and Western Europe greatly benefited from it. Economic growth, especially in the 1950s and 1960s, was remarkable. Even in the darkness of the first and second oil shocks (1973–1974 and 1979–1980) the US leadership maintained a solid grip on the economy and softened the impact of the crisis by kick-starting the recycling of petrodollars, a scheme that funneled the surpluses of oil-producing countries toward Western investment.

Paradoxically, when the final aim of the Cold War, the lifting of the Iron Curtain was achieved, the post–World War II order disintegrated, and the state lost control of the market. Politics no longer dominated economics. It was at that point in time that the economy ceased to be of service to citizens and became a feral force, oriented exclusively toward making a quick buck at the expense of consumers.

The events that symbolize the beginning and the end of the Cold War, the Marshall Plan, and the fall of the Berlin Wall, mark the bookends of the complex relation between politics and economics and well explain the transition toward rogue economics.

THE SEX WALL

Highway E-55, which runs along the Czech-German border, is known as the Highway of Love. This miserable stretch of asphalt hosts the largest concentration of prostitutes in Europe. Women from the former Soviet Bloc stand along the side of the road, offering their bodies at rock-bottom prices: half an hour for 35 euros, 45 without a condom. Only the sex industry of Dubai matches such prices. Yet Highway E-55 is not unique. The former border between Eastern and Western Europe is crowded with the accoutrements of the trade: a cluster of sex markets, brothels, and curtained kiosks replacing the imaginary Iron Curtain.

Throughout the 1990s, prostitution proliferated on the routes leading to the boundaries with Western countries. The symbolism is shocking: "The fact that the borders are open gives sex work an air of internationalism, especially in the Western borderland where the 'encounters of nations' take place. Here, sex work is exported to the countries of Western Europe."[4]

Some of the women who work along the borders are not prostitutes, but sex slaves. They have been purchased at specialized markets located in the vicinity of the old East–West divide. The infamous Arizona Market, in northwestern Serbia, is well known among international pimps. It resembles a nineteenth-century American gold-rush town, hence the name. Tucked behind a stretch of road nicknamed Arizona Highway, which runs near the Croatian border, the market has been nicknamed the Wal-Mart of Serbia because it was constructed with the support of American troops at the end of the Balkan civil war. Traders come to the Arizona Market to buy women. "They order the girls to take off their clothes and they are standing in the road naked [. . .] Men walk up, touch their flesh, inspect their skin and even look into their mouths before they make a bid."[5]

The biggest player in the prostitution racket involving Slavic women is the Russian Mafia. Ironically, many Russian pimps are from Chechnya. "I was traded by a group of Mafiosi from Chechnya," reveals Eva, a former prostitute who was freed with the help of a client. "They came to Odessa pretending to be wealthy businessmen on holiday. They offered me a job as a shop assistant in one of their boutiques in Moscow; they even showed me a picture of the shop. I heard so many stories of Ukrainian women who'd been lured by Russian criminals into prostitution, but I thought, these people are from Chechnya . . . I was bought and sold several times at the Arizona Market by many traders: Russian, European and even Arab. I became merchandise; yes, this is what we are, products for the global village."[6]

Highway E-55 and the Arizona Market are recent outlet malls of the new global prostitution industry, the joint venture between the two oldest professions: prostitution and international trade. For more than fifteen years, its most popular products have been prostitutes and sex slaves from the former Soviet Bloc. The sex-for-sale wall, which today runs along the old East-West divide, is one of the by-products of the fall of the Berlin Wall. It is also one of the first manifestations of the return of rogue economics, a feral force unleashed by the twentieth century's greatest economic transformation: the dismantling of Communism and the rise of globalization.

Before the fall of the Berlin Wall, prostitution in Communist countries had become virtually nonexistent. Though the practice was not banned, governments usually marginalized the world's oldest profession. Demand was low. Sexual habits were extremely liberal, and contraception and abortion were readily available, so that men had less need to rely on hookers. Supply was also low. Full employment guaranteed that everybody had a salary, a situation that greatly reduced the pool of women willing to make a living by selling their bodies. Communist prostitutes catered primarily to foreigners, most of them businessmen, who ventured across the East-West divide. In the early 1980s, for example, in Budapest, men could meet prostitutes only in two nightclubs. Both were forbidden to Hungarians and to visitors from the Soviet Bloc. In Moscow, "friendly" women paraded their wares outside the entrances of hotels frequented by foreigners. Unlike their Western European counterparts, Communist prostitutes managed their own profits; pimping was a serious crime.

The dismantling of Communism boosted prostitution because it plunged the population of the former Soviet Bloc into poverty, women in particular. By the mid-1990s, unemployment among Russian women had reached 80 percent, up from virtually zero during the Soviet regime. Women also made up over 80 percent of the population of single-parent, single-income families.[7] By 1998, more than half of Russian children under the age of six lived below the poverty line, most of them in single-parent households. Against this back-drop, many women became prostitutes to feed their children. For them, the choice was between indigence and sleeping with the enemy.

A strong correlation also exists between the supply of Slavic prostitutes and female unemployment; to an extent, they show identical geographical patterns. Employment in former Communist countries was distributed according to the industrialized and regional structure of the command economy. In Russia, for example, women accounted for 83 percent of the workforce in the textile sector. The textile industry was located in specific regions, such as the Ivanovo Oblast, northeast of Moscow, in Cheboksary, and in the Chuvash Republic, in Central Russia. Under the Soviet regime, these areas became known as women regions.[8] From 1990 to 1994, there was a 67 percent decline in textile production. Hundreds of thousands of women ended up on the dole in the above-mentioned areas, which pimps and human traffickers targeted for their dirty businesses. Today, these are sadly known as "hookers regions."

As early as 1991, an abundant supply of Slavic women flooded the Western market. "Before the fall of the Berlin Wall, mostly German girls worked as prostitutes in Germany," recalls Stephen, a sixty-year-old overweight German pimp who is also known as *der Prinz,* the prince. "Now it's not like that anymore. The market has expanded, and it has become more international. Many women come from Poland and Russia, but they all speak German, because we want all of them to do so. Customers today are not only looking for sex, they also want a girl who can talk to them and create an atmosphere. They want a drink, to have a conversation, to have a show, not only bam bam bam."[9] Stephen started working in the German sex industry forty years ago, with a few girls on the street. Today, he is considered one of the top sex-businessmen in Berlin, though he won't disclose how many clubs he owns.

In the 1990s, the supply of highly educated Russian and Eastern European women became a unique phenomenon in the prostitution industry. Until the arrival of Slavic women, pimps had to fish in a pool of unsophisticated people, predominantly poor Asian girls. It soon became apparent that educated women commanded higher prices and thus produced greater profits. As illustrated by the Hollywood movie *Memoir of a Geisha*, intelligent, cultured, and sharp prostitutes command a premium. Again, the peculiar economic structure of the Soviet system offered pimps the possibility to pocket such bonuses through commercializing highly educated Slavic women. In Russia, besides textiles, "women's jobs" were concentrated in medicine, education, science, planning, and accounting, all of which were particularly badly hit by the economic crisis of the 1990s.

The pool of Slavic women, considered unique, boosted demand beyond expectation. "At the beginning of the 1990s, the business was not only good, it was excellent," recalls Michael, a thirty-year-old German pimp who owns several sex bars in Berlin.[10] "Men just could not have enough of these women. They saw them as exotic. You could make a fortune out of the sex industry. I would make something like 3,000 euros per day and after a while I had become very rich."[11]

The prostitution business, like any industry, responds to the laws of economics and particularly to supply and demand. Though the defeat of what Ronald Reagan dubbed the Evil Empire forced millions of Slavic women into the global sex market, this event alone proved insufficient to create a new market. The marketeers and pimps filled that void, building an Eastern European meat market around the new merchandise to attract customers. "In 1989 it started with pimps that had two, maybe three girls in a car. And later they bought houses on the highway E-55. [By 1997], there were girls . . . all along the side of the road in a huge line," recalls Jaromir Jirasek, a physician in Dubi, a Czech town not far from Dresden.[12] As the economic crisis of the former Soviet Bloc deepened, the marketeers of sex could rely on an endless supply of new, healthy Slavic women. "When one [prostitute] got ill they just replaced her. That's it,"[13] explains Dr. Jirasek. Today Dubi, which runs along Highway E-55, hosts hundreds of brothels and strip joints.[14]

NATASHAS

Israel represents one of the largest importers of Slavic prostitutes and various sources estimate that one million Israelis visit a prostitute every month.[15] According to the Israeli Parliamentary Inquiry Committee, "[S]ome 3,000 to 5,000 women [from the former Soviet Bloc] are smuggled to Israel annually and sold into the prostitution industry. [. . .]The women work seven days a week for up to 18 hours every day and out of the NIS120 (US$27) paid by customers, they are left with just NIS20 ($4.50). Ten thousand such women currently reside in about 300 to 400 brothels throughout the country. They are traded for about $8,000 to $10,000 each."[16] The magnitude of the business, even at the outset of the trade in Slavic women, is clearly illustrated by the large profits from prostitution that have been laundered in Israel; from 1990 to 1995, for example, about $4 billion was invested in Israeli banks. Another $600 million was laundered in real estate.[17]

At the root of the growth of prostitution in Israel are cultural and religious factors. Israeli men, like most men, have a soft spot for tall, blond, Slavic women, whom they indiscriminately call 'Natasha.' Men would "walk into the parlor and with a stupid grin on their face call out 'Natasha!' like we were some kind of Russian dolls," recalls Marika, a Russian woman trafficked to Israel.[18] Demand is particularly high among Haredim, the most conservative Orthodox Jews, many of whom are regular clients of brothels. "When you go to the area of the Stock Exchange or the Diamond Exchange, you see a lot of prostitution and a lot of very, very religious men, because these men need sex but the women in their society cannot give it to them when they want it. They also cannot masturbate because they cannot waste their sperm. So they have to do it with a woman," explains Nissan Ben-Ami, codirector of the Awareness Center, an NGO specializing in the trafficking of women and prostitution in Israel.[19]

Several Israeli sources confirm that the influx of Russian Orthodox Jews, again a phenomenon related to the dismantling of the Soviet Union, unexpectedly boosted the local prostitution industry. "Many had links with the Russian Mafia, who in the early 1990s controlled almost the entire racket of Slavic prostitutes. They helped make deals with local pimps," admits a policeman from Tel Aviv. Michael, the German pimp, confirms that as soon as the Berlin Wall came down, the Russian Mafia took over the trade of the new merchandise. "Back in the nineties it was the Russians who brought the new girls to Berlin."

Armed and criminal organizations are also involved in this multibillion-dollar business. In Germany, where prostitution has been legalized, there are many ways to get a cut of the sex business. "Hamburg and Berlin are controlled by the Lebanese Mafia," explains Michael. "There's nothing you can do about it. You have to pay for their protection. Those Arabs show up at your bar and ask for the money. If you say 'no,' they nudge their mobile phone in front of you and tell you that a whole bunch of fellas armed with Uzi submachine guns will come within half an hour. So, what do you do? You pay them; that's all I can say. In Cologne it's a different matter, the PKK (Kurdistan Workers Party) controls the business. Again, they are not directly involved in prostitution, but brothels and sex bars must pay them for protection."

The interdependency between the prostitution industry and armed groups is also apparent in Israel, a country at the core of the war on terror. Slavic prostitutes and sex slaves reach Israel via the Gaza Strip, often with the cooperation of Egyptian and Palestinian criminal gangs. Ildiko, a twenty-two-year-old student from Hungary, was smuggled across the Balkans to Egypt. "I landed at Alexandria and was met by a Russian who took me to the desert and handed me to a Bedouin. There were six other girls, all from Russia. We trekked across the desert for days until we reached the border."[20] Ildiko entered Israel across a short trail that separates the city of Rafah from the Israeli-Egyptian border. North of Rafah lies the Gaza Strip. "Rafah is only a few hundred feet from the Egyptian border. Its southernmost houses serve as gateways to a maze of tunnels dug by Palestinians and Bedouins from Sinai. These are conduits for terrorists, drug dealers, and human cargo traffickers, who smuggle women to be sold as prostitutes in Israel and the West Bank."[21] Privately, terror experts from various Israeli organizations voice their concern about the involvement in the sex trade of criminal organizations that have ties with terror groups. It is undeniable that, to satisfy its citizens' insatiable desire for Slavic women, Israel is sleeping with the Arab enemy.

Without major changes in morality, the extraordinary growth in the global supply of Slavic prostitutes and sex slaves could never have been matched by an equally remarkable international demand. Today, modern globalized society tacitly condones prostitution. "Prostitution [. . .] has been re-branded as an extension of the entertainment industry. And studies suggest that one in 10 British men—2.3 million—has already been entertained," stated the *Sunday Times*.[22] Nobody wants to miss out on the fun; everybody wants to be part of the new game in town. "Once there was a guest who came in and asked for a show to be performed by a number of girls. He sat there and had his show, without touching the girls or anything. He just sat there," recalls Stephen, the Berlin pimp. "And the funny thing is . . . he was blind."

The philosopher Roger Scruton points out that "when sex

becomes a commodity, the most important sanctuary of human ideals becomes the market. That is what has happened in the past few decades, and it is the root fact of postmodern culture."[23] In the West, the shift in morality led to the acceptance of what can be defined as middle-class prostitution. Trading of sex through escort agencies and through personal ads placed on the Internet is the most common vehicle to commercialize the new product among the middle class. "Type 'female escort' into Google UK and you get 760,000 hits."[24] Most sites belong to small- to medium-size companies set up in the 1990s.

If the marketing of "sex for sale" boosted demand, the glamorizing of prostitution facilitates the luring of Slavic women into the sex industry. Hollywood blockbusters, such as *Risky Business* and *Pretty Woman*, project an entirely fictional image of prostitution. According to several NGOs that work with Slavic women who have been tricked into prostitution by sex traffickers, many women naively believe that by becoming hookers they will meet Mr. Right, as Julia Roberts did in *Pretty Woman*.[25]

Happily-ever-after stories about prostitution happen only in Hollywood scripts, but they sell books and films because they make the middle class comfortable with its acceptance of "sex for sale." Plenty of publishers and filmmakers remain eager to feed the suburban appetite for "amusing" fairytales about prostitution, essentially making money out of women's misery and desperation.

ROGUE ECONOMIC ILLUSIONISTS

The "sex for sale" culture, like the American Dream, is based on a web of illusions. A cleverly constructed mirage exists wherever prostitution is in high demand, as shown by the insatiable appetite of German men for Slavic women, is indispensable, as in the case of Israeli Orthodox Jews, and is ultimately acceptable and enjoyable. In reality, prostitutes today, as ever, remain in demand because many men are unable to have sex without purchasing it; prostitutes become palliatives, substitutes for real women willing to give themselves for love. Above all, prostitution represents a multibillion-dollar business based on the ruthless abuse of women (in 2006, the estimated annual value of global prostitution equalled $52 billion).[26] This exploitation springs from the illegal nature of the business. In such countries as the Netherlands, where prostitution has been legalized for decades, the degree of exploitation is lower: there are fewer pimps, prostitutes pay taxes, receive medical and social security benefits, and have police protection.

Like the promoters of the American Dream, the marketeers of the global prostitution industry act like great illusionists who sell not only products but also a new lifestyle. The pimps of globalization altered middle-class morality and Slavic prostitution and sex slaves became the accessories of a new, permissive culture, one in which sex can be sold and bought freely by consenting adults and even children. On PornoTube, for example, people can watch teenagers take off their clothes in front of their friends' mobile phones. On Baazee.com, an Indian website owned by eBay, the video of two adolescents having sex in the school bathroom was put on sale by a student friend. But is society really better off embracing the culture of "sex for sale"? Is this illusion beneficial to those who populate the sex market, as the American Dream was to the Europeans and Americans? The marketization of the dream helped lift the old continent from the ashes of the war and boosted the growth of the United States economy, it was advantageous to both buyers and sellers. In sharp contrast, the rise of the global sex industry works against suppliers and consumers of love.

Leaving morality and economics aside, let's now look at sexually transmitted diseases and fertility rates. In Russia in

1994, the incidence of syphilis was 81.7 per 100,000 inhabitants; by 1995 it had reached 172, and in 1998 it had risen to 221.9.[27] By 2002, Russia's syphilis rate was one of the top ten worldwide, putting the country in the same league as AIDS-plagued nations in sub-Saharan Africa. The trend shows health standards reverting back to nineteenth-century levels, when Russia suffered from a similarly high incidence of sexually transmitted diseases. To understand the magnitude of the current epidemic, consider that in 1997 one out of every 75 Estonians had syphilis, compared with 2.5 cases per 100,000 people in the United States.[28] Russia also suffers from one of the fastest-spreading rates of HIV. The epidemic has really just begun, with most individuals infected between 1999 and 2005,[29] and it is likely to spread worldwide. The World Health Organization fears that Slavic women contaminate clients everywhere.

Sexually transmitted diseases badly affect fertility rates, and Russians have among the lowest fertility rates in the world.[30] While a solid statistical correlation between the collapse of fertility rates, the dramatic decline in Russian birthrates, and the rise of the global prostitution industry does not exist, radical changes in morality caused by the culture of "sex for sale" have unquestionably affected the attitudes of Russian women to life. "A 1997 survey of 15-year-old [Russian] schoolgirls found that 70 percent said they wanted to become prostitutes, while 10 years before they wanted to become cosmonauts, doctors and teachers."[31] Increasingly, Russian women do not want to have a family and children. They must find ways to survive, and prostitution seems a good option. "The collapse of Communism in the early 1990s only made the population more egotistic and led to a profound moral crisis, which continues to these days," concludes Viktor Erofeyev, a Russian author.[32]

The sole winners of the "sex for sale" culture are the marketeers of sex, the pimps of globalization, skilled rogue-economics illusionists. Vicious criminal gangs and corrupt politicians from Russia and the Balkans have pocketed billions of dollars and established themselves in the global economy by trading Slavic women. From early 1998 until mid-1999, for example, Semion Mogilevich, a Ukrainian-born crime boss involved in prostitution, drug trafficking, and investment scams, laundered $10 billion through the Bank of New York.[33]

The relation between the fall of the Berlin Wall and the booming prostitution industry in the West underscores the perils of undervaluing the consequences of major economic transformations. The entry of the former Soviet Bloc into global capitalism saw a political system dismantled without a clear plan for its replacement. Thus entire nations plunged into deep poverty and political anarchy; inside the void created, economic predators, such as the pimps of globalization, blossomed.

As described in the following section, "democratic" Russia has emerged through rogue economics in the role of Dr. Frankenstein's monster. The process of democratization promoted by the West fostered undemocratic economic forces that guided the country's transition from Communism to global capitalism. This phenomenon is well illustrated by the shocking linkages between beauty pageants, pop concerts, and the monetarization of the Russian economy.

BEAUTY QUEENS AND CONVERTIBLE RUBLES

Privatization in Russia was the economic translation of Mikhail Gorbachev's perestroika. Regarded as the former Soviet Bloc's entry ticket into a nascent global capitalism, privatization also became the price of membership in the country club of democracy. Encouraged by Western advisers such as Jeffrey Sachs, the IMF, and the World Bank, and supported by Western politicians, perestroika soon became synonymous with rapid economic change. Economic reforms took the lead over political transformation. Today, many economists agree that the absence of ad hoc regulations, implemented by a solid political class, unleashed a variety of rogue economic forces. "They basically liberalized the economy without setting up the institutions that were supposed to control and guide the transition to a market economy," remarks Miklos Marshall, regional director of Transparency International (TI) for Europe and Central Asia.

Following in the footsteps of British Prime Minister Margaret Thatcher, in 1987 and 1988, Mikhail Gorbachev launched an ambitious privatization program. The main obstacle was the non-monetary nature of the Soviet economy. Officially there were two currencies: rubles and *beznalichnye*. Rubles were in circulation only inside the USSR and were used by the population. Domestic and CMEA (Council for Mutual Economic Assistance) commercial transactions, i.e., those between members of the Soviet Bloc, were cleared in *beznalichnye*, which was a mere accounting unit, nothing more than paper money. The supply of *beznalichnye* was plentiful, since it consisted simply of a state authorization to buy and sell. The Soviet economy, centrally planned, operated outside the rules of the market. The state fixed prices of goods because the state owned all the means of production, which included factories, mines, and the like, as well as all the products. The state remained the sole employer, and in turn, workers, i.e. the Russian people, owned the state. No one needed real money within such a system because the state performed both buying and selling functions.

Cash in the form of rubles, however, had a real monetary value, primarily because rubles were exchanged and used in the black market to buy and sell hard currencies and to purchase any kind of product or service that could not be found on the official market. Communist economies constantly suffered shortages of products because planning proved unable to mimic or even to gauge the market. Officially, Communist governments considered the black market illegal, but leaders looked the other way because it performed valuable tasks (and often lined their pockets). The black market and the informal economy, therefore, functioned according to market laws, but both were rife with small-time crooks, corrupt officials and party members.

Beznalichnye could not be converted into cash rubles because the Central Bank would not exchange them. They could, however, be traded on the black market. Their value was, understandably, much less than the value of rubles; the official rate was one ruble to ten *beznalichnye*.

As early as 1987, it became apparent that newly privatized companies that wanted to trade abroad needed rubles and could not afford to use the black market for a steady supply of liquidity. Cash was also needed to set up efficient self-financing schemes, the lifeline of small private firms. Although the government could allocate plenty of *beznalichnye* to these firms, there was no place to exchange them. The black market proved too expensive, the Central Bank was cash poor, and the nonexistent Russian treasury could not issue government bonds to raise funds for conversion.

Against this scenario, at the end of 1987, Gorbachev allowed Komsomol, the Communist youth league, to convert *beznalichnye* into rubles. In effect, he turned its members into the Russian treasury, hoping that they would come up with arrangements for conversion without state supervision. Scientific activities, which included organizing beauty contests and pop concerts, qualified for the conversion. These concerts and pageants soon became part of the clever plans of rampant young Russians to amass large fortunes, among them Mikhail Khodorkovsky, then president of the Komsomol youth club at Moscow University.

In 1987, Khodorkovsky transformed his youth group into the Center for Scientific Technical Creativity for Youth. Its main businesses became organizing beauty contests and rock concerts. The scheme was simple. Khodorkovsky accepted payments in *beznalichnye* from people willing to attend beauty contests and pop concerts. He then converted the *beznalichnye* into rubles or hard currency by exchanging them with export companies (primarily timber firms) that had plenty of foreign exchange. The hard currencies were used to import computers from Western countries, which were then sold in Russia for *beznalichnye,* thus allowing Khodorkovsky to net a sixfold profit for each ruble.[34] The *beznalichnye* were then converted into rubles or hard currency using the same tricks. For each transaction, Khodorkovsky pocketed a profit. He set up hundreds of such transactions simultaneously. "I invented several financing methods that were broadly used and that in the best days allowed me to conduct up to five hundred contracts for scientific research simultaneously. Five thousand people were working there."[35] Had the conversion been handled by the Treasury or the Central Bank, Khodorkovsky's profits would have boosted the government's earnings. Instead, they seeded the ground for his fortune.

Beauty contests offered the Russian Mafia a great opportunity to establish a solid prostitution racket. "At that time in Russia everybody knew what the Mafia was up to. Beauty contests were the ideal recruitment ground for prostitutes and sex slaves," admits a former banker who, during the transition years, worked for the European Bank for Reconstruction and Development (EBRD). "Girls would be duped with the prospects of a great career on the big screen and then end up in brothels in Israel or Dubai or in Western Europe. People like Khodorkovsky simply handed the merchandise to the Mafia on a silver dish. He knew that his beauty contests were nothing more than meat markets, where pimps and human traffickers could target their victims. He also knew that what he was doing was legal and was making him very, very rich. Did he care about the girls? Of course not. Those contests were money spinners, and he needed a lot of money for his next scheme."[36]

Although he provided opportunities for the Mafia, Khodorkovsky was not directly involved in the prostitution racket. He had a much bigger fish to fry: Russia's vast energy resources.

The key question remains whether the IMF and the World Bank, which supervised the privatization of Russian assets, had any idea that perestroika and privatization had turned a bunch of ruthless would-be oligarchs into the Russian Treasury, allowing the Mafia to profit from new rogue businesses, such as prostitution. If they did not, they were grossly unqualified to lead the transition of a Communist economy into globalized capitalism. "No one else was qualified either . . . this was virgin territory. . . . Moreover, at that time, the primary objective of the West was to privatize as fast as possible, in order to make the transition irreversible," admits Bart Stevens, former head of communication at the EBRD.[37]

Privatization took a major turn in 1992, when President Boris Yeltsin announced that Russia was about to become a stakeholder society. The wealth of the nation was going to be divided, like a cake, into three parts: one part to the state, which would retain a controlling interest in the newly privatized enterprises; one to foreign investors; and the rest to the people. On October 1, 1992, the state donated to each citizen vouchers equivalent to 10,000 rubles (about $60 dollars, the average month's salary). Vouchers could be exchanged for shares in former state companies. Vouchers could also be saved, bought, or sold. Yet very few Russians knew what to do with them.

From 1992 to 1994, Russia suffered a major economic crisis. The ruble-to-dollar exchange rate fell from 230 to 3,500. The devaluation, coupled with double-digit inflation, wiped out people's savings. More than one-third of the population fell below the poverty line.[38] Not surprisingly, United Nation statistics show that 1992 marked the first peak in the supply of Slavic women and sex slaves in Western Europe.

People were desperate, and to feed their families they resolved to sell everything they had, including the vouchers.

Khodorkovsky and the other oligarchs secured 90 percent of the vouchers by setting up stalls where people could exchange them at a fraction of their value. According to a poll conducted for the Russian newspaper *Isvestiya*, by the end of the 1990s, only 8 percent of Russians had exchanged the vouchers for shares in the companies they worked for. The oligarchs used the vouchers to become minority shareholders in the newly privatized Russian enterprises.

By 1995, Russians had realized that capitalism had made them poorer, not richer. Official Russian economic statistics indicated that the GDP had declined by roughly 50 percent. The state was broke, and salaries and pensions went unpaid. As people grew nostalgic for the old Communist regime, Yeltsin faced the prospect of defeat in the 1996 election. To secure victory, the Russian president brokered a deal with the oligarchs. The state agreed to auction its controlling interests in the privatized state enterprises in exchange for loans to pay wages and pensions. Thus the loans-for-shares scheme was born, and Yeltsin bribed his way to reelection. "Here we had a corrupt government in desperate need for cash and the so-called 'banks' owned by the oligarchs making a deal. The government needed cash to pay pensions, etc., so it used its shares in the state-owned companies as collateral to receive loans from the oligarchs' banks. As expected, the government was unable to pay back the loans, so automatically the shares went to the oligarchs' banks. Once again, everything was absolutely legal."[39]

After Yeltsin's reelection, the oligarchs received their rewards for their support. Khodorkovsky, for example, became the sole bidder for Yukos, Russia's third-largest oil company, which he bought for about $300 million, a fraction of its value. The magnitude of the bargain became apparent only in 2003, when Russian prosecutors froze 44 percent of Yukos' assets, equivalent to $10 billion.

ROVING BANDITS VERSUS STATIONARY BANDITS

The late American economist Mancur Olson would describe Russian oligarchs and the pimps of globalization as "roving bandits. "Roving bandits will take all they can carry, since they care nothing for their victims and expect to rob still others tomorrow."[40] Oligarchs and pimps became the robber barons of Russian wealth. The former stole assets, the latter women's bodies and souls. The profits they made were reinvested, not in Russia, but in Western countries. "Privatization accompanied by the opening of the capital markets, led not to wealth creation but to asset stripping," confirms Joseph Stiglitz, former Chief Economist of the World Bank and best-selling author of books on the economics of globalization.[41] In the 1990s "Russia suffered the greatest theft of resources that has ever occurred from any country in a short period of time, $150 to 200 billion in a decade. This is the low end of the figure which goes as high as $350 billion," calculated Raymond Baker, senior fellow at the Washington-based Center for International Policy.[41]

By 1998, when the ruble collapsed and the IMF and the World Bank put together a $22 billion rescue package, the oligarchs were well positioned to funnel the new funds abroad through well-established networks. "What happened was that the very same day the loans were transferred, the oligarchs, who had plenty of rubles which they had collected by converting *beznalichnye,* bought all the dollars at a very cheap rate from the Central Bank. The government was happy to sell them because it needed rubles to meet the payments of salaries and pensions," explains Transparency International's Miklos Marshall. "Within hours the oligarchs deposited the dollars abroad, in offshore accounts in places such as the Cayman Islands and Cyprus, making a fortune with money that was supposed to defend the ruble exchange rate." The outflow further weakened the Russian currency and plagued the economy.

The oligarchs orchestrated the progressive pillaging of Russian national wealth, and by doing so, they created the ideal conditions for Russian pimps and mafiosi to prey upon Russian women. After the 1998 crisis, NGOs registered another peak in the supply of Slavic women for the global sex industry.

"But being a free market, there was nothing illegal in what the oligarchs were doing," admits Miklos Marshall. From a free-market standpoint, their behavior was also perfectly logical. "An oligarch who had just been able to use political influence to garner assets worth billions after paying only a pittance, would naturally want to get his money out of the country. Keeping money in Russia meant investing in a country in deep depression, and risking not only low returns but having the assets seized by the next government, which would inevitably complain, quite rightly, about the 'illegitimacy' of the privatization process."[42]

The fiasco of Russia's entry into the country club of democracy and its failure to achieve economic prosperity shocks hardly any reader of the writings of classical economists who warned politicians about the perils of uncontrolled markets. More than two centuries ago, at the outset of the Industrial Revolution, Adam Smith wrote in *The Wealth of Nations*:

> Commerce and manufactures can seldom flourish long in any state which does not enjoy a regular administration of justice, in which the people do not feel themselves secure in the possession of their property, in which the faith of contracts is not supported by law, and in which the authority of the state is not supposed to be regularly employed in enforcing the payment of debts from all those who are able to pay. Commerce and manufactures, in short, can seldom flourish in any state in which there is not a certain degree of confidence in the justice of government.[43]

Under current circumstances, many would argue that Russians lives were better under Communism, even when the people were ruled by Josef Stalin, a man described by Olson as a stationary bandit. "Stationary bandits, who monopolize crime in a particular area, have to consider whether excessive greed today will lead to frustrated greed tomorrow. They have an incentive to moderate their appetites in order to allow their victims the modicum of prosperity needed to trade and accumulate wealth. Thus, stationary bandits have an encompassing interest in the welfare of those who live on the territory they control. They will even provide wealth-generating public goods, including, above all, the public order that reduces the investment-discouraging activities of roving bandits."[44]

Most analysts today agree that Russian President Vladimir Putin fits the mold of a stationary bandit, one who is now trying to strip the oligarchs of their assets. Privatization proved but a fleeting moment in the history of Russia. It never led to democracy or to economic prosperity; instead, it fostered a generation of roving bandits. Fifteen years after the fall of the Berlin Wall, Putin is on his way to recreating the power of the Soviet Union.

Against this scenario, one should ask the uncomfortable question: should we have dismantled the Soviet Union within the new framework of globalization if what we have today represents a harsher replica of the old regime? Many Russian women, among the biggest victims of the post-Cold War experiment in globalization, would probably say no. With the advent of rogue economics, they largely became sexual merchandise.

The comparison between the Marshall Plan and the fall of the Berlin Wall illustrates the problems of globalization in a world ruled by rogue economics. In the global economy, it is increasingly difficult for politics to regulate the market. Measures taken in one country, including political changes, can trigger a chain reaction with devastating global consequences for several others. Who predicted that the Soviet Union would disintegrate without a fight? Who could have foreseen that the fall of the Berlin Wall would have boosted the global sex industry? That the privatization of Russian economy would have kick-started the pillaging of its resources and created a generation of oligarchs?

People remain equally unaware of rogue economic interdependencies. Those who flocked to East and West Berlin to take down the Wall with their bare hands were motivated by the desire to end a long and painful period of separation, to heal a divide that for decades had tortured the soul of a continent and plagued its existence. Yet, for millions of Eastern European and Russian women, their worst nightmare had only just begun.

In the euphoria of the moment, nobody, not even distinguished economists, could foresee that the Wall was a mere symbol. Knocking it down proved nothing more than historical gloss; beyond it, there was a complex, predatory economic system nurtured and fed by the political rigidity of the Cold War. It desperately needed new markets, and nobody, not even the architects of the destruction of the Soviet system, could control it. In the political vacuum that was created, rogue economics transformed globalization, the brainchild of Reaganomics, Thatcherism, and modernization, into an economic mutant.

The fall of the Berlin Wall at the end of the Cold War, like the Marshall Plan at the beginning, had the scope to create new, larger markets for Western economies by funneling funds to reshape less-developed regions. The former failed because the market had broken the chains of politics. Economics had become a rogue force and, as we shall see in the following chapters, it was ready to reshape the globe.

CHAPTER TWO

NOBODY CONTROLS
ROGUE ECONOMICS

"I place economics among the first
and most important virtues, and public debt as the greatest danger to be
feared."

Thomas Jefferson

Meet Mr. and Mrs. Jones, children of the post–World War II
American Dream. They live in a suburb of a midwestern
town, but this is as close to the Dream as they've come. Mr.
Jones is a carpenter who, during the recession of the late
1990s, traded in his benefits to keep his job in a local construction company. Mrs. Jones is no domestic goddess. More
likely, she is overweight and overworked. Employed as a nurse
at a nearby hospital, in her spare time she assists neighbors
without medical insurance. The occasional tax-free extra cash
is crucial to make ends meet. In 2006, the couple's household
income was $46,326, $2,000 lower than in 2001, the year the
previous recession ended. They have $3,800 in the bank,
$8,000 of credit card debt,[1] and no stocks or bonds; they
reside in a $160,000 house, with $90,000 still left on the
mortgage.[2] Husband and wife shop at Wal-Mart, eat at
McDonald's, and regularly buy lottery tickets in the hope of
winning their way out of the middle class. That is Middle
America's overwhelming new Dream.

In fifty years, less than the lifetime of one generation, the
American Dream has turned into a nightmare. Wage stagnation, bankruptcy, and income inequality are at the root of
such a transformation. What is not often discussed is that the
impoverishment of America's middle class has accelerated

during the last fifteen years, triggered by the fall of the Berlin Wall and fostered by the advent of the global economy. Ironically, the two crucial victories of the Cold War, one political, the other economic, plunged the populations of the defeated Soviet Bloc into poverty and laid the groundwork for the socioeconomic decline of Middle America, the backbone of the victorious United States.

THE COMMUNIST CURSE

The dismantling of the Soviet Bloc kick-started the deflationary global era: prices fell everywhere, as did wages in the industrialized world. Deflation was prompted by the influx of former Communist labor into the global economy. While the world cheered at families crossing the Iron Curtain heading West toward freedom and prosperity, industrialized economies were ill equipped to absorb the new supply of labor. There were simply too many people and not enough capital to employ them. Alan Greenspan, the maverick former Chairman of the United States Federal Reserve, who served three American presidents, agrees that the end of Communism "brought billions of cheap laborers on to the [international] scene. This was highly deflationary,"[3] primarily because in order to secure jobs, Eastern Europeans and Russians accepted wages well below Western standards. This process led to the first wave of reductions in European salaries. America did not escape this trend. From 1989 to the mid-1990s, US real median income, that is, the wages of those sandwiched between the rich and the poor, fell considerably.

The influx of workers from the former Soviet Bloc marked only the beginning of a long-lasting, exceptional surge in the global supply of labor. Over the last fifteen years, not just Russians and Eastern Europeans, but also Chinese and Indian workers, people previously employed in closed and sometimes sealed-off economies, gained entrance into the internatio economy. Richard Freeman, a Harvard labor economist, estimated that in the early 1990s, the global labor supply doubled.[4]

With the fall of the Berlin Wall, Mr. and Mrs. Jones, as well as their European equivalents, had to compete for jobs with the newcomers. Competition was fierce because corporations successfully began tapping into these large pools of cheap foreign labor, and to cut costs, they outsourced jobs and relocated production abroad. "Western workers saw jobs disappear under their noses," summarized an Italian trade unionist. Foreign competition was so ruthless that to secure employment, workers in industrialized countries forfeited benefits. In unified Germany, for example, unions agreed to reductions in salaries and longer working hours to prevent companies from relocating production to Eastern Europe. The absence of a global social contract, of a solid legislation that regulated minimum wages and workers' benefits internationally, greatly reduced the bargaining power of Western labor.[5]

Among the industrialized middle class, people like Mr. and Mrs. Jones are the ones who suffer the most. While American social benefits and welfare have been cut to the bone, Europeans still enjoy high "social wages," such as education, healthcare, and housing facilities provided or subsidized by the state. The prospects for future generations look even gloomier. As long as it continues to be cheaper to produce abroad than in the domestic market, wages in the industrialized world will continue to stagnate. The impoverishment of the middle class may last for decades, until salaries in the developing world catch up with income in the West. "Richard Freeman estimates that if Chinese wages double every decade, as they did in the 1990s, they will reach the levels found in the advanced countries today in about thirty years. Absorbing the labor forces of other countries could take a little longer but the transition could be completed in forty to fifty years, at which point, presumably, Western wages will start rising again and the balance between capital and labor will be restored."[6] Ironically, the dissolution, not the rise, of Communism is the curse of Western labor.

Higher education will not shield future generations of Westerners from their destiny: to be globalization's new proletariat. "Indonesia, China, India . . . have more than doubled university student enrolment in the 1980s and 1990s. . . . by 2010 [China] will graduate more PhDs in science and engineering than the US."[7] These people are becoming part of the global supply of labor at every level. While the initial impact of the doubling of the labor supply was felt only by unskilled workers, skilled labor is beginning to fall prey to offshoring and outsourcing. "From January 2001 through January 2006, [for example] United States employment in the information sector declined by 17 percent; jobs in accounting and bookkeeping and in computer systems design shrunk by 4 percent and 9 percent respectively."[8] Over 750 multinational firms have already set up research and development facilities in China. Accountancy, medical diagnostics, and information technology are also beginning to be relocated to China. Industrialized economies are losing their monopoly in research, innovation, and technology.

Economists have underestimated the consequences of offshoring, in particular its disruptive effect on industrialized countries. "We have so far barely seen the tip of the offshoring iceberg, the eventual dimensions of which may be staggering," noted Alan Blinder, a former vice-chairman of the United States Federal Reserve.[9] Economists mistakenly thought that offshoring would be beneficial for free trade, a key factor to boost international exchange of goods in the global era, and an addendum to David Ricardo's theory of comparative advantage. Ricardo, a nineteenth-century economist, argued that nations have an incentive to trade with each other by specializing in the manufacture of goods that cost less and by abandoning production of those that cost more in comparison to other countries. Ricardo used the example of England and Portugal. Both nations manufactured wool and wine, but producing wine was cheaper in Portugal, while making wool was less costly in England. By specializing in manufacturing and trading wine and wool respectively, both Portugal and England ended up better off.

The comparative advantage is the backbone of international trade, and offshoring and outsourcing are crushing it (from 1989 to 2006, United States foreign trade in goods and services shrunk to 12 percent). "Offshoring is an example of companies obtaining absolute advantage by combining high-tech capital with low-cost labor," a formula pioneered by China, explains President Reagan's former Assistant Treasury Secretary, Paul Craig Roberts.[10] China's overwhelming and unchallenged absolute advantage revolves around an endless supply of cheap labor, a resource so powerful that it has stripped industrialized economies of their comparative advantage. The rogue nature of this phenomenon has already altered trade relationships between China and the United States. The US is the largest recipient of Chinese exports, but instead of trading its goods back to China, the US exports its debt.

The system is simple. A river of dollars flows from America to China, creating a dollar-denominated surplus in the Chinese trade balance. To offset the trade surplus, China runs a capital account deficit with America, i.e. it buys US treasury bonds and increases dollar-denominated reserves.[11] Visually, we can imagine two identical flows of dollars crossing the Pacific, one moving westward to buy Chinese goods and one heading eastward to purchase US Treasury Bonds.

Ironically, China, a Communist country, has been financing both the trade and the budget deficit of the United States to avoid revaluing its currency, an action that would make its products less competitive in the US. America has welcomed such a strategy "to keep consumers and voters happy and the economy afloat."[12] A similar stratagem was at the core of the petrodollar recycling of the 1970s, when disequilibrium in the trade balance of oil-producing and oil-importing countries were matched by opposite capital flows. Yet, that process was beneficial for the world economy because it softened the impact of the first two oil shocks. The peculiar interdependency between America and China may damage world trade. So far, China's comparative advantage, its cheap merchandise, has been matched by America's comparative advantage: consumption. This voracious spending ranges from the American middle class's pathological consumption to the staggering government deficit to bankroll President George W. Bush's global "war on terror." The question is what will happen when China's domestic market is able to absorb the bulk of its production. Then, will the comparative advantage between the two countries disappear? Ricardo would argue that, more than comparative advantage, what we have today is America's economic codependency with China. If this analysis is correct, the development of a strong Chinese domestic market might well cause a major economic crisis in the United States and in the rest of the world.

AMERICA IS GOING BROKE

The dismantling of Communism can be compared to the melting of the North Pole's ice cap: cheap labor flooded the global market and redesigned the economy of entire continents. But the most pernicious outcome is the advent of rogue economic interdependencies. The fall of the Berlin Wall shook the fundamentals of economics to the extent that the stagnation in Western real wages did not curb consumption. On the contrary, from 1989, United States and European consumer spending rose to historically high levels, thanks to falling interest rates. A chart of US and European interest rates throughout the 1990s resembles a ski slope.[13]

After double-digit interest rates and the economic slow-down of the 1980s, cheaper and cheaper credit produced global euphoria. Joseph Stiglitz even renamed the decade the Roaring Nineties. Encouraged by an aggressive credit industry, the world went wild on spending. From credit cards to mortgages, borrowing became readily available under unprecedented conditions. John, a builder in South London, collected eleven credit cards. "I kept getting offers of new cards in the mail. All I had to do was to fill the form and send it back. After a week I received a new credit card."[14] When one card reached its limit, John used another.

Cheap and easily available credit encouraged people to spend money they did not have. In the United States, from 1993 to 2004, consumer debt—including credit card payments, bank loans, and car financing—skyrocketed from $800 million to $2 trillion, equivalent to about 3 percent of the world's economy. By 2006, Americans' outstanding debt was three times the country's GDP. Strained by debt repayment, people like the Joneses resorted to revolving accounts, paying outstanding credit card debts over time at interest rates well above bank rates (by 2006, more than half the US adult population, 115 million Americans, was on revolving accounts.)[15]

Banks were as generous as credit card companies in granting loans. In the 1990s, America and the United Kingdom paved the way to easy mortgages. Key monetary policies were behind cheap mortgages.[16] Since the fall of the Berlin Wall, the Federal Reserve has systematically cut interest rates to the bone to fend off crises linked to the globalization of America's economy; this policy had dramatic consequences for household debt and consumer spending. By 2006, for example, mortgage borrowing in the United States had reached $7 trillion, equivalent to 10 percent of the world's economy. "Today we are living with the legacy of such policies, including a bubble in global capital flows and a bubble in US housing markets," explains George Magnus, senior economic advisor at the UBS financial-services firm. "America's is now fast bursting apart."[17]

Borrowing took place without adequate asset backing. In 2005, for example, 40 percent of American mortgages required zero down payments. "This has been the only time in my life when you did not need a down-payment to buy a house, you just needed a job," said J. Ronald Terwilliger, chairman of Trammel Crow Residential, which has built over 200,000 homes across America.[18] These are very risky transactions, as proven by the sharp rise in bankruptcy everywhere in the West.[19] Far more than Islamist terror, insolvency is plaguing the Western world. In 2006, British individual bankruptcy rose by 55 percent, and in the first half of the year alone, banks in the United Kingdom wrote off 3.3 billion pounds of bad debt.[20] But it is in the United States of America that insolvency is growing faster than anywhere else. In 2006, the growth rate of bankruptcy was 1.5 percent higher than the rate of growth of the GDP.[21] It is no secret: America is going broke.

Ironically, a segment of the credit industry is booming, thanks to the surge in insolvency, one of the rogue consequences of the Federal Reserve's long-term policy of low interest rates. Data show that in the United States, "in 2005, businesses that specialize in debt for collection purchased $66 billion in delinquent credit card accounts. That amount represented a golden opportunity for debt collectors, but something entirely different for an estimated 8 million credit card users—who were targeted for repeated phone calls, dunning letters, lawsuits, wage garnishment, property seizure, and sometimes even arrest as a result of their credit card debt."[22]

The mortgage industry is at the core of the high number of bankruptcies. Housing foreclosure is by far the most common form of bankruptcy, and Colorado has the highest rate in the United States. In 1996, seven hundred Denver residents lost their homes because they could not honor their mortgage repayments; in 2006, the figure had jumped to four thousand. State authorities are convinced that there is a direct correlation between house foreclosures and the ready availability of loans in the state.[23]

Within this trend, several mortgage brokers have joined the ranks of globalization outlaws. "Until 2006, mortgage brokers have not been so concerned about repayment of the loan because they got their cut, which is a percentage of the mortgage, when the property was bought," explains a Montana real estate agent. "Banks are not so concerned either. When housing prices rise at a phenomenal pace and demand is strong, they can turn around repossessed properties quickly and even make a profit." Often, bank managers alert developers and buyers, who are their clients, of a forthcoming foreclosure so that these can approach the owner and purchase the property before it is auctioned by the bank. Glacier Bank in Kalispell, Montana, for example, has used this strategy for properties in nearby fashionable Whitefish. Often, the new buyer purchases the property with a mortgage from the foreclosing bank. As interest on the outstanding debt is paid before the principal, banks often net a profit from repossession.

If readily available cheap loans have been a strong incentive to purchase expensive houses, the "feel good" factor of owning a home is often an important element in borrowing more than one can afford. "We [Americans] sell home ownership as a cure for all our problems; this is creating a lot of instability," explains Jacky Morales-Ferrand, director of housing for Denver's Office of Economic Development.[24] The "feel good" factor of owning a property is particularly strong in families with children, where the parents want to leave their kids some assets. The credit industry has been skilled in tapping into this market, presenting home mortgages as an essential component of the idyllic middle-class family.

On the contrary: Middle American parents with children should refrain from borrowing, because they are more than twice as likely to go bankrupt than any other segment of the US population.[25] Projections for the future are even bleaker. Elizabeth Warren, a professor at Harvard Law School, warns that by the end of this decade more than 5 million families with children will file for bankruptcy. "That would mean that across the country nearly one of every seven families with children would have declared itself flat broke, losers in the great American economic game."[26]

A WEB OF ECONOMIC ILLUSION

The middle-class family was at the core of the postwar American Dream. A cocoon of American values, Middle American households symbolized the superiority of the American way, because they encapsulated all the key elements of the Dream: financial stability, high morality, happiness, progress, and above all, homogeneity. The Dream was the culmination of the Founding Fathers' vision of the new state:

> We, the People of the United States, in order to form a more perfect Union, establish justice, insure domestic tranquillity, provide for the common defense, promote the general welfare, and secure the blessings of liberty, to ourselves and our posterity, do ordain and establish this Constitution for the United States of America.

The American Dream was just that: a dream. One income earner driving a shining Ford to work, a beautiful housewife enjoying electric gadgets, two smart kids biking to school through a neighborhood of identical streets, all these images made up an illusion conjured up by the marketers of the Dream. Yet in the postwar collective imagination, it seemed real enough to exist. For nearly sixty years, economic prosperity has made it possible for Americans to hold on to this fantasy and for the rest of the world to maintain the illusion that the middle class held the key to the land of opportunity. Hurricane Katrina smashed this powerful image, exposing the nation's real nature: a land without adequate infrastructure to save its own people from a hurricane, a country plagued by widespread poverty and vast inequality. The world listened in disbelief to people describing their surreal ordeal, too poor to rent a car or to buy gas to flee the city. For the first time in post–World War II history, Mr. and Mrs. Jones were absent from the picture. Impoverished and heavily in debt, New Orleans's middle class had sunk into poverty.

How is it that American and foreign observers of Katrina's devastation did not notice that the economic decay of the "winner of the Cold War" had begun more than a decade earlier? That the fall of the Berlin Wall had unleashed a variety of rogue economic forces that had progressively eroded the wealth of Middle America and blocked social mobility? Economics, not severe weather, had stripped the Dream, revealing its inconsistencies and exposing its fake nature. Today, Middle America and the world are equally unaware that rogue economics, not neoconservative politics, is at the core of its current nightmare; poverty, bankruptcy, and above all, income inequality are finishing off the middle-class family.

In the new economic environment of Middle America, two incomes are often not enough to support a family. Parents are caught in what Elizabeth Warren defined as the "two incomes trap": they face higher costs because their social wages, i.e. benefits, have disappeared. A large percentage of any family's income goes to meet mortgage payments for expensive houses located in a declining number of good school districts; another portion covers health insurance and savings for future college expenses, which have gone up 78 percent over the last decade.[27] Couples with children also need child care, they require help with their kids when they are sick, and they must have a second car. In 2006, Kaysa Cobb, an executive at an image-consulting business in Miami, with two small children, spent monthly $520 for her infant daughter's child care, $340 for her car payment, and $400 for the family health-insurance premium.[28] And every month, these important payments are in arrears because the Cobbs can hardly make ends meet.

Yet Mrs. Cobb earned $39,000 in 2006. Her husband, a library assistant, had a salary of $21,000. Their joint income exceeded the 2006 median household income of $46,326. To earn extra cash, Mr. Cobb moonlights as an usher and maintenance man at a cinema for $5.45 an hour (barely above the $5.15 minimum wage), and Mrs. Cobb considered working weekends as a shop assistant in a big department store.[29] Since 2001, moonlighting has been booming in America. According to the United States Department of Labor, in 2006, between 7 and 8 million people—about 5 percent of those employed, or one in seventeen Americans—held more than one job.[30] The majority are married, most in their late thirties or early forties, with children. The highest percentage of people working multiple jobs is located in Midwestern states, where Mr. and Mrs. Jones reside.

Ignorance of the world we live in is the offspring of the web of economic illusions we inhabit, a maze of smoke and mirrors that alters reality and prevents a clear reading of events. Until Hurricane Katrina brought New Orleans' social decay into American homes, people associated the city with Mardi Gras and thought of it as a sort of adult playground along the lines of Venice and Las Vegas. Fictional environments expand in times of harshness because economic degradation erodes civil society and alters people's perception of their own surrounding. Since 1989, rogue economics has been blurring reality and shaping a progressively unreal environment in America and the rest of the world.

Thomas Mann captured the economic erosion of reality in his short story "Disorder and Early Sorrow." The story describes a day in the life of Dr. Abel Cornelius, a professor of history during the Weimar Republic, the time of Germany's bout of hyperinflation. Mann attributes the dissolution of authority in the world he portrays to the monetary madness of the Weimar Republic. "[I]nflation eats away at more than people's pocketbooks; it fundamentally changes the way they view the world, ultimately weakening even their sense of reality. In short, Mann suggests a connection between hyperinflation and what is often called hyper-reality."[31]

Today, Middle America is in the grip of hyperdebt, a phenomenon that produces effects similar to hyperinflation. Debt erodes income in the same fashion that inflation reduces the value of paper money, forcing people to lower their standard of living. Mann depicts the way in which "Cornelius and his family live in a world in which they do not have desserts anymore, they have dessert substitutes [*ersatz*]. Forced to economize by inflation, they can no longer afford the real thing."[32] America's middle class is equally victim of a pervasive cheapening of the world. It has stopped buying steaks and has moved to hamburgers; when it is unable to afford fresh hamburgers, it will buy frozen ones; and so on, sliding down the quality ladder, constantly seeking a cheaper substitute, *ersatz*.

Inflation changes the way people think because it forces them to live for the moment; hyperdebt produces an identical effect. American middle-class families cannot plan holidays, birthday parties, even a future for their children, because they do not know if tomorrow they will still have a home. Fear of insolvency and bankruptcy becomes an obsession, and people must devote all their energies just to keeping their heads above water. Mrs. Cobb is reminded every day of her family's economic strains on the way home from work, when she picks up her husband and children. "In bumper-to-bumper traffic the conversation revolves around how they can make their lives better: How can they cut costs? Should her husband go to community college? Where can they afford to live?"[33]

Thomas Mann describes the Cornelius household as scattered with unrepaired items; a sink, for example, has not been fixed for two years. Hyperinflation has made repair jobs and spare parts obsolete, because it is impossible to keep pace with rising prices. Hyperdebt is preventing middle-class Americans from fixing their homes; they simply do not have the necessary cash.

As economic harshness tears society apart, people fall into an existential trance, and they become confused. "Sometimes, I wonder," Mrs. Cobb told the *Washington Post,* "is my life normal?" Against this scenario the media provide an illusory, positive world within which to take refuge. False hopes are manufactured, such as the widely publicized high rate of growth of the US economy. Yet, they are mere illusions. A seminal work produced by Ian Dew-Becker and Robert Gordon, two American economists, shows that from 1997 to 2001, the bulk of growth has enriched corporate CEOs, including former members of Enron's board of directors, superstar actors, athletes, media moguls, and so-called celebrities.[34]

"Mann senses the connection between the world of inflation and the world of the modern media. The government creates an illusion of wealth by tampering with the fiduciary media; the communication media similarly contribute to the creation of an all-pervasive world of fairytales. Writing in the 1920s, Mann is already aware of how modern technology and the increasingly mediated character of modern life create new possibilities of deception."[35] The media help society to sink into manufactured fantastical illusions to cope with a world in ruins. Against all odds, Americans believed President George W. Bush's reassurances that reducing taxes for the rich would benefit the poor. Slavic women are duped by Hollywood films into becoming prostitutes in the belief that they will be the next "Pretty Woman."

As reality fades, so do old values. Acquiring a degree, getting a job, and having a family merely replicate the bleak destiny of the middle class; there's nothing to gain. Instead, people become obsessed with celebrities, whose exceptional life stories are junk food for thought, supplied by newspapers and TV. At supermarket checkout lines, American shoppers are bombarded by pictures of celebrities splashed on the covers of magazines. They are beautiful, fit, and smiling, and readers cannot but dream of joining them. In "Disorder and Early Sorrow," a young man fantasizes about becoming a famous actor. Today, he would dream of winning the *Big Brother* contest or of competing on *American Idol*.

Reality shows help viewers daydream and deny their own realities, let alone the realities of others in other countries, whose lives rarely get even a consideration in anyone's Nielsen ratings. Moreover, you don't even have to pay actors now, because the actors have become the fantasy seekers themselves!

The impact of hyperdebt mimics that of hyperinflation. It alters the connotation of reality, forcing people to embrace illusions in order to cope with socioeconomic decay. The hope is that what Middle America is experiencing will not open the gates to total madness. When the Weimar Republic finally collapsed, hyperreality was instrumental in the rise of the Third Reich. The perils of Nazism were grossly undervalued by a population that had lost the ability to distinguish fantasy from reality.

THE RETURN OF THE GILDED AGE

To watch America's economic decadence unfold, we have to break through the web of economic illusions presented by politicians and the media. Traditional measures of the US economy have been rosy. In 2006, GDP was a respectable 3.1 percent, unemployment was 4.5 percent, and inflation was still tame at 2.4 percent. Income inequality in the US, however, had reached levels unseen since the 1920s, when the gap between rich and poor peaked and social mobility had become a slippery downward slope to poverty. The reason is simple: the rich and the superrich have been eating most of the economic pie.

Today, income inequality is growing at a rate not seen since the Middle Ages, when economies were trapped inside the feudal system and "the archbishop of Salzburg, owned a third of the gross social product in the region in which he lived."[36] To visualize the magnitude of the gap between the middle class and the superrich, let's use the tool of Dutch economist Jan Pen: the income parade.[37] Imagine a national parade where the population is arranged by height according to their income. Those with a median income are 1.70 meters tall, while those with the lowest income barely reach 1 meter, which represents the poverty line. Below the meter marks are the super poor. The parade starts with them. As the people march, the levels increase, but very slowly. It is only at the very end, when the last 1 percent of the population arrives, that we notice an extraordinary jump in height. Football (soccer) managers like Sir Alex Ferguson, who earn $6 million, are 300 meters tall, relatively tiny in comparison to David Beckham, who reaches a height of 3 kilometers. The parade ends with the giants, who are several kilometers tall, such people as Stephen Schwarzman, chief executive and cofounder of the Blackstone Group, the world's largest private equity firm, who in 2006 earned $2.5 billion.

The acceleration of income inequality is one of the unreal consequences of rogue economics; not only has politics been unable to prevent the widening of the gap between the superrich and the rest of the population, it has actually facilitated it. Fiscal policy, for example, one of the traditional tools to redistribute wealth, has privileged the rich versus the poor. From 1980 to 2004, the share of pretax income going to the top 1 percent of the United States population rose from 8 to 16 percent. Over the same period, the share of pretax income of the top 90 to 95 percent earners remained flat at 12 percent.[38] This means that taxation has become regressive; the lower the income, the higher the share of taxes.

Income inequality has also been fast growing in Europe, with the widest gap between rich and poor to be found in the United Kingdom. From 2004 to 2007, the number of poor people in the United Kingdom has risen from 12.1 to 12.7 million. In 2006, British corporate profits were the highest since 1965, but they were distributed less equitably than in the past. In the first half of 2006, the pay of directors of leading companies rose by 28 percent, yet median weekly wages adjusted by inflation fell by 0.4 percent.

According to Goldman Sachs, profit margins of corporations have been rising steadily since 1989, reaching an all-time high in 2006, thanks to the decline in labor's share of national income. This phenomenon is linked to the exceptional surge in the global supply of labor. "As the law of supply and demand suggests when labor outstrips capital, the price of labor falls and returns to labor, i.e. real wages, stagnate while returns to capital, i.e. profits, soar," explains George Magnus. Without ad hoc policies to prevent income inequality, wealth accumulation will continue to occur primarily among corporate bosses, investment bankers, and celebrities; this situation will go on for at least the next fifty years, until wages in developing countries catch up with wages in the West.

Shockingly, it is the increase in salaries, not the return on investment, that is enriching globalization's superrich. What makes their wealth soar are not sudden jumps of the share prices held in their portfolios, but rising fees received for their work. "The growth of global corporations and markets allows 'superstars,' whether in business, finance, sport, law and entertainment, to apply their talents across a much bigger base, increasing the economic return to their skills."[39] This phenomenon is by no means limited to corporate CEOs. Alex Rodriguez of the New York Yankees is the highest-paid baseball player in history. In 2006, he earned $22 million, "four times what the top player, Bobby Bonilla, earned in 1993 [. . .], 44 times the average wage of a professional baseball player. Mr. Bonilla earned only 14 times [the average wage of his peers]."[40] Though some baseball experts might argue about comparing Alex Rodriguez to Bobby Bonilla, since Rodriguez really is a superstar and Bonilla was never considered one, most people would agree that salaries in professional sports, and baseball in particular, have gotten out of hand.

Global notoriety and the underlying forces of technological change seem to justify the fact that a growing percentage of all the football or movie tickets that are purchased now goes to fund the salaries of superstars, which range from a few million to tens of millions of dollars. "Globalization expands the market into which a talented individual can apply his or her skills, while technology permits companies to grow to ever larger scale."[41] On the opposite side of the earning spectrum we find people involved in the same businesses on a daily basis, from those who cut the grass of football fields to managers of movie houses: employees who put the show together. Their salaries have been eaten away by increased global competition, and they earn less in real terms today than they did decades ago. To obtain basic modern necessities, a middle-income earner would have to work more hours today than was the case five, ten, or fifteen years ago. Globalization has broken the link between productivity and real earnings at the local level, unleashing a novel economic interdependency.

Today, those who are nostalgic for the American Dream should look at the Nordic countries, where the middle class still exists and where income inequality has been curbed by ad hoc policies. Only in the Scandinavian countries can we find the type of social mobility that reflects the underlying force of the motto, "America is the land of opportunity." While in the United States and in the United Kingdom children of poor and rich families are likely to remain poor and rich respectively, in the Nordic countries they have the same chances to succeed.

A paper published by the National Bureau of Economic Research in the United States warns that income inequality in America is returning to the point at which it stood more than a century ago, during the so-called Gilded Age of the 1890s, when the divide between rich and poor peaked. In 1899, American economist Thorstein Veblen, an eccentric individual who held strong opinions about the decadence of American society in his own time, renamed the Gilded Age's superwealthy the "leisure class" and showed them engaged in "conspicuous consumption."[42] For Veblen, American society had gone beyond industrialization and was driven by nothing more than pleasure and consumption. The leisure class was composed of people who had lost the principles of hard work of the Victorian age and were unmoved by corruption.

World War I was a mere interlude for the leisure class, which at the end of the conflict went straight back to its consumerist habits. F. Scott Fitzgerald captures well this hedonistic and unethical world in *The Great Gatsby*, a story of greed and unlucky love set in the Jazz Era of the Roaring Twenties.[43] Gatsby and those who shared his glitzy life were crooks, stockbrokers, movie stars, and famous sportsmen— the equivalent of today's celebrities—"inhabiting a fluid, mobile society." They paid a great deal of attention to consumerism, which had corroded American idealism to the extent that the Founding Fathers' "liberty and pursuit of happiness" became a series of choices about where one plays golf or what shirt to buy. As pointed out by Veblen, what matters to the leisure class is not the ownership of the means of production, as Karl Marx argued, but the ownership of the means of consumption.

Today, a new class of celebrities and billionaires, people who do not mix with common individuals, is reaping the benefits of the global economy. The formation of transnational capitalism, driven by finance and speculation, is underpinning globalization's new leisure class by robbing the middle class of its equitable share of new wealth. History warns that extreme income inequality can be disastrous. Professor Tony Atkinson, a leading expert on income distribution, showed that in the 1980s, inequality in the United Kingdom increased far more than it did in any other European country. Eventually, the high degree of income inequality deepened the British recession of the early 1990s, by far the most serious slowdown in economic growth experienced by a European country in the post–World War II era.[44]

The Gilded Age led to World War I and the Roaring Twenties ended with the crash of 1929, which triggered the Great Depression. A decade of wild unemployment, it evidenced the peril of keeping the wealth of nations in the hands of a few people. Luckily, the British economist John Maynard Keynes came to the rescue. He suggested, along with massive government intervention in the labor market, the introduction of new policies to redistribute wealth and to encourage share ownership among the population. Today, such measures will be insufficient to tame the feral nature of rogue economics.

THE RETURN OF THE GREAT GATSBY

Social decay traps the American middle class within a web of illusions. Its members live in the prison of fantasy, unaware of the reasons their standard of living is deteriorating. There is only one way to survive such an ordeal: to fantasize. And only one way out: to escape. The young Gatsby inhabited a similar environment; surrounded by insurmountable socioeconomic barriers that insulated him from the world of the superrich, he took refuge in a dream world. Fitzgerald's West and East Egg, poor and rich neighborhoods of the Roaring Twenties, symbolize the divide between Gatsby's miserable life and his desire and determination to be rich. Gatsby is unaware of income distribution, of the fact that the spectacular wealth of East Egg is at the root of the poverty of West Egg; he is equally uninterested in social reform, which at the time was considered a utopian concept. In the novel, rich and poor are separated by an unbridgeable gap, which is symbolized by the water between them. Only a miracle, a stroke of luck or, as in the case of Gatsby, a tenacious determination that does not stop at anything, including crime, could close it.

Mr. and Mrs. Jones are governed by similar feelings when they watch celebrity shows on TV. The short distance to their TV is inversely symbolic of the planetary distance between their sitting room and the world populated by the superrich. Like Gatsby, they do not want to change the world they live in. All they desire is to escape it by being miraculously catapulted into the elitist ranks. Marx would say that neither Gatsby nor Mr. and Mrs. Jones are conscious of their conditions; Thomas Mann would say that they are confused about who they are and what is happening. Both, however, would agree that ignorance is what they have to battle.

Ignorance makes Gatsby mistake wealth for happiness, so that his quest for money justifies everything, including his breaking the law. Today, Middle America and the middle classes of the industrialized world have fallen victim to the same malaise. "Money is at the heart of contemporary Italian culture and people think that it is normal," says Francesca Comencini, director of *A Casa Nostra*, a film describing how Italy has mutated into a country of widespread venality and immorality. The quest for money has pulverized moral and ethical barriers, facilitating the spread of rogue economics. Yet nobody is conscious of this reality. Italians are not aware that they have misplaced their moral compass and lost their ethical soul, explains Comencini. *A Casa Nostra* reproposes Veblen's analysis of the barbarization of everyday life caused by the rise of the leisure class. The danger is that values, once lost, may never be fully recovered.[45] *A Casa Nostra* is a kaleidoscopic interplay of stories that center on the attempts by Italian high finance to take over a bank. The movie is set in Milan, the Italian financial capital, but it could have been filmed in London, the global financial capital. It is to London, in fact, that Gatsby's gaze would stretch across the water today. Chelsea, Hampstead, Belgravia, the London neighborhoods where the highest concentration of the global superrich lives, are the modern East Eggs.

"New money" is the lifeline of the hedonistic capital of Tony Blair and Gordon Brown's New Labour; this money was accumulated primarily through the pernicious mechanisms of rogue economics that, while impoverishing the Western middle class, enriches a small elite. London's European flavor gives its rich neighborhoods the same patina of elegance and class that characterized East Egg's old money. The modern Gatsby, however, would not be a misfit in Chelsea, a nouveau-billionaires' ghetto, where in 2006 house prices appreciated 1,893 pounds per day.[46] Gatsby would be at ease in the streets of this life-size Monopoly board, because they are populated by people like him. His peers are Russian oligarchs, European footballers, Chinese and Indian tycoons, actors, TV and pop-music stars, and financiers, who over the last fifteen years have managed to pocket a disproportionately large share of new wealth. These are the undisputed winners of the global era.

After 1989, the modern "leisure class" moved to London to take advantage of an old Victorian fiscal law. "The law was designed to protect the profits of British plantation owners across the Empire, from the West Indies to Africa and India. They could maintain British residency and move their domicile, i.e. their fiscal residency, abroad where they had their businesses. Therefore they were taxed only on the income they brought back to England while the rest was tax free," explains Grant Woods, former director of Coutts, where the Queen and the British aristocracy bank.[47] The identical principle is today applied to new billionaires residing in London. The rogue nature of the British fiscal system makes it possible for those who pocket a large share of the new global wealth to avoid taxation at home. "When I was at Coutts," Woods continues, "I personally restructured the portfolio of several Russian oligarchs taking full advantage of this legislation. To get British residency is very easy. It is sufficient to deposit in a UK bank a large sum of money and leave it there." Money is not an obstacle for globalization's *nouveau riche,* especially when considering that, by moving to the United Kingdom, people can avoid taxation in their country on billions of dollars. Only Americans cannot benefit from this law, because the United States taxes its citizens on global income.

Ironically, 9/11 encouraged global billionaires to relocate in London. "The tough financial legislation introduced in the United States after the attack ended up penalising Caribbean offshore facilities. To this, one should add, the US monetary authorities' global monitoring of dollar transactions. The pound and the euro, therefore, suddenly became very attractive as investment currencies. That explains why they became the favorite currencies for hedge funds," adds Woods.

Today, Fitzgerald's Gatsby would have made his fortune as a crooked hedge fund or private equity manager, in a fashion reminiscent of the main character of *A Casa Nostra.* Similar to the profiteering bootleggers of Prohibition, aggressive and unethical groups of hedge funds are today among the most powerful of globalization's outlaws. They are the bullies of finance, using the size of their portfolio to crush industries and circumvent legislation. In Comencini's film, behind the glitzy life of Milan's high finance lurks the callous power of those who control it: corrupted financiers. Tracking corruption among hedge funds is hard because they are unregulated. An extremely powerful creation of the global era, commanding vast pools of money, they elude national monetary and financial controls.[48]

Size and lack of regulation allow hedge funds to reshape the global financial market to their advantage, as has been the case of the derivatives market. Derivatives, or futures, originally had the objective of protecting commodity traders from fluctuating exchange rates.[49] They were essentially a sort of insurance against risk. Today, derivatives have taken on a life of their own and are used as financial and accountancy tricks to avoid taxation, cover up for bad management, bypass legislation, alter balance sheets, and speculate. A well known example is Enron, a company that used derivatives to hide its fraudulent daily business.

The move of hedge funds into the derivatives market is intimately linked with the globalization of the world economy. In 2005 and 2006, for example, the economic rise of China created an unprecedented commodities boom. Once regarded by the United States as a docile manufacturing colony, China is now the world's largest consumer of steel, copper, and tin, and the second-largest importer of petroleum, helping to push prices to record levels. Against this background, hedge funds have speculated heavily in the commodity markets, pushing prices even higher.

More recently, hedge funds have targeted the equity market, inventing a new practice: private equity. Private equity can be described as leveraged buyout of public companies to remove them from the stock market and put them in private hands, thus reducing the degree of supervision of these businesses. Public companies are also frequently bought to be dismembered and each section is sold separately to the highest bidder. Employees are generally fired, and assets are stripped. The International Monetary Fund (IMF) and prominent economists are wary of potential shocks to a system that is becoming increasingly opaque because of private equities' practices.

Hedge funds and private equity managers are the final frontier of global capitalism. They use money to produce money, via a pernicious multiplier of cash that does not produce new wealth. The mechanism follows the "2 and 20" rule. Gatsby's wealth was accumulated following a similar paradigm at a time when America was meant to be dry. The fund manager collects 2 percent of every $1,000 an investor parts with, and if the fund is profitable, he skims another 20 percent from the top each year. The rest of the money goes into the Clearing House margin account[50] or sits at a brokerage house to collect interest, ready to be moved into the next money-making adventure. No investment in the underlying goods takes place, no improvement in industry performance is achieved, and no real economic growth follows, because the cash does not go into real investment.[51] Money accrues to hedge fund managers much as Gatsby's clients drain bottles of liquor. But while Gatsby's business was illegal, the hedge funds' behavior is primarily unethical.

In his analysis of high finance during the Gilded Age, Thorstein Veblen wrote that businessmen were the latest manifestation of the leisure class because they did not produce goods and services but simply shifted them around while taking a profit. One could argue that hedge funds and private equity shift large sums of money away from real investment, and in doing so, they perpetuate the imbalance between the global supply of labor and capital. Veblen even compared businessmen to barbarians: both used prowess and competitive skills to make money from others, and then lived off the spoils of conquests rather than producing goods themselves.

Engaged in conspicuous consumption, the twenty-first-century leisure class is turning Western capitals into gigantic, exclusive shopping malls. While the new wealth of industrialized nations is increasingly consumed instead of being invested, India, China, and all emerging markets are expanding capital and labor so as to industrialize, in a determined bid to catch up with the West. Soon, they will be supplying most of the products sold in the new urban malls of the modern leisure class. This process will last until emerging markets become able to absorb the bulk of their own production. At that point, Western consumption will lose its comparative advantage, and trade will fade away. Western labor will become the proletariat of the world, and Western economies will finally become conscious of their own decay. But if the impoverished Western middle class is unaware of this scenario because it is trapped inside the market matrix, the web of economic illusions which alters reality, the leisure class is blinded by its own hedonistic quest. Both are deeply ignorant of the rogue nature of the world they inhabit.

The Jazz Era of Fitzgerald's Gatsby was the playground of the superrich and of big-time crooks, the outlaws of that era. Prohibition played into the hands of organized crime, which, thanks to the staggering profits of rumrunning, bought its way into political office. Income inequality was rampant, and poverty was on the rise. The leisure class did not anticipate the end of the Gilded Age because it believed that it could control the economy. But 1929 wiped out this fantasy. Though we cannot compare Al Capone–type gangsters with the callous financiers who today control high finance, nor the opportunities created by Prohibition with outsourcing and offshoring, a modern-day parallel can be drawn with the pimps of globalization and the oligarchs who channel their dirty profits into high finance. These people believe that they are above the state and that they are the masters of the economy. History will prove that they are mistaken. The array of mutations of capitalism since the fall of the Berlin Wall seems to confirm that no one, not even high finance and organized crime, can control rogue economics.

CHAPTER THREE

THE END OF POLITICS

"Man is essentially political."

Antonio Gramsci

On a crisp fall day in 2003, a swarm of cars from the Italian Guardia di Finanza (customs and excise police) drove into the Port of Gioia Tauro, in Calabria. Set on a rare sandy beach along the rocky southwest shores of Italy, the port stretches deep into the territory controlled by the *n'drangheta*, Calabria's criminal organization. With 3,000 ships and 3 million containers per year, Gioia Tauro is the third-largest port in Europe and the eighteenth in the world. It specializes in transhipment, which is the transfer of cargoes from large ships (50,000 tons) to smaller ones. That morning, however, the Guardia di Finanza's cars did not head for the international docks but drove straight to the local port. The policemen stormed a boat that had just arrived from South America while the crew prepared to unload its cargo of marble blocks.

As the *finanzieri* pierced some of the blocks and extracted mysterious containers from within, the crew looked on in astonishment. The cylinders appeared to be stuffed with a type of white cheese. A closer look, however, revealed their true nature: hermetically sealed bags of cocaine, each weighing one kilogram and numbering 5,500 in all. The captain's documents revealed that Miguel Diez, a fake import-export company set up by the Colombian drug cartel, had chartered the ship; the buyers of the cargo were Lavormarmo and Marmo Imeffe, two marble companies of Vibo Valenzia, a Calabrian town near Gioia Tauro. The blocks were supposed to be delivered to a local mine owned by Vincenzo

Barbieri and Francesco Ventrici, both members of the Mancuso *n'drina*, a local *n'drangheta* family. The shipping company, the Danish Maersk Line, had no idea of the true nature of the cargo; neither did the crew, nor the captain.

The discovery of the cocaine came at the end of a three-year sting operation code-named Decollo (take-off), conducted jointly by the ROS (Reparto Operativo Speciale) of the *carabinieri* and the Guardia di Finanza and involving the cooperation of the antidrug squads of several countries. Yet the operation's success emerged largely from tips provided by an informer—a rare opportunity when dealing with the *n'drangheta*. The informer had revealed how, when, and where the cocaine was going to be delivered.

What happened that day proved the exception to the rule. For in Italy, as everywhere else, for each discovery of illegal cargo, hundreds go unchecked. At Gioia Tauro, only a fraction of incoming containers are scanned because of the time and prohibitive expense required. The core of the problem, however, goes well beyond the insufficiency of routine port inspections; it is intimately linked to the *n'drangheta*'s restructuring, from a national organized crime ring to a "full-service provider" for a variety of criminal organizations. "Gioia Tauro is the life-line of the new *n'drangheta*, which supplies international crime with the global infrastructure to go unpunished," admits one of the undercover agents involved in Operazione Decollo. "If the cargo of marble had been delivered, the *n'drangheta* would have sold the cocaine through its large network of *n'drine* in Europe and possibly in the former Soviet Bloc. The same network also launders the profits and invests them in legitimate businesses. In exchange, the organization keeps 30 percent of the value of all the merchandise it handles. This sum represents its profit margin. No other criminal entity offers this type of service. The *n'drangheta* has gone beyond crime; it has cornered the global market in the supply of illegitimate infrastructure. It offers to its clients a full package, from transoceanic smuggling to portfolio management."[1]

GLOBAL CRIME, FULL-SERVICE PROVIDER[2]

The *n'drangheta,* offspring of Cosa Nostra, has a long history, dating back to the unification of Italy as a nation. Founded in 1860 by a group of *picciotti*—members of the Sicilian Mafia, who, expelled from their native island by the new northern rulers, crossed the strait of Messina and settled in Calabria—*n'drangheta* originates from the Greek word *andragathía,* which means loyalty and courage, two characteristics that helped its founders' rise to power.

Always maintaining a very close network around its members, using intermarriage as the main glue of the organization, until the late 1980s, the *n'drangheta* grew primarily within the borders of Italy. Unlike Cosa Nostra, in the past it never looked across the Atlantic but consolidated a strong presence in Italy, creating a network of *n'drine* along the Italian peninsula. Thus, its geographical identity has always been a strong feature. Resorting to corruption and intimidation and always keeping a very low profile, the *n'drine* bullied their way into Italian institutions, from banks to industries, from local authorities to state enterprises. In the 1970s, thanks to the successful penetration of the Freemasons, the *n'drine* established direct channels to the judiciary and political parties. Giacomo Lauro, one of the organization's few defectors, revealed that several bosses became masons to maintain a permanent presence inside the country's institutions.

In its internal structure, too, the *n'drangheta* differs from its forebears. Unlike Cosa Nostra, it does not have a pyramidal configuration but can be described as a federation of *n'drine,* "autonomous in their territory."[3] Today the *n'drine* scattered around the world are part of a collective entity, still linked to the geography of their homeland, but without a functioning inner circle like Cosa Nostra, so that the organization cannot be beheaded nor challenged from within. Heads of the families meet once a year to discuss business and make plans. Decisions are then implemented by the bosses in their own territory. For the *n'drangheta*, the inner circle is essentially a concept, an idea far removed from the daily functioning of the *n'drine*.

Today, Italian authorities believe that the *n'drangheta* encompasses 160 families and 6,000 people in Italy alone; globally, there are as many as 10,000 members who operate from Sidney to Cali, from Brussels to Miami. Intermarriages guarantee a high degree of cohesion, which prevents infighting among the *n'drine* and secures loyalty.

Historically, the organization always worked underground, away from the limelight. The *n'drine* shunned the spectacular public killings adopted as a publicity tactic by the Sicilian Mafia, opting instead for low-key executions and assassinations, as, for example, in August 1991, when they killed Judge Antonio Scopelliti on behalf of Cosa Nostra. Secrecy has always been the cardinal rule of the *n'drangheta*, which created a secret society, known as the Santa, within its own framework.[4] Even the media have managed only sporadic and superficial coverage of its activity. The cult of secrecy continues to this day. "The *n'drangheta* is like the dark side of the moon," said Julie Tingwall, Florida's district attorney, referring to the proliferation of *n'drine* in the United States; "it is invisible."[5]

Despite their differing tactics and profiles, the *n'drangheta* emulates Cosa Nostra in its code of conduct. The *n'drangheta*'s ballads are encrypted in violence and celebrate the lifestyles of its members with such titles as "Who Fails Pays," and "Blood Cries for Blood."[6] All those who challenge or do not submit to its authority pay with their own lives as well as the lives of their loved ones. Betrayal demands the punishment of the extended family, including ritualistic and barbarous executions. The loyalty and integrity of the global network rests on what the French sociologist Emile Durkheim described as "mechanical solidarity,"[7] a collective consciousness entrenched in likeness and similarities.

Mafia associations first emerged through the mutual recognition of "institutional similarities, including parallel features in the organizational model, culture, and normative rules."[8] Cosa Nostra, for example, represented the nineteenth-century tribal response of the Sicilian peasantry to Garibaldi's military conquest of the island. Mechanical solidarity holds particularly strong in primitive societies and fades away with modernization. The intermarriage rule of the *n'drine*, strictly adhered to for over a century, secures a strong tribal identity, an ethnic extended family, if you will. At the same time, it prevents change. "The familiar bond has not only worked as a shield to protect secrets and enhance security, but also helped to maintain identity in the territory of origins and to reproduce itself in the territories where the family has migrated," states an Italian government report.[9]

Unlike the Sicilian Mafia, the *n'drangheta* never attempted to become a political force. Its main aim has always been the control of the local economy. *Il pizzo*, a monthly protection fee imposed on every business, including churches, inside the area under its control, symbolizes such domination. As discussed in the following sections, the strong emphasis on economics versus politics was instrumental in the transition of the *n'drangheta* into a full-service provider for global crime.

THE CHALLENGE OF GLOBAL CRIME

In the early 1990s, the dismantling of the Communist system led to the outbreak of civil wars in the former Yugoslavia. Chaos replaced politics. This phenomenon affected both legal and illegal businesses. Vicious ethnic infighting along the former borders of the country, for example, blocked traditional smuggling routes across the Balkans. The *n'drangheta* saw new opportunities in this exceptional situation and convinced Albanian, Bulgarian, Turkish, and Islamist smugglers to make a detour to Calabria, across the Adriatic Sea in order to expand their businesses. From Turkey and Albania, products and people were smuggled to the Calabrian coasts, which soon became the new illegal entry point to Europe. By the time the war in the Balkans ended, these activities boomed and the old routes never reopened. New international business ventures for the *n'drangheta* represent yet another of the unintended and pernicious consequences of the fall of the Berlin Wall.

The ability of the *n'drine* to adapt their network to the post–Cold War new economic and political landscape, to fully exploit the opportunities of the dismantling of Communism, facilitated the metamorphosis of Calabrian organized crime. Unlike Cosa Nostra, always highly politicized, the *n'drangheta* refrained from fighting the newcomers on its own territory. Instead, it encouraged them to bring their dirty businesses inside its Italian enclaves. Thus, it adapted to new, exceptional circumstances. In the early 1990s, for example, it began establishing close links with the Colombian cartels to profit from a fundamental shift in drug habits in Western countries. Because of the spreading of AIDS, heroin consumption had suffered a sharp decrease, while demand for cocaine was booming in Europe.

From Balkan smugglers to Latin American drug cartels, the *n'drangheta* forged profitable joint ventures throughout the 1990s. Using its expertise and key position inside the Italian economic infrastructure, it helped its partners to penetrate and profit from the European market. Territoriality remains the key to organized crime, and in a globalized economy the geography of crime expands exponentially. Local criminal organizations are presented with new international opportunities almost daily, as shown by the recent transformation of the Camorra. Over the last few years, this Neapolitan organization has internationalized its dirty business by entering into joint ventures with the Chinese Triads operating in Italy. Competition from local criminal organizations prevents the formation of an international, centralized network similar to Cosa Nostra's twentieth-century monopoly on crime across the Atlantic, but it encourages economic alliances. The new model of globalized organized crime, therefore, revolves around business ventures between foreign and local crime. This is the paradigm followed by the *n'drangheta*.

"Rather than aspiring to establish a control over the territory, the *n'drangheta* invests the proceeds of its illegal activities abroad to service its clients," as stated in a 2000 Italian parliamentary report on the activities of the *n'drangheta* in Germany, Eastern Europe, and Australia.[10] During the 1990s, members of the *n'drine* moved abroad to establish hubs from which to supervise the smuggling activity and set up money-laundering centers for their clients. Spurred by demand for their services from new clients, they soon expanded beyond Europe. Across the globe, the organization replicated the highly integrated network that had succeeded in Italy. It expanded inside the community of Calabrian emigrants who had relocated in the wake of World War II, and at the same time it internationalized its cadres. "Children of the bosses enrolled in European and American universities to gain degrees in law, accountancy, and finance. Many ended up taking residency in Monaco, Luxemburg, Switzerland and several other tax heavens from where they created complex money laundering schemes," says Vincenzo Spagnolo, an Italian investigative journalist.[11] In 2000, for example, the Italian authorities unveiled a large operation that stretched from Italy to Switzerland and Germany; it involved several banks, among them Deutsche Bank in Milan. The *n'drina* of Giuseppe Morabito, also known as *Tiradritto* (go ahead), conducted money laundering, banking fraud, and bond cloning (issuing of false bonds) in Russia, Poland, Malta, Spain, and Lithuania.

The ability to exploit external, unpredictable factors, like the new economic conditions created by the dismantling of the Soviet Bloc, coupled with the progressive weakness of state actors, made the transformation of the *n'drangheta* possible. Recent studies have shown that mafias emerge in "modernising societies that are undergoing economic expansion but lack a legal structure that reliably protects property rights or settles business disputes."[12] This explanation rings true in the case of the *n'drangheta*'s monopolization of money-laundering activities in Europe. The introduction of the euro was not accompanied by a harmonious and homogenous antimoney-laundering legislation on the Continent. As explained in the following section, against this background, George W. Bush's "war on terror" projected the *n'drangheta* into the Olympus of global crime by shifting the epicenter of money laundering from the United States to Europe.

EUROPE: LAUNDROMAT TO THE WORLD

Until 9/11, the bulk of the $1.5 trillion generated by the illegal, criminal, and terror economies was laundered in the United States and in US dollars.[13] Because 80 percent of this economy is washed clean in cash, money had to physically enter the United States. The main entry came through offshore facilities and shell banks located in the West Indies. In October 2001, the US Congress approved the Patriot Act, legislation that greatly restricted civil liberties in America. Its financial section drastically reduced money laundering inside the United States and in dollars. For example, US banks and US register banks no longer can do business with offshore shell banks. In addition, the Patriot Act gave American monetary authorities the right to monitor dollar transactions throughout the world. Today, it is a criminal offense for a US bank or a US-registered foreign bank not to alert the authorities of suspicious transactions in dollars anywhere in the world.

The Patriot Act succeeded in blocking the entry of dirty and terror money into the United States, but, because it applied exclusively to the United States and only to US dollar transactions, it did not curb terrorist financing, criminal activity, and money laundering abroad. These dirty businesses simply shifted to Europe, where the newly unified European currency offered organizations already involved in money laundering, such as the *n'drangheta*, unexpected opportunities for growth. "The entering into force of the Euro facilitated the transport and exchange of cash within the EU preventing law enforcement authorities from establishing the geographical origin of these illegal proceeds," admits a Europol source who requested to remain anonymous. Data from the Guardia di Finanza show that from 2001 to 2004, money-laundering activity in Italy increased by 70 percent. The introduction of the euro also reduced the cost of money laundering. "In the old days, the *n'drangheta* used tourist exchange outlets[14] to wash dirty profits in various currencies. These outlets proved costly, 50 liras per dollar, as well as time consuming," explains Colonel of Italian Guardia di Finanza Cesare Nota Cerasi.

Today, money laundering gets done by moving bulk cash from one country to another at rock-bottom prices. The absence of a European Union regulation, requiring the reporting of cash movements entering or leaving the European Union countries, facilitates these bulk shipments.[15] "Bulk shipment allows organized crime to identify and reach fertile geographical areas where it is easier to inject cash into the legal banking system. The unregulated European market offers a sort of shopping list of best offers to avoid detection," says the Europol source. Recent data from Europol demonstrates that since 2001, we have seen a general increase of cash movements within the territory.

In 2005, during Operation Chub, the United Kingdom Customs and Excise Services in Dover intercepted a refrigerator truck traveling from the United Kingdom to Southern Europe. About 3.5 million pounds in cash were found inside the truck; this money, allegedly originated from drug trafficking, was destined for reinvestment in the real-estate sector of such countries as Spain, Italy, and Greece. Northern European real-estate agents also confirm that they are often approached by suspicious buyers willing to complete large purchases in cash. Operazione Decollo revealed that the *n'drangheta* planned to use the profits from the sale of Colombian cocaine in Spain to buy properties in Belgium and Holland for the Colombian Cartel.[16] "The lack of efficiency of the European money-laundering system is particularly apparent in the real-estate sector, because local land laws are not updated to anti-money laundering international standards," explains the Europol source. "In addition, local land registers cannot communicate with each other across borders; therefore it is impossible to verify if somebody has bought properties in different jurisdictions."[17]

The Patriot Act also prompted the Colombian drug cartel to find new smuggling routes. The cartel feared the monitoring of dollar transactions not only in the United States but internationally. The key problem became not how to launder dirty profits but how to transfer cash denominated in dollars from one country to another. Essentially, the cartel did not know how to invest US dollars without alerting American monetary authorities. A Sicilian immigrant in Colombia found the solution to all the cartel's problems. Sicilian-born Salvatore Mancuso, the head of the AUC—the paramilitary Colombian terrorist organization—introduced the cartel to the *n'drangheta*. "Mancuso became the link, the 'go-between' for the two organizations," explains Vincenzo Spagnolo.[18] The *n'drangheta* offered the drug barons a full service inside Europe: from drug smuggling to money laundering to legitimate investments in euros, something that nobody had been able to provide before.

The absence in Europe of a legislation similar to the Patriot Act, coupled with the presence of several offshore facilities, proved advantageous for the *n'drangheta*'s new illegal activities. "Real estate investments' profits in euros generated in Belgium, for example, can be transferred to Bogotá without any screening," notes the Europol source. Thus, not only did the Patriot Act not curb money laundering, it even prompted the Colombian drug cartel to expand its smuggling activity in Europe and gave the *n'drangheta* the ability to consolidate its presence as global crime's full-service provider.

END OF FREEDOM

The intermarriage rule is at the core of what Hannah Arendt would call the "apolitical nature" of the *n'drangheta*. Belonging to a group is a natural phenomenon, she writes, because "people are part of it by birth, always,"[19] but constituting a group is something very different from being born a Jew, a Muslim, or a member of a Mafia family.[20] Politics requires a relationship that goes well beyond personal affiliation, deeply entrenched in common interests and centering on freedom of choice. Not genetic needs, but cosmopolitan and universal requirements, belong to everybody. Humans are political animals, concludes Arendt, and freedom is the reason that they live together in political organizations at all. Without it, politics as such would be meaningless.[21] It follows that politics ends where freedom dies and violence begins.

Inside the territories controlled by the *n'drangheta*, there is not freedom of choice, not even among the members of the *n'drine*. These tribal enclaves exist outside politics and are ruled by violence. According to Arendt's allegory, they resemble deserts. "The desert is composed of all the things in the world that can weaken a wretched cosmopolitan soul—conflict, misery, countless human beings and destinies. [. . .] The danger is that one eventually and regrettably becomes so used to the desert that one ends up adjusting and feeling at home there."[22] Humankind remains an adaptable animal, and history has multiple examples of how easily humanity can survive without freedom of choice, to the extent that it becomes unaware of the meaning of freedom. This trait clearly applies to members of the *n'drangheta*, who have no knowledge of life beyond the political desert they inhabit. Arendt would say that they remain acosmic, totally ignorant of the political universe that surrounds them. Born and raised within the socially claustrophobic *n'drine,* forced to intermarry, the only life these people know is the one imposed on them by their own family.

The absence of politics, however, does not prevent the *n'drine* from doing business. While politics requires freedom of choice, economics does not. When opportunity knocks, people do business with each other, "no questions asked." All seek their own advantage: to improve their economic standard, to accumulate wealth, to become rich and powerful either in a democracy or in a totalitarian regime. Profit is the sole motor of economics and business blossoms in failed states, in Yeltsin's Russia, as shown by the wealth of the oligarchs, and even in Hannah Arendt's desert. By nature, these economic systems are highly exploitative.

Politics, as freedom of choice, then remains the sole force able to prevent economic and social injustice. This is why in her critique of Marx, Arendt resolutely stands against the subjugation of politics to production.[23] Economics, for the German political philosopher, is nothing more than an instrument for improving politics, for enhancing people's welfare; it promotes progress and development, just as modern medicine improves our physical health and technology facilitates communication. The task of economics, therefore, is limited. Any departure from this paradigm transforms it into a rogue force, a powerful exploitative mutant.

Arendt's vision of the relationship between politics and economics is based upon the observation of the rise to power of Nazism in Germany. She witnessed the disintegration of the Weimar Republic under the corrosive propaganda of Hitler and of his cronies. These men manipulated Germany's economic crisis into a powerful tool, eroding democratic institutions and brutally crushing opposition. In the hands of Nazism, economics became a sinister power.

Equally traumatic economic transformations, such as economic globalization and the dismantling of Communism, have unleashed rogue economic forces once again. This shift was possible because political participation failed to keep such changes in constant check. Arendt would admonish that "commercial globalization ought to be accompanied by political and legal control over commerce, in the form not only of elite bodies, such as the World Trade Organization or the World Economic Forum, but also of spaces where citizens can debate and to some extent shape the trade practices that affect their lives."[24] Citizens require opportunities to voice their concern and express their opinion and leaders, for their part, must listen and act accordingly. The heartbeat of politics can only reflect the nation's will, which manifests itself in a clear and loud voice, drowning out the whispers of pressure groups, corporate moguls, and religious fanatics.

The main task of the nation-state that emerged in Europe and North America in the nineteenth and twentieth centuries was to fulfill the will of the people, nothing less than that.[25] Created to pursue national interests by seeking an equitable distribution of resources among the population, the nation-state is the pillar of modern politics. Hannah Arendt would argue that when such a state disintegrates, when chaos supplants the central government, politics vanishes; citizens lose their freedom, and violence replaces authority. But what about economics? Is economics also a casualty? Not necessarily. Economics, we all know, can thrive in the political desert of anarchy. For example, after the fall of the Berlin Wall, tribal, apolitical organizations such as the *n'drangheta* have profited from the spreading of rogue economics inside the former Soviet Bloc.

THE MUTRAS: WHAT WRESTLERS AND MAFIOSI HAVE IN COMMON

Three key factors—structure, speed, and secrecy—in combination played a pivotal role in the metamorphosis of the *n'drangeta*. In one decade, the organization proved able to export abroad the network it had established, tested, and consolidated within the borders of Italy for over a century. This phenomenon took place under the nose of foreign police and antismuggling units, which were unaware of the organization's power. The Guardia di Finanza, for example, managed to convince the Dutch authorities to cooperate in Operazione Decollo only after a cargo of small arms heading for the United States appeared at Gioia Tauro. "We got the Dutch on board when we proved that the *n'drangheta* was smuggling arms for its Colombian clients. Until then, they thought that it was exclusively a Calabrian organization," explains Colonel Cesare Nota Cerasi.[26]

Ultimately, the metamorphosis of the *n'drangheta* took place because of the successful geographical transplantation of the *n'drine*, coupled with the weakness of the state apparatuses in the areas targeted by the organization and by its clients. In other words, "the inability of the state to govern significant transformation in the economy [. . .] can lead to mafia entrenchment."[27] Great opportunities arise for crime when politics fails to keep economic changes under control, as happened during the dismantling of the Soviet Bloc. Black markets always thrive in times of chaos; well-organized black markets flourish.

The transition from Cold War economics to market economics left large regions of the world unguarded. In the newly created political void, Arendt's allegorical desert, organizations with a strong geographical network found it easier to reap the benefits of the globalized market economy by reproducing or expanding their networks outside the boundaries of the law. Often, they filled the vacuum created by the absence of state authority by offering protection to various legal and illegal actors. In doing so, they guaranteed the survival of the economy that inevitably became a rogue force.[28] We see this process clearly in the case of the criminalization of the Bulgarian nomenklatura, the core members of the Communist party.

The example of Bulgaria can be taken as the template of the political transformation of the former Soviet Bloc. What happened in Bulgaria also took place in many other former Socialist states, including the Central Asian Republics. The criminalization of the nomenklatura was a necessary step to maintain control of the economy and, in the process, of the survival of entire countries. Contrary to what many believe, the fall of the Berlin Wall did not take the nomenklatura by surprise. In 1979, following the Soviet military involvement in Afghanistan, the KGB had predicted that within the next decade, the Communist system would collapse. "The nomenklatura had ten years to restructure itself and to take advantage of the inevitable transition toward capitalism. In 1982, members of the Bulgarian ruling elite began developing joint ventures with Bulgarian state enterprises and fictitious foreign firm[s] located offshore. To fund these partnerships, they borrowed money from Bulgarian state banks, funds that they moved offshore," reveals a former member of the Bulgarian Mafia. "This process accelerated toward the end of Communism. Between 1987 and 1988, these fictitious joint ventures swallowed about $10 billion of Bulgarian state finances. By 1989, when the Berlin Wall came down, the nomenklatura had transferred and secured the bulk of Bulgarian monetary wealth to offshore accounts."[29]

During the following decade, money generated by stripping off the Bulgarian state wealth funded the transformation of the nomenklatura into a criminal organization, which fostered and eventually merged into the local Mafia. Money stolen from the state helped to transform old Communist networks, including secret services and sports teams, into novel criminal networks. These new networks provided the necessary infrastructure to take control of the domestic economy.

The emerging Bulgarian Mafia, for example, transformed sports teams into their bullies and bodyguards. The tribal "Communist" structure of such networks facilitated this transition. During the Cold War, the most popular terrains of confrontation between the two blocs often involved Olympic Games and world championships. Sports sublimated the clash between two ideologies: Communism and capitalism. The Soviet world venerated successful athletes as modern celebrities. Boxers and wrestlers, in particular, were extremely popular because they symbolized the physical, muscular superiority of Communism vis-à-vis decadent capitalism. The state took good care of them, granting them unique privileges as the pride of socialism. They trained in ad hoc academies where they grew up and resided. "They had a rudimentary education, having spent their life inside gyms and sports centers. They were divided according to sports: wrestlers, weightlifters, canoeists, etc. Sport created a reference group of friends, and identity based upon the cult of power."[30] Though originating from different ethnic and social backgrounds, these sportsmen had a very strong sense of belonging and loyalty to their group. Their identity reflected and defined their assigned role inside the Cold War dichotomy, through physical confrontation with Western athletes. This tribal *esprit de corps* featured the same mechanical solidarity, or collective consciousness based upon likeness and similarities, of the *n'drine*.

With the fall of the Berlin Wall, Communist gyms lost state funding, and athletes lost their special status, a place to live, and their assigned roles. Yet, the end of Communism did not destroy their loyalty to the group. "After the disintegration of the social structure and the atomization of society, boxers, wrestlers, weigh-lifters, etc., mostly people who came from the lower social strata of the Bulgarian population, remained united, taking care of each other. Solidarity among them continued to be very strong."[31] Unemployed and without marketable professions, but with a high degree of cohesion, these athletes were easy prey for the emerging local Mafias, which used them to construct a vital, cohesive, and loyal support network.

In Bulgaria, members of the Mafia offered former champions money, fast cars, women, and new social status. Their post-Communist roles now meant intimidating the population and making sure people understood who ruled the country. "In Sofia you could spot them easily: they were huge, mostly ugly men, often dressed in black, wearing sunglasses," says Zoya Dimitrova, a Bulgarian investigative journalist.[32] Known as the *Mutras*, or "ugly faces," these athletes recruited to be Mafia strongmen did not prove unique to Bulgaria. A similar phenomenon took place in Russia, where the local Mafia enrolled, along with athletes, veterans of the anti-Soviet jihad, the so-called Afghanzy, who in addition to physical strength possessed an in-depth knowledge of arms.

THE CRIMINALIZATION OF THE BULGARIAN NOMENKLATURA

"In Bulgaria, the period between 1990 and 1995 was marked by chaos, illegal trading, and a non-functioning state," explains Zoya Dimitrova.[33] Against this background, extortion, especially in the private and public transportation sector, became one of the first profitable businesses for the emerging Mafia. The Mutras provided the basic support structure for this activity.

After 1991, vehicles from the West could easily be smuggled into and traded within Bulgaria, a country that for years had suffered a chronic shortage of automobiles. As contraband of cars skyrocketed, so did car theft. The Mafia not only took charge of smuggling operations but used the Mutras to sell "fake car insurance," a form of extortion to protect people from theft.[34] "People were forced to subscribe. If you refused to pay for the insurance, the Mutras took your car or they would burn it. They forced people to pay protection money for anything, including insurance to get compensation if aliens stole your cars. The ex-Communist leaders were behind this racket, they were at the top of the pyramid. Most of them were from the Bulgarian secret services, with good connection to the KGB."[35]

The racket of smuggling vehicles soon expanded. The next step established a monopoly on contraband in the neighboring countries by taking over commercial and passenger transportation. "The Mafia controlled all means of transportation. The single pre-1990 state carrier SOMAT was supplanted by a host of smaller transport companies run by Mafiosos."[36]

Smuggling filled a huge need while fulfilling a bona fide business opportunity. The fall of the Berlin Wall had created a chronic shortage of all types of wares: from consumer goods to industrial materials. Until 1989, 85 percent of Bulgarian trade had taken place within the Soviet Bloc. The collapse of the Soviet Union ended this trade flow and brought the domestic economy to a halt. With the borders wide open, and in the total absence of a functioning state, illegal trade replaced import-export flows and became the sole form of sustenance for the population. Thus, the nomenklatura and the Mafia supplanted the economic tasks of the state with their own criminal businesses.

By early 1990, the Turkish smuggling route had become the most convenient and profitable commercial pathway. Shockingly, destitute women facilitated this illicit trade. In 1989, the expulsion of Turkish minorities in Bulgaria gave rise to the peculiar phenomenon of the *vodachka*, or women-guides.

Kicked out of Bulgaria, these desperate women had no way to support themselves and their families. They resolved to facilitate smuggling between their country of ethnic origins, Turkey, and their country of birth, Bulgaria. They worked as interpreters for smugglers and would use any form of corruption, including sexual services, to facilitate the entry of contraband materials into Bulgaria.

Smuggled goods were openly exchanged in gigantic wholesale markets. The most important one, Illiantzi, in Sofia, emerged in the early 1990s. Merchants and smugglers from Serbia, Montenegro, Macedonia, Bosnia, and Albania plied their trade there. The Bulgarian Mafia, which at the time had begun developing the insurance racket, also took over the market. It provided protection to the *vodachka* and to the traders, who often were robbed by local gangs on the motorways to Sofia.[37]

The Mafia also corrupted the police and border authorities. "In the mid-1990s, I worked as a policeman, but left after seeing all the corruption," says a former Bulgarian policeman. "We arrested a lot of people, but they would just pay my bosses, and be free again. Sixty percent of my fellow policemen turned to the other side and now work for shadowy organizations. The reason: the salary with the police was 350 leva, or 175 euros. A Mafia boss would give you 1000 leva (500 euros) per month to be his bodyguard. I was also offered such a salary, but I refused. That's why I left to become a taxi driver."[38]

By the time the United Nations imposed the embargo in the Balkans, the so-called Yugo embargo (1992 to 1995), to isolate war-torn areas, the Bulgarian Mafia controlled most of the smuggling routes to the West from the Balkans and was ready to profit from the embargo. "The Yugo embargo on oil and arms trafficking in the region was a crucial source of profit for the Bulgarian Mafia. It was during the embargo that the Mafia consolidated its financial power. It got rich smuggling oil and weapons. The oil came from the Black Sea, the weapons from the former Soviet Bloc," explains Tihomir Beslov, an expert on crime with the Center for the Study of Democracy in Sofia, Bulgaria.[39]

Paradoxically, during this period, the booming oil and arms traffic kept the monetary infrastructure of Bulgaria afloat. "Most of the profits from arms sales physically came to Bulgaria from Serbia via Macedonia," explains Kolyo Paramov, chief auditor at the Bulgarian National Bank.[40] "The Serbs did not use Macedonian banks because they did not trust them. Serbian banks such as First East International Bank and Elitbank made a lot of money from these activities, as well as from the export of Serb currency to Swiss banks. They carried out the money in cloth military bags. Once, DEM 16 million [equivalent to $8 million] was loaded on planes as valuable packages. That was regarded as a legal banking operation. On average, about $10 to 12 million were physically taken out of the country daily, while during the Communist regime, capital flights had been virtually nonexistent." Large sums of money also found offshore homes. "From 1993 to 1994 about $1 billion was transferred abroad. Without these funds the Bulgarian and Serbian Mafia could not have become strong and rich. Bank accounts were opened and closed all the time. Firms were registered, they functioned for one or two days, then they were closed down and new firms were incorporated. Nobody could start legal actions against these people because they controlled the police, the judiciary and had the politicians in their pocket."[41]

The criminalization of the Bulgarian nomenklatura exhibits all the key characteristics of the metamorphosis of the *n'drangheta:* a network with a strong mechanical solidarity that shows solid tribal cohesion, and an "enlightened" leadership that understands the need to adapt to the changing political climate caused by the end of Communism and the outbreak of war in the Balkans. Both networks also possess the ability and willingness to fully exploit the advent of a global market economy. The endemic weakness of state actors to keep economic change under control facilitated the task of these networks. Their transformation took place against a background of protracted violence and because of it. Indeed, violence made the exploitation of new opportunities possible and kept the economy afloat, proven by the fact that the smuggling of arms and oil in the Balkans fed the Bulgarian money supply. Above all, violence supplanted politics; in the case of Bulgaria, the Mutras terrorized the population. Eventually, violence erased the meaning of politics, i.e. freedom of choice, from people's minds. Thus, the honest Bulgarian policeman resolved to abandon his profession and became a taxi driver. As Hannah Arendt would say, people grew accustomed to life in the desert.

THE END OF POLITICS

The rise to power of the *n'drangheta* in the murky universe of global crime stresses the unpredictable consequences of key political victories, such as the end of the Cold War, and policies, such as the Patriot Act, in a world in which economics has been progressively globalized and politics has remained entrenched within national boundaries. During major transitions, illegal businesses, which have at their disposal large service networks, can supplant national economies, while the policies of powerful governments can serve to empower organized crime. Against this scenario, we cannot avoid posing the question: has politics died?

According to Hannah Arendt the answer is no. She would argue that even in the depth of the desert there remain oases, and even "if the oases are destroyed by sandstorms or an excluding world, there are still watering-holes to keep mind and soul together." Eventually the oases will replenish themselves, fed by underground water. The defeat of Nazism confirms such optimism. Arendt's unshakable hope springs from the belief that politics remains a natural dimension to humankind. It is part of our nature to seek freedom. "The oases exist free of political relations" and cannot be destroyed by the failure of one political system. When our nation is forced into the desert, "what goes wrong is the politics of our pluralistic existence and not what we can do or create as individuals: the isolation of the scientist and the artist, the intrinsic, world-less relations between people as it exists in love and, in some cases, friendship. When one heart reaches out to another, like in friendship, or when the world around them goes up in flames, like in love. Without the preservation of the oases, we would not know how to breathe."[42] Hannah Arendt is adamant that human as political animals have in themselves the emotional, intellectual, and material strength to win freedom time and time again.

The world we inhabit today is different from the one observed by the German political philosopher. In a globalized world we find it almost impossible to draw the geographic boundaries of politics. Attempts to do so can backfire. The Patriot Act backfired, damaging America's main ally, the European Union, by shifting the epicenter of money laundering from the United States to Europe. In a globalized world, the divide between positive and negative is constantly blurred by economic interests. China's abysmal human-rights record did not prevent it from gaining membership in the World Trade Organization. The G-7 became the G-8 while the oligarchs stole the wealth of the nation from their own people. Globalized politics goes well beyond nations' high ideals to the extent that it can become a vicious, highly unpredictable battle for economic power. Arendt's analysis centers on the nation-state as the ideal form of government. But since the fall of the Berlin Wall, the nation-state has been eroded by unexpected rogue economic interdependencies that have prevented politics from reaching its objectives. No one had anticipated such an outcome. Those who actively worked for and produced the dismantling of Communism, politicians from both sides of the Iron Curtain, did not envisage that their decisions would backfire to such an extent that rogue economic forces would enslave entire nations. President Ronald Reagan did not plan for Middle America to become impoverished because victory over the Evil Empire flooded the global labor market with cheap labor.[43] Yet this is exactly what happened.

Paradoxically, in the globalized world, the national boundaries of politics, the element that guarantees freedom of choice to citizens, are the biggest obstacle to the success of domestic policies. George Bush and the neoconservatives naively believed that the Patriot Act represented the best deterrent to terror and criminal money. They did not realize that monitoring dollar transactions globally could not curb money laundering, because in a globalized economy other currencies exist, other offshore facilities operate, and other financial avenues are open to dirty business both inside and outside normal channels. While politics is still entrenched within the nation, economics has gone global, and in the process has broken away from the constraints of domestic politics. Against this scenario, the relationship between politics and citizens needs to be renegotiated and redefined along the lines of new economic and political equilibrium. As discussed in the epilogue, any new social contract today would have to be the result of a major revolution triggered by globalization.

The extent of global restructuring, however, shows us that profits generated by rogue economics do not always come from independent networks operating outside the law. In fact, political systems presenting fundamental similarities with such networks can share the benefits of rogue economics, as proven by the emergence of Communist China as a global capitalist giant. These new systems represent a variation on what Philip Bobbit, a historian of nuclear strategy who has served in the White House and the Senate, and on the National Security

Council, terms market-states—political entities that have departed from the traditional role of protectors of citizens to embrace a more "entrepreneurial" role. "Whereas the nation-state based its legitimacy on a promise to better the material well-being of the nation, the market-state promises to maximize the opportunity for each individual citizen."[44] Thus, some nation-states have adapted to the new economic climate and in doing so, have altered the relationship between politics and the individual.

Since the end of the Cold War, the transition from nation-state to market-state has been characterized by the struggle for supremacy between politics and rogue economics. The outcome remains uncertain. But if Hannah Arendt is right, people do have the power to win this battle, to prevent the death of politics, and to renegotiate the social contract. But to do so, they must become conscious of living in the desert and begin irrigating it with new ideas. The first step requires breaking through the economic illusions created by rogue economics. Only then will people be able to exercise their choices and renegotiate the terms of their engagement in politics.

CHAPTER FOUR

LAND OF OPPORTUNITY

"Let China sleep."

Napoleon Bonaparte

Western history is the history of idealism. Its culture rests on the theoretical formulation of a model. In *The Republic*, Plato constructs what he regards as the ideal form of government using myths and fantastical images that bear no relation to reality. Once created, the ideal model is implemented in the real world. Following in Plato's footsteps, all Western philosophers, including Hannah Arendt, have argued that as long as a concept can be formulated intellectually, it exists in the real world and, therefore, can be implemented. This implementation process is known as *modeling*.

Politics exist as a direct product of modeling. It requires the intellectual formulation of the best possible model, or the ideal form of government, as Plato would say, and its implementation, i.e. the willingness to replicate it in the real world. Modeling forms the roots of the nation-state and of the constitutional state, both products of the Enlightenment, a period that gave rise to an infectious passion to perfect political systems. Constitutions are sets of ideal rules that govern the functioning of a state, norms that its citizens must respect. Often, the application of the ideal model requires force, even major upheavals, as seen in the case of the French Revolution.[1] Modeling also proves crucial in the creation of the market-state. One can consider this newly assembled state to be the political adaptation of "supply-side economics," in which the political role of the state is stripped to the bone.

Modeling encounters serious problems in situations that cannot be fully comprehended rationally or logically; this hap-

81

pens when mathematical patterns cannot be formulated. It is in the domain of chaos, therefore, that Western thinking fails. War is, perhaps, the area where these limitations are most apparent, as pointed out by von Clausewitz, who wrote that European culture cannot think in terms of war.[2] As we shall see, Chinese culture thrives on chaos.

"A CRISIS IS AN OPPORTUNITY TO RIDE THE DANGEROUS WIND."

Victory on the battlefield often depends on circumstances, not on strategy, as Tolstoy reminds us in *War and Peace*. On the eve of the battle of Austerlitz, he writes, Austrian and Russian generals review their plan, which they deem the ideal military strategy. They are confident that Napoleon will be defeated; his army is far away from his military bases, it is smaller than the Austro-Russian coalition, it has been retreating for days, and it will fight from a disadvantageous position. Napoleon, on the other hand, seems unconcerned about the battle, to the extent that he does not even develop a plan of action. He arrives at the battlefield early in the morning in a good mood. He is in love, reveals Tolstoy, and he is drenched in the optimism of all young lovers who know their love is returned. While the enemy troops begin the difficult maneuver to encircle Napoleon's army, a thick fog suddenly sets in, blocking their vision. Austrian and Russian soldiers, officers, and generals are lost. They cannot apply their complex plan because they are unable to see where they are going. Blinded, the coalition army plunges into chaos. An unpredictable circumstance, that is, the fog, has turned the tables. Napoleon improvises and takes full advantage of the situation. He attacks the enemy while blinded by the fog, destroys its defenses, and wins the battle.

Sun Tzu, the Chinese author of *The Art of War*, would say

that Napoleon behaved like a Chinese general. He exploited the existing situation, adapting his strategy to it. A crisis, the fog, became an opportunity to ride the dangerous wind and win the battle. In Chinese culture, modeling is pointless because it requires ideal circumstances that have nothing to do with reality. Instead, victory arises from searching for and adapting to favorable factors from which one can fully profit, such as the fog at Austerlitz.

Written in the sixth century BC, *The Art of War* clearly illustrates the philosophical foundation of Chinese culture, which proves antithetical to European modeling. While Western philosophy strives to adapt reality to the ideal, conceptualized model, in Chinese culture, such a model does not exist. Reality emerges as the product of circumstances, and as such, it changes constantly. Thus, the fog at Austerlitz becomes the point from which to construct victory, not the exceptional event that leads to defeat. It follows that nothing in Chinese culture is permanent, from the buildings that are erected with perishable materials and are in constant need of rebuilding, as was the case of the Forbidden City, to business contracts. "For a Westerner a contract is a contract, but in China it is a snapshot of a set of arrangements that happen to exist at one time," writes Tim Clissold in *Mr. China*, a book recounting his failure to do business in China.[3]

The heart of Chinese civilization beats to a series of events from which to take advantage. This philosophy constantly blurs the boundaries between what Western culture defines as legal and illegal. In 2004, when China's voracious demand for steel exploded, manhole covers started to disappear all over the world. "The first displacements were felt in Taiwan [. . .] the next were in other neighborhoods, such as [in] Mongolia and Kyrgyzstan [. . .]. More than 150 covers disappeared during one month in Chicago. Scotland's 'great drain robbery' saw more than a hundred vanish in a few days. In Montreal, Gloucester and Kuala Lumpur, unsuspecting pedestrians stumbled into holes."[4] Chinese merchants purchased the manhole covers from local thieves, then cut them and shipped them to China; buyers did not even blink at the words "City of Chicago" marked on their steel. Traders and buyers needed steel, and somebody had supplied it at irresistible prices. For all they cared, this transaction was only good business.

Circumstances, not ethics or morality, guide the Chinese wise one, who will think in terms of global process, as described in the Chinese classic, the *I Ching*. Circumstances also guide the general and the strategist, who will think in terms of confrontation to protect their people. Both will work with current events and within the restraints imposed on them, recognizing that life remains a temporal and spatial process dictated by circumstances and chaos. History has no transcendental meaning, it represents a collection of unique moments.

Western culture, on the contrary, thinks in terms of transcendental aims that explain, justify, and ultimately require the formulation of ideal, permanent models. This concept is deeply rooted in many religions: Jews march toward the Promised Land; Muslims aspire to enter paradise; Christians wait for the resurrection of the dead; Christian fundamentalists dream of Armageddon; and suicide bombers seek martyrdom. Life becomes meaningful only in relation to its final, transcendental goal, and history serves as the long march toward it.

Western history repeats itself for the simple reason that, generation after generation, people strive for the same ideals. Western society has encoded rogue economics in its social DNA for the same motive. Rogue economics resurfaces at times of great transformation because Western governments program politics to achieve such idealistic, often utopian, goals and nothing else. Each time politics fails, rogue economics takes over.

As described in the previous chapters, the fall of the Berlin

Wall triggered political chaos. Against this disorderly background, Western politics proved incapable of fulfilling the final aim of the Cold War victory: the democratization of the former Soviet Bloc. Modeling failed, and rogue economics blossomed from the unpredictable, messy economic circumstances arising from the dismantling of Communism. The winners were globalization outlaws, the pimps of globalization, Russian oligarchs, the *n'drangheta*, and the Bulgarian nomenklatura; these are people who adapted themselves and their networks to the new, exceptional, unforeseen circumstances. Without knowing it, they applied the principles of Sun Tzu.

Has Western political modeling become obsolete in the globalized world, a world ruled by rogue economics? If so, does the Chinese model better suit conditions for this new world? The answers may rest in the mysterious rise to power of the ultimate market-state, Communist China.

CHINESE LATERAL THINKING

China remains a mystery to many Westerners because of its cultural uniqueness. China's geographical isolation has greatly influenced its originality and intellectual diversity. Though, historically, foreign powers, such as the Mongols and the Manchu, made China the object of conquest, China's superior civilization had successfully assimilated them.[5] For twenty-five centuries, China followed a strong, unique cultural path. It constructed an empire and a formidable economy. Until 1820, China and India were the world's biggest economies, producing up to 80 percent of the world's GDP. Britain's industrial revolution ended their supremacy.[6] Because of its isolation, China built its civilization with the cement of what the West would call "lateral thinking." This explains why China does not fit into any Western intellectual standard; it has blossomed entirely "outside the box."

Only at the end of the nineteenth century did China finally have to confront and interact with a culture equally developed as its own: that of Europe. Dragged into violent confrontation with European powers, China had to come to terms with European cultural models (languages, philosophy, science, and history) that constituted forces of progress, and with revolution as a political tool. For the first time, China became subjugated by an equally developed civilization, in many fields even superior to its own. This event understandably proved a deeply traumatic experience.

The Chinese answer to Western hegemony became Mao's Long March to power, a masterpiece of Chinese lateral thinking. In a country shaken to the bone by European cultural colonization, Mao applied a Western political model to free his people: he unleashed a revolution. Thus he fought European powers with tools imported from their own civilization. He embraced the Bolshevik revolution, a Marxist model, and adapted it to Chinese circumstances. He applied essentially an industrial model to a peasant community. Borrowing heavily from Marxist theory and celebrating the concept of class struggle in a nonindustrialized country that had no concept or understanding of class consciousness, Mao redesigned China.

The transformation of Marxism into Maoism, i.e. the Chinese adaptation of a Western model, succeeded because Mao never lost touch with China's soul; Chinese civilization was essentially based upon a peasant society, still tinged with feudal customs, where nationalism outpaced Marxism as a driving force. This background permitted Mao to form an alliance with the nationalist Chiang Kai-shek to defeat the Japanese army in World War II. Unlike his close allies, the leaders of the Chinese Communist Party, who visited and studied in Europe, Mao never left his homeland and, therefore, remained forever "uncontaminated" by the West. As his ancestors, he rejected modeling but used Western political tools as instruments to maneuver events as they unfolded. Thus, the alliance with Chiang Kai-shek allowed him to claim victory in the eyes of the population and to establish power with unique credibility.

THE FIRST PARADOX OF THE CULTURAL REVOLUTION

Once in power, Mao began the ambitious process of shaping a new Chinese identity, which became the foundation of modern China. The task required the creation of a homogenous cultural context, deeply Chinese but cleansed of old, obsolete habits, customs, and traditions, as well as of foreign influences. He used the instrument of the Cultural Revolution.[7]

The Cultural Revolution plunged China into a decade of utter chaos and anarchy. Mao did not foster this situation accidentally. He created the conditions he needed, those he knew best, to carry out his task. "I love great upheavals," he admitted in the summer of 1966, when he launched the Cultural Revolution. He shut down schools and universities, displaced and publicly humiliated millions of people, and persecuted ethnic minorities. "Between 400,000 and a million people died in the resulting violence, the government for the most part ceased to function, and China conveyed the appearance, to the outside world, of a state that had gone completely mad."[8] Yet, against this exceptionally chaotic background, Mao and the Gang of Four went to work.[9] They purged the party, shaped the nation's identity, and drew China's contemporary geographical boundaries along the borders of Imperial China. In effect, they constructed a unique, exclusively Chinese historical and geographic reality.

As suggested by Sun Tzu twenty-five centuries earlier, Mao acted as a general on the battlefield and turned European colonization to his own advantage. Capitalism became the *casus belli* to achieve what generations and generations of Chinese warlords had unsuccessfully attempted to obtain: the reclamation of the borders of the old empire. To secure such an ambitious goal, Mao had to reinvent China's historical memory, to rewrite tales of wars among regions, and to erase tales of geographical fragmentation inside the borders of the ancient empire. He did it with an iron fist because he saw history as a malignant cancer. In the words of one of the scholars of the Cold War, John Lewis Gaddis, Mao applied to this cancer "the most potent chemotherapy available."[10]

To Mao, history was not the transcendent force of progress found in European culture, but a temporal and spatial sequence of unconnected events. Thus, the centuries between the old empire and the advent of Maoism were forcibly "wiped away to change people's perception of history."[11] This surgical operation hermetically joined China's ancient imperial past to its present.

Through a process of "historical recycling," Maoism became the natural evolution of imperial China in its modern version. "When I was a child, in the early 1980s, I used to listen on the radio to the great classical Chinese novels which recount the historical legends of the Shang-Zhou, Han, Three-Nations, Tang, Song, Ming and Qing dynasties. These stories made me aware of the greatness of China and of its people. To a certain extent they instilled in young Chinese people, like me, a sense of superiority vis-à-vis the rest of the world," explains Burley Wang, a Chinese researcher in Guangdong Province.[12] Yet Chinese children had no knowledge of China's power struggle with European powers in Central Asia. When asked about the Great Game, the ruthless nineteenth-century struggle among China, Russia, and Britain to control the natural resources of Central Asia, Burley admits that, until he went to MIT, he had never heard of this confrontation.

The Cultural Revolution exemplified a deeply traumatic process that altered the past, adapted the present, and shaped the future in order to recreate China's imperial power. This, in a nutshell, is the first paradox of the Cultural Revolution, the violent, brutal incursion into China's history in an attempt to reproduce conditions that had made the country a world power. Moreover, Mao's recycling of history does not rank high as a unique occurrence in China. On the contrary, this process has been an integral part of Chinese civilization since Emperor Qin Shi Huang unified the country in 221 BC. Since then China has witnessed multiple political crises, acts of mass violence, sacrifice, and cultural cleansing. Chinese history has repeated itself many times.

To return China to its imperial hegemony, Mao not only had to rewrite the past, he had to create the Maoist future. "Smash the old world. Establish a new world," reads one of the famous slogans of the Cultural Revolution. On the poster, a young, hammer-wielding Red Guard smashes classical Chinese texts, the statue of Buddha, and the crucifix.[13] This image encapsulates the true nature of the revolution, evoking a total cultural makeover. The Cultural Revolution, in fact, "called for a comprehensive attack on the 'four old elements' within Chinese society: old customs, old habits, old culture, and old thinking."[14] The destructive rage was soon out of control, affecting all artistic expression, including craftwork. "There was a bow maker in Beijing," recounts Chi Fing Kuong, a Chinese student in London, "his family was killed because bow-making was regarded as a traditional art and had to be destroyed."[15]

The Cultural Revolution also targeted "anyone who had had Western education or dealings with Western businessmen or missionaries, and all intellectuals who could be charged with 'feudal' or 'reactionary' modes of thinking."[16] Thus, Mao erased the European conquest of China from people's memory. Purging those who had known China before the Revolution of 1949 added legitimacy to the regime. The removal of any sense of what had come before Maoism and after the empire implied that a regime, such as the current one, had always ruled. Maoism became the blueprint for old and new China.

Since young people carried out the task of smashing the old world, the Cultural Revolution also represented a generational struggle. "The youth needed little urging from Mao to rise up against their parents, teachers, party cadres, and the elderly, and to perform countless acts of calculated sadism. For years the young had been called on to lead lives of revolutionary sacrifice, sexual restraint, and absolute obedience to the state, all under conditions of perpetual supervision. They were repressed, angry, and aware of their powerlessness."[17]

By becoming engaged in their own futures, the young became the vanguard that destroyed the past and recycled history. Today, modern China is closer than we think to the China of the Cultural Revolution, because those who carried out that upheaval now rule the country. The revolutionary past of these rulers explains why "people in power think that China as a whole has not changed or made any progress since Maoism. They think that criticism of the Cultural Revolution would rock the system. To them the soil and institutional conditions that produced the Cultural Revolution cannot be changed and cannot be criticized," explains Xu Youyu, a research officer of the Institute of Philosophy at the Chinese Academy of Social Sciences.[18]

The Cultural Revolution brought the politics of violence back into the Chinese psyche. For contemporary rulers, the 1960s generation of Red Guards, politics means violence. In 1989, following the brutal repression of the student protests in Tiananmen Square, it became apparent that the violence of the Cultural Revolution was endemic in Chinese politics. Political participation is an alien concept in Chinese culture, one that holds equally true for the old imperial China and for Communist China. Power is achieved and maintained only through violence and force. This reality was recently illustrated by the massacre at Dongshou.[19]

On a breezy evening in December 2005, thousands of Chinese security forces surrounded the hamlet of Dongshou, a fishing village near Hong Kong. They tear-gassed terrified residents who had gathered in the main square to protest. At about eight o'clock in the evening, live ammunition replaced the gas, scattering the soil with corpses. The incident in Dongshou was the latest in a series of protests that had engulfed the surrounding countryside, particularly in the heavily industrialized eastern provinces of Guangdong, Zhejiang, and Jiansu. Residents wanted to peacefully protest the forced and uncompensated expropriation of their land to build a coal-fired power plant; they also voiced concern about the additional pollution that the complex would generate. This expression of public dissent met with brutal repression not only from legitimate forces but also from criminal gangs. Later, villagers revealed to a correspondent for the *International Herald Tribune* that, in addition to security forces, the authorities had enlisted thugs from local organized crime groups to crush the protest. "They had knives and sticks in their hands."[20]

The massacre of Dongshou illustrates one of the many repressive measures taken by the Chinese government to dampen people's desire to participate in key economic decisions that affect their lives. In line with the role of the market-state, the Chinese government sees itself exclusively as a source of opportunity for individuals, not a protector of citizens: thus, the forced land expropriation and the lack of concern about the increased pollution. The "opportunistic" nature of the market-state is compatible with Chinese thinking because circumstances, not modeling, dictate actions. In Dongshou, the heavily industrialized area needed energy to boost productivity, and coal was available in the region. In turn, the government provided the infrastructure to build a power plant. The people's protest was an impediment and therefore had to be crushed.

THE NEW EMPEROR WEARS RED CLOTHES

The politics of violence became the platform upon which Mao reconstructed the cult of the emperor. He sent millions of students to the countryside to homogenize the nation through violence. They offered a new reading of history, a recycled version of the truth. Mao's geographic narrative, in fact, demanded the invention of fictional histories to shape collective memory, as well as the construction and representation of official state history at the expense of the truth. This process prepared the ground for Mao's personality cult.

In sharp contrast to what occurred in the Bolshevik revolution, Mao's personality cult became the modern version of the cult of the emperor. The Cultural Revolution purged the political party, which is essentially a Western institution, and transformed all political power into the administrative apparatus of Mao, similar to the Chinese emperor's administration. In creating this situation, Mao also prevented the assimilation into the Chinese culture of a key concept of Western politics, that of political participation. He blocked China's transition into a nation-state, and as we shall see, he instead facilitated its metamorphosis into a totalitarian market-state.

Even today, Chinese culture lacks a definition of politics. "The word politics was first heard from Europeans in the nineteenth century. The character in Chinese was imported from Japanese but the meaning is unclear as it implies also the role of administration. I do not recollect a definition from my education," explains Burley, "but I can say that politics should be regarded as a kind of activity which involves society to keep it alive, though I would prefer to use the word administration instead of society because politics is not a tangible thing, rather it is a sort of pattern." For the Chinese masses, Communism remains as obscure a concept as politics. "From primary school, we have been told that according to Karl Marx's theory, Communism is society's natural evolution. Yes, we believe that, and I believe it too, though I know nothing about it," admits Burley.

The Cultural Revolution promoted a new narrative wherein ancient myths justified Mao's imperial status. Mao used traditional Chinese fables and his interpretation of them to legitimize violent state action. Mao was often referred to as *Mao Wansui*, whereby "*wansui*" means "to live long" or, literally, "ten thousand years."[21] Mao was the new emperor. "China was an 80 percent peasant society. Peasants had no idea of politics. Politics belonged to the Emperor, who was the son of God, a man whom nobody ever saw, who never came out of the Forbidden City," says Angie Junglu Lai, a Chinese student in London.[22] The emperor represented an idea, a concept, and this served as unifying mental glue in a country as vast as China. As long as the emperor remained invisible in his forbidden city, the Chinese people could picture him as they wanted and where they wanted. As with the *n'drangheta*'s conceptualization of the inner circle, the emperor's "intangible" status promoted the acceptance of the system within a large geographic network.

The unfamiliar status of politics coupled with its violent nature strengthened the taboo of politics in the eyes of Chinese people. Politics became "forbidden," as "forbidden" as the space where it took place, the residence of the emperor.

"GET RICH"

At the beginning of the 1990s, China liberalized the sale of blood. Collection centers for its commercial use opened everywhere. In the province of Henan,[23] the local authorities decided to launch a campaign to buy blood from the population of 90 million people to sell it to the biotechnology industry. The liberalization had two goals: to attract foreign capital and to sell the blood at home and abroad. The Department of Health signed an agreement with the regional Red

Cross and a local company arranged for exports to South Korea.

The sale of blood soon proved a good business. Peasants eagerly sold it because they received 50 yuan per 400 cc, a considerable sum of money in a poverty-stricken area, equivalent to almost a month's salary. Demand for plasma proved particularly strong. Plasma was obtained by using centrifuges to separate if from the red and white blood cells, as well as from the platelets.

In the absence of any health regulation or control from the central government, the Chinese blood industry blossomed. Needles, for example, were used several times over without sterilization. Beijing neither supervised nor intervened to make this sector any safer. In line with the market-state parameters, the Chinese government simply gave the green light to businesses to march on. Thus, blood money created new opportunities, but lack of government supervision and scientific ignorance soon transformed a potentially "good" business into an epidemic of AIDS. This happened when blood-collection companies decided to reinject the "left over blood from the separation of the plasma" to donors for the cost of 5 yuan. Leftover blood from hundreds of donors thus was mixed into the centrifuge process before being reinjected into them. If one donor had a disease, all the others became infected. By 1994, the epidemic had engulfed the entire region. After several reports from local doctors, the central government ordered the blood centers in Henan to close, but the local authorities ignored the order. Only in 1995, when the first case of AIDS surfaced in Beijing, did the central government put some pressure on the local authorities of Henan. By then, however, AIDS had begun its own deadly march through China.

The AIDS epidemic came as a direct consequence of Deng Xiaoping's motto: "get rich," the unshakable creed of China's totalitarian market-state. Introduced in 1992, during Deng's historical southern tour, the exhortation to get rich proved the Chinese answer to Tiananmen Square. Deng understood that, to keep political power in the hands of the party, China needed to grow economically. He liberalized the economy and urged people and institutions to attract foreign capital. While getting rich was allowed, challenging the power of the party was not. Thus, by opening the economic valve, Deng once again maintained the Chinese cultural taboo on politics.

Deng, like Mao before him, applied Chinese lateral thinking masterfully. As Mao had recycled history through the Cultural Revolution, so Deng recycled Mao through the liberalization of the economy. In 1978, he declared that "Mao had been right seventy percent of the time and wrong thirty percent." This dictum became party doctrine. Among the "right" things Mao had done were reviving China as a great power, maintaining the Communist Party's political monopoly, and opening relations with the United States as a way of countering the Soviet Union. Among the "wrong" things was Mao's embrace of a disastrously administered command economy. With this pronouncement on percentages, Deng won himself room to pursue a very different path.[24]

Deng's new path "involved experimenting with markets at local and regional levels, after which Deng would declare whatever worked to be consistent with Marxist-Leninist principles."[25] Liberalizing the blood industry and commercializing plasma, for example, came under this umbrella. Through this process of adaptation, economics became open to the small businessman, who could now enter into contracts with foreign firms without first having to ask permission. They could honor, or not, such contracts as they pleased. Markets went completely unregulated as the business "of getting rich" entered virgin territory.

The transition from Mao's China to Deng's market-state implied the deregulation of the economy and nothing more, as China had never existed as a nation-state. Moreover, the central government had never really protected its citizens, but rather it had oppressed them. "Chinese do not expect anything from the state, they are happy just to have the opportunity to make money," explains Angie Junglu Lai. The central government of Deng's new China therefore represented an improvement, a step up from the Mao era, because it provided economic opportunities for individuals.

Deng's reforms meant that the totalitarian market-state offered people the opportunity to make enough money to free themselves from the slavery of poverty. In doing so, the market-state stipulated with the population a new social contract, the first ever produced in China. While the state opened economic avenues, the population refrained from involving itself in politics. Chinese enthusiasm for making money supplanted any bad memories of Tiananmen Square. It did so to such an extent, in fact, that today even those activists who took part in the Tiananmen democracy movement deny its violent repression.[26]

Deng's social contract is a simple and straightforward *do ut des*. It does not involve any industrial or labor legislation. Western manufacturers operating in China are often those who impose Western labor legislation, such as minimum wage and weekly working hours, to Chinese workers. Many in China regard these standards as an impediment to achieving Deng's goals. No wonder, then, that Chinese workers are the first to break Western labor rules. Ron Chang, the Taiwanese general manager of Shoetown Footwear Co., which supplies Nike and employs 15,000 workers in Qingyuan, Guangdong, says that he regularly loses skilled employees to rival factories that break the rules imposed by Western manufacturers. "Workers are eager to put in longer hours than he offers, regardless of whether they get paid overtime rates."[27] In the absence of tough government controls, competition is rampant.

As in Bulgaria during the 1990s, China today has become fertile territory for globalization outlaws. Yet, Chinese workers do not define exploitation as Western workers do. This circumstance may sound paradoxical in a Communist country, but China never assimilated Marxism; it became indoctrinated with its Chinese mutation, Maoism. Class consciousness belongs to a system, an industrialized system, that has basically conquered extreme poverty. China still has a long way to go to achieve this goal. Thus, the tragedy of Henan can also be explained in terms of extreme poverty. Poverty made people sell their blood, and poverty infected them with AIDS.

Moreover, poverty lies at the root of Chinese cheap labor practices and exploitation; the Chinese people remain less concerned about exploitation than with acquiring the means to feed their families. As put by Pierre Haski, the deputy editor of France's *Liberation*, "behind the industrialized, glitzy coastline, there are rows and rows of poor Chinese peasants waiting for their turn to join globalization. They will work for what may look like a few cents, for what we regard 'exploitative salaries,' but for them is the beginning of the road to riches plotted by Deng."[28]

The extraordinary work ethic of the Chinese encapsulated in the statement "working hard, as hard as possible, is what Chinese do,"[29] also intimately suggests a convenient approach for forgetting the horrors of the Cultural Revolution. Nations often internalize deeply traumatic experiences by associating them with politics; politics thus becomes taboo. Post–World War II Germany serves as a case in point. "West German commentators and politicians have often regarded the Nazi past as an ineluctable burden, one beset by and working through the mystical force of taboo."[30] Equally China remains entrenched in the grip of her historical denial. Why else is the majority of nongovernmental historiography on twentieth-century China written by European and American authors? This phenomenon also proved the case with German historiography for many years following World War II.

The process of "overcoming" the trauma takes place on the economic level through hard work. Achieving material wealth through hard work becomes a cathartic experience, which frees people from the ghosts of the past. While the memory of the Holocaust became an impediment, a constraint for German political culture, the nation cleansed itself from the Nazi nightmare by working exceptionally hard. In 1950, the rate of growth of German industrial production was 25 percent, far outstripping the economic expansion of any other country in war-torn Europe. Also by that time, Germany's economy was larger than that of the United Kingdom; such was the focus on hard work and self-denial inherent in the psychology of the Germans at the time.[31]

A similar situation of self-denial and hard work provided the psychological orientation necessary for the rampant economic expansion China underwent in the decades following the Cultural Revolution. This development has seen China's economy grow to the point of making the country close to a superpower.

From 1978 to 1994, Chinese per capita income tripled. Gross domestic product quadrupled. Exports expanded by a factor of ten. By the time Deng died in 1997, the Chinese economy had become one of the largest in the world. The contrast with the former Soviet economy could not be more shocking. Despite high oil prices, the Soviet Bloc showed no growth at all in the 1970s and actually contracted during the early 1980s, plunging into deep recession in the 1990s. This indictment was one from which Soviet leaders never recovered. "After all," Mikhail Gorbachev commented ruefully in 1993, "China today is capable of feeding its people who number more than one billion."[32] Russia, sadly, was not.

Deng Xiaoping encouraged China to cleanse itself of the ghosts of the past by achieving material wealth. This process found its application in the trial of the Gang of Four, a crucial ritual that once again recycled history. By sacrificing the Gang of Four, Deng preserved the myth of Mao, and with it, China's identity.[33]

China's historical and emotional baggage—the horrors of the Great Leap Forward, Mao's failed economic and social plan to increase industrial and agricultural production—and the horrors of the Cultural Revolution became the yin and yang of Chinese attitudes toward politics and economics. The baggage of the past became a political constraint, while getting rich was an economic enabler. China's love affair with global capitalism thus became the counterforce to the painful memories of the Cultural Revolution.

MAOIST TRIBALISM

In 1968, Ma Bo, a student at Beijing University, departed for Mongolia. He joined the millions of young students who enthusiastically embraced Mao's exhortation to move to the countryside to destroy the past and build a new future. "In 1968 a raging tide of youth, a raging tide of hot blood, a raging tide of innocence surged toward the countryside, the mountains, and the vast wilderness," writes Ma Bo in the opening passage of his book, *Blood Red Sunset*. "Not an eastward crusade, yet history was about to be written; not a mass migration, yet tens of thousands of households would taste the bitter fruit of parting; not a battlefield incursion, yet a volunteer army, solemn and purposeful, was on the march."[34]

China's survival after the dismantling of Soviet Communism proves that no revolution can succeed "unless there is also a revolution in men's minds."[35] Yet this goal depends on the ability of the state to control the nation's spaces; thus people like Ma Bo had to carry the revolutionary message to the farthest corners of the country. For a totalitarian regime emerging from a revolution, territoriality is as paramount as it is for organized crime. Territoriality proved equally important for imperial China. A state unable to assert a geographic presence in one or any of its vast territories faces the possibility of resistance.[36]

Mao understood that the strength of China has always been a matter of space. Size mattered more than history, and thus the Cultural Revolution needed to reclaim the imperial borders. Historical amnesia became the platform from which he launched a hegemonic, violent incursion into Chinese space. "Not only were frenetic attempts made to break conclusively with the past, but geographic interaction on a scale probably unparalleled in modern Chinese history took place."[37]

Regionalism, the great enemy of the Chinese empire, became the great foe of Maoism. Resistance often grew in rural areas where local governments proved weak and easily replaced by powerful warlords. Mao countered this problem by making full use of the Red Army and of the students. Soldiers and students like Ma Bo brought the regional groups under the ideology of the Cultural Revolution and linked them to the Party Central Committee in Peking.

"[Mao] allowed regional autonomy to grow only to a certain point and then, in the Cultural Revolution, cracked down on semi-independent 'kingdoms.'"[38] Regionalism challenged Mao with a potential paradox: while he needed a small degree of regional autonomy, in order to ensure that the ideology of the party remained in the minds of people isolated from the centers of power, this autonomy could not grow so much as to threaten the legitimacy of the state. The balance depended on the dissolution of the urban/rural divide. "For a long time the Chinese were divided into two groups, those living in the city and those living in rural areas," explains Burley. The Cultural Revolution reduced the cultural distance between the two.

Mao's "Chinese road" confirms the importance of drawing people and space in their entirety into the process of building a different society outside politics through the recycling of history and through violence. "This process is conceived as a multidimensional one, [. . .] implying the production in space of a variety of goods as well as the production of space as a whole, the production of a space ever more effectively appropriated."[39] Thus, the Cultural Revolution did not represent only a social exercise, but above all, a geographical one. Unity of space mattered as much as social unity. The privileging of this spacial unity, the geographical unity of the Chinese empire, over a historical identity became the second paradox of the Cultural Revolution. This crucial factor underscores the evolution of a Chinese geographical identity rather than a Chinese cultural identity.

Modern Chinese identity, therefore, has deep roots in the geographical space occupied by the Chinese people. When asked what it means to be Chinese, Burley provides first of all a geographical distinction: "The Chinese are those living in Chinese society. The mainland and Taiwan area can be categorized into one group, while those living in Hong Kong and Macao and Chinatowns in the world could be categorized into a second group. People in the first group could be described as peaceful, diligent, generous (even if sometimes they have to pretend to be), wisdom chasing (at least they think they are), easily content with the environment, reputation-oriented." One can draw a parallel with the collective identity of the *n'drine* scattered around the world. The Chinese seem to share a similarly strong geographical orientation. The successful reclamation of China's imperial geographical borders, not its history, customs, and culture, therefore, gives continuity to Chinese civilization. "When in 1980 I began primary school, I was told what a great country China is. We are one of four great ancient civilizations together with ancient India, Egypt, and Babylon. While the other three have in fact been eliminated, China is still the Great Red Cock, standing in the east of the world," summarizes Burley Wang.

By undermining regionalism and recycling history, the Cultural Revolution ensured the uniform development of society across all of the nation's spaces. But to do this, individualism could not impinge on the collective and homogenized Chinese identity that focused, above all, on the common cause. Maoism became the common ground of the new society. "Mao was hailed as the 'Great Helmsman,' 'the Reddest Red Sun on Our Hearts.'"[40] Thus, one could argue that a sort of "mechanical solidarity,"[41] a collective consciousness based upon likeness and similarities, developed inside Maoist China. The Cultural Revolution imposed on the population institutional similarities, including parallel features in the organizational model, culture, and normative rules and similar characteristics to Mafia organizations such as the *n'drangheta*.

This process took place against a new social background, one that displayed strong tribal features. In the attempt to homogenize society, Mao and his Communist clique effectively set China on the road to tribal identity. People had a dress code, a uniform, and a little red book of Mao's sayings, identical throughout the country. Mao introduced new rituals. "Each day began [for the Red Guards] with a 'loyalty dance.' You put your hand to your head and then to your heart, and you danced a jig—to show that your heart and mind were filled with boundless love for Chairman Mao."[42]

Children became indoctrinated with tribal loyalty to Maoism. "As a child I joined China's youth pioneers group. Later at fourteen, I joined the China Communist youth group. The two groups are considered the human resources ladder for the Chinese Communist Party," explains Burley. Teachers were instrumental to the assimilation of Maoist tribalism. "I remember that my first teacher in primary school told us that there are three main things in our life: join the China's youth pioneers group when you are a kid, China Communist youth group when older, finally [be] an honorable CCP member."

In the science-fiction novel *The Diamond Age*, Neal Stephenson describes China as a country where geography has conquered history.[43] History has become nothing more than a cultural resource, shaped according to the needs of a particular group, and is the social glue of a postmodern tribalism that is defined by the territory of the tribe. In the book, China has two main tribes, the Victorians, who inhabit the extremely wealthy coastline, and the impoverished Celestial Kingdom, trapped in the interior of the mainland. In Stephenson's masterpiece, China does not historically progress as a nation, as Western culture would describe all civilizations, but as an organic cultural system constructed around a well-defined territory. China comes to represent the ultimate spatialized identity.[44]

In *The Diamond Age*, an endless pattern of recycling traps history in an effort to adapt memories to the needs of the tribe. Thus, history is held hostage to a cultural geography, an ultra-stable geographic identity of "Chineseness." In reality, the recycling of history as well as subordination to geography feeds Maoist tribalism. Tribalism forms an important link to imperial China because it allows the maintenance of a selection of the "accessories" of the past that contribute to the definition of modern "Chineseness." At the same time tribalism created an insurmountable geographical and intellectual barrier between China and the rest of the world. This explains why as recently as 2003, in the Mu Zhen Liao area of Beijing, young people chose to wear "classical" and "traditional" Chinese dress, modeled on garments worn in imperial China, when they were going out, instead of the latest Western fashions, as might have been expected.[45]

In the context of China's controversial love affair with globalization, tribalism keeps the influence of foreign cultures at bay. "Westernization of young people is the biggest cultural clash modern China is experiencing," complains Angie Junglu Lai. Tribalism contributes to the antagonism with Western culture. It feeds the Chinese belief that the West wants to conquer it once more. "I hated *Wild Swans*. It is a book written to please Westerners," she remarks, implying that the author of the famous account of the Chinese Revolution and Mao's China had purposely misrepresented her country.[46]

The successful ascension of China into the Olympus of global capitalism demonstrates three key characteristics reminiscent of the Bulgarian nomenklatura and of the *n'drangheta*'s tribal networks: first, a background of long-lasting violence sets the stage, shaping people's perception of their limited roles in society, preventing political participation, and turning politics into a taboo; second, an "enlightened" leadership directs the network to reap the benefits of major changes, as in Mao's manipulation of the European hegemony leading to the Cultural Revolution and Deng's opportunistic embrace of capitalism creating China's market-state; third, a strong unity of space, not history, lies at the root of the network's tribal identity, with geography as its cohesive force. While the metamorphosis of the *n'drangheta* and the criminalization of the Bulgarian nomenklatura took place amid the endemic failure of state actors to keep economic change under control, Deng's government purposely withdrew from the political arena, freeing economics from the constraints of politics. This decision allowed China to take full advantage of globalization and to blossom within the sphere of rogue economics.

Deng's economic *laissez faire* reflects China's unique approach to politics. A culture not enslaved by modeling, China sees itself free to be shaped by circumstances, and most recently by rogue economics. China's remarkable success story in the midst of globalization seems to confirm that in the new world ruled by rogue economics, politics is nothing more than an accessory to business and economic opportunism. That opportunism has displaced the ethics and morality of the nation-state.

CHAPTER FIVE

FAKE IT

"If you haven't got it, fake it! Too
short? Wear big high heels, but do
practice walking!"

Victoria Beckham

In November 2005, police sized 16,000 bottles of fake Chanel
No. 5 perfume. The shipment had landed in Antwerp from
China, and customs officers immediately renamed them "Chinel
No. 5."[1] The buyer, a Chinese importer, had paid 10,000 euros
for the entire cargo, which according to Chanel, was worth 1.2
million euros. The staggering difference between the price of the
bogus and of the authentic, however, has as much to do with the
"heavy-duty" marketing tactics of the international perfume
cartel to keep prices artificially high as it does with the spreading of the knockoff industry.

In the spring of 2006, the French antitrust authority cited
several cosmetic companies, including L'Oreal, Chanel, Christian Dior, Yves Saint Laurent, Estée Lauder, and Clinique, "for
colluding in maintaining high prices to the detriment of consumers."[2] The French authorities fined these companies a
total of $64 million for breaking European Union antitrust
laws. The price-fixing tactic they used, called police pricing,
involved the cartel's imposing an identical high retail price in
every shop that stocked its perfume. For this practice to work,
discounts are fixed by the cartel, and if shops grant higher
reductions they cease to have access to products. Valéry, a
Parisian cosmetics shop assistant, confirms that inspectors
from the various brands carry out spot checks to make sure
that shops do not discount products. The maximum price
reduction allowed is 10 percent.[3]

Famous brands also artificially create scarcity in order to maintain high prices, as can be seen in the case of the Chloé Paddington handbag. Buyers must sign up for a waiting list at Chloé's shop in Paris to purchase the 900-euro handbag. While this practice represents a legitimate marketing strategy, such tactics also boost the counterfeit industry. Shop assistants at Chloé admitted that while waiting their turn on the list, buyers often purchase fake Paddington handbags on eBay for a third of the cost of the original.

Ironically, the aggressive marketing strategies of Western corporations benefit the counterfeit industry. Luxury brands' high prices lie at the root of the strong demand for fake designer goods.

RECYCLING HISTORY

China is the lifeline of the international industry of bogus products. Italian authorities estimate that one in every two counterfeit products sold globally comes from China. China's love affair with knockoffs springs from its endemic recycling of history and not, as many believe, from the spreading of the illegal economy. Geographical and historical elements differentiate replicas from originals. While fakes are available everywhere, originals remain rare.

Furthermore, originals have a history. A painting, a statue, a monument, as well as a Chanel haute-couture dress, have a unique past. This past consists of the creative process that shaped it. When we admire, touch, or wear a particular object, we remain conscious of its special quality because the life of the original, much like a diamond's structure, is encoded in its history. We sometimes refer to this as the "aura" of a product, that special glow "imbedded in the fabric of tradition."[4] Western concepts of intellectual property find their philosophical justification in the uniqueness of the aura, which cannot be replaced, or stolen, because it represents the soul of the original.

The advent of the mass market has created a global demand for replicas; the millions who cannot afford the original are happy to settle for a copy. "Every day the urge grows stronger to get hold of an object at very close range by way of its likeness, its reproduction." At the same time, globalization has shrunk the world, fostering "the desire of contemporary masses to bring things 'closer' spatially and humanly."[5] Modern technology satisfied this exceptional and consuming craving for fakes in almost real time. Indeed, the reproduction process has become cheaper, easier, and more readily accessible than ever before. Replicas are plentiful, inexpensive, and well tailored to satisfy today's obsession with having direct, immediate access to products.

Fakes, imperfect clones of the original, are stripped of that special aura, which is constantly recycled during the reproduction process. Unlike the original, however, knockoffs are widely available and accessible to the masses. This is the trade-off between the original and its replicas.

The recycling of the "aura" maximizes the global availability of originals. Culture, too, has not escaped this globalization trend. The success of the blockbuster *The Da Vinci Code*, for example, well illustrates the appetite for widely available recycled art history and religion. Similarly, historical novels satisfy readers' desire to rapidly consume junk history and culture as an escape mechanism. Culture has become a commercial product, and modern technology makes its fictional version cheaply available to the masses everywhere, from airport bookshops to supermarkets, from websites to cinemas.

Authenticity, for its part, has become a fugitive because it is encoded in time and not in space. While authentic products are unique and spatially confined, every forgery begets yet other forgeries, all of them sold globally. Against this background, we can begin to understand why the cultural justification of piracy comes so easily to postmodern China. Originally, copyright and patent legislations were devised in foreign countries based on concepts totally alien and culturally incomprehensible to the Chinese people. Piracy in China remains a way of economic life inextricably linked to centuries of historical recycling. Once history is written and rewritten to fit the needs of the power of the moment, reality evaporates. The value of its accessories, from works of art to music, from literature to fashion, including the "aura" of the original, also vanishes, and unique ideas and objects find themselves easily replaced by piles and pyramids of cheap replicas. Unsurprisingly, the Chinese confuse the original with its replica. "Today people buy counterfeit wines [and liquors] with fake banknotes, then they come and complain to us," says the president of the consumer association of Changsha, in Hunan Province. "The same phenomenon took place during the Cultural Revolution. False revolutionaries denounced phony revolutionaries, who then appealed to the Central Committee of the Communist Party to be rehabilitated. Things seem different today but the same story continues to be repeated. China is infested by forged products; this is our social pathology, which started well before the Cultural Revolution."[6]

When Deng Xiaoping announced his famous "get rich" slogan, he unleashed an economic revolution that spurred a permanent recycling of products and ideas. Fake festivals, presented as ancient traditions, for example, were staged as a way to attract foreign capital. The *ersatz,* or substitute, came to define a whole range of pirated consumer products made in China. Foreign films illegally pirated and shown in Chinese cinemas continue to roll without people knowing or particularly caring that they are not watching the original. Quality suffers when everything becomes a reproduction of a reproduction, including reality, but who cares as long as everything remains cheap and widely accessible?

Deng's motto did not rock the political boat, which remained firmly in the hands of the party, because technological development enriched the counterfeit industry, which is a branch of rogue economics. Modernization and economic development did not promote the democratization of the society, but prepared the ground for rampant capitalism. One can draw a parallel with the twentieth-century technological revolution, when Fascism and Nazism channeled innovation into ways to sustain expansionary conflicts instead of improving people's lives. The Italian-born Futurist movement even described this phenomenon as the aesthetics of war.[7]

Counterfeit products and the landscape that surrounds them, from the huge wholesale markets of Southern China to the dollar stores of America, have become the aesthetics of rogue economics, equally celebrated in China and the West. When asked by Sang Ye, the author of *China Candid*, if piracy is illegal, a top programmer in Thieves Alley in Beijing, China's Silicon Valley, replied: "Piracy is not such a bad thing. The Four Dragons (Hong Kong, Taiwan, South Korea, and Singapore) have attained wealth and prosperity thanks to piracy."[8] Who has never bought a fake designer watch or handbag made in Hong Kong?

Drunk on this propaganda, people believe that by embracing the commercial recycling of Western products they will improve their lives.

In a similar fashion, today China is consumed with the urge to destroy and rebuild the physical landmarks of the past, as decades ago the Cultural Revolution wiped away the historical ones. Entire suburbs are bulldozed daily, only to be reconstructed soon after. Taxi drivers in Beijing, notoriously bad at remembering streets, must now deal with new roads and buildings, constructed almost overnight. The Chinese see everything new as "better," a testimonial to modernity and development, but design and quality remain very poor.[9]

So far, the Chinese have proved luckier than the Italians and Germans were in the 1930s and 1940s. China's economic development, however, also suffers from income inequality, widespread corruption, rising crime rates, high levels of prostitution, an AIDS epidemic, severe air pollution, and exploitation. "Every time you pick up a newspaper today, it is filled with scandals, crimes, murders. The crime rate in China is rising in direct ratio to economic growth, or possibly even faster," the Chinese director of *Lost in Beijing*, a film about everyday life in China, told the *Financial Times*.[10]

The advent of rogue economics and the pivotal role played by China may suggest that global society falls into the same trap that, in the 1930s, turned technology into an evil force, when "instead of draining rivers, society direct[ed] a human stream into a bed of trenches; instead of dropping seeds from airplanes, it drop[ped] incendiary bombs over cities."[11] Any such gloomy scenario, however, remains premature. As discussed in this book's Epilogue, China may instead develop the ability to offer the world a new social contract, one that will tame globalization outlaws. But before such an extraordinary outcome takes place, China and its people have to go through the pains and perils of rogue economics.

THE CHINESE MAFIA

Organized crime now flourishes on the fringes of the Chinese counterfeit industry. The Triads, the Chinese Mafia, are involved in the shipment of bogus products from China, as well as in the trafficking of cheap Chinese labor. This growing industry is booming and has direct links to the proliferation of Chinese sweatshops in the West. Paris, for example, is one of the European hubs of the Chinese bogus industry and hosts the largest number of Chinese illegal immigrants in the European Union. A 2006 report published by the International Labour Organization (ILO) puts the number of Chinese illegal immigrants in France at 50,000, 70 percent of whom live in Paris, the rest in eastern and northern France. The influx of Chinese illegal immigrants is rapidly becoming cause for concern all over Europe. In Italy in 1980, there were 730 Chinese immigrants, both legal and illegal; by 2004, the Italian NGO Caritas estimated that the number had grown to 100,000. According to Europol, Chinese migrants have become the fastest-growing ethnic group to reach Europe, and by far the cheapest to employ.

The ILO confirms that the first destination for Chinese immigrants has shifted from the United States to Europe, simply because the cost of smuggling Chinese immigrants to the United States has doubled, compared to Europe. In addition, applicants seeking refugee status receive more generous treatment in European countries.[12]

Since it remains almost impossible for Chinese immigrants to acquire visas to European Union countries, they rely chiefly on underground networks of human-smugglers, who charge 10,000 to 20,000 euros per person for the journey. Often, having received illegal passage to Europe, the immigrant spends two to ten years of indentured servitude to pay off his or her debt. The ILO estimates that 75 percent of Chinese migrants who have illegally entered France owe anywhere from 12,000 to 20,000 euros to their traffickers.

Traffickers take a cut of the immigrants' salaries directly from the employers. For this procedure to be possible, traffickers requisition migrants' ID cards and passports at the beginning of the voyage and later hand them over to the employers in Europe. "The most common scenario is for the person's identification documents to be confiscated by the smuggler, who gives them to the employer, who then pays the worker's wage to the trafficker to reimburse the debt," explains Gao Yun, a lawyer with the ILO. "The trap closes around them: it will take them from two to ten years to reimburse their debt. From that moment on, the migrants enter an underground ethnic economic network that is difficult to define. They make themselves invisible through fear of arrest."[13]

Every year, Chinese criminal organizations smuggle tens of thousands of Chinese workers into Europe. Their lives appear to us as the Asian twenty-first century versions of Charles Dickens's characters: men, women, and children struggling to make ends meet during the Industrial Revolution. Often criminal gangs, in partnership with Chinese manufacturers based in Europe, lure the migrants to Europe. In early 2006, a detailed Italian antidrug-unit study showed the ways that human smuggling from China takes place through a two-tier system. Chinese-based organizations supervise the transcontinental shipment of people, while locally based Chinese groups manage the transit points of the "human merchandise" to the countries of destination. Today, Moscow and Malta serve as the most popular transhipment points.

Sometimes, the entry into a European country is legal; European governments grant work permits to Chinese workers on the basis of employers' legitimate requests. After a few weeks, however, these immigrants can be fired and forced to work, often for the same employer, in the black market. In other cases, they reach Europe with regular passports and tourist visas, which are confiscated by the traffickers at the border. Passports and visas are then sent back to China, so that it appears that the "tourists" have returned home. Without regular documents, immigrants must work in the black market to survive.

In Europe, the majority of illegal immigrants end up working in the $80 billion garment industry. Italy and Spain have become primary destinations. Paris is another. Mr. Li, one of globalization's transplants, lives with his wife and young daughter in a room ten meters square on the outskirts of Paris. Husband and wife work at their sewing machines night and day. Mr. Li stocks a few bottles of wine that he occasionally gives to neighbors to stop them complaining about the noise of the machines that run all night long. The last link in the subcontracting chain, Mr. Li collects garments that have already been cut and sews them together at his home, nonstop.

Chinese enterprises benefit from cheap Chinese labor at home and abroad, inside the very markets that they want to conquer with their bogus products. The Italian anti-Mafia unit confirms that the extraordinary competitiveness of Chinese businesses in Europe is directly related to cheap Chinese labor employed in the black market. This practice includes the growing business of counterfeiting logos. Chinese fake goods are smuggled into Europe, where they receive their final touches, including the sewing of counterfeited logos. The products range from designer clothes to toys and bathroom accessories.

Ironically, while Chinese migrants come to Europe seeking a better life, they repatriate the profits of their hard work. Because Chinese businesses tend to avoid using the formal banking system, most of the revenues are kept in cash, and therefore do not get taxed. The Italian authorities have estimated that at least 34 percent of the vast wealth generated by Chinese enterprises in Italy is tax free and returns to China in cash by way of couriers. Other methods include the use of an informal banking system similar to the *hawala*, which was created in the tenth century to protect Arab merchants from bandits as they traveled along the Silk Road to China.

BIOPIRATES

Western corporations use the concept of intellectual property to battle those who counterfeit their products. In the West, a complex system of patents and trademarks protects original ideas and guarantees that their commercial exploitation remains in the hands of those who have produced them. But in a world ruled by rogue economics, the patent system can become a double-edged sword, as shown by the proliferation of "biopirates."

Biopirates, the modern-day version of the profiteering white hunters, raid Africa for that continent's profitable biological organisms. We find traces of these organisms in our clothes, in our beauty products, even in our laundry detergent. The American multinational Genencor International, for example, has taken from the lakes of the Rift Valley, in Kenya, a bacterial microorganism used in the production of blue jeans. When they are mixed with laundry detergent, these bacteria fade the cloth used to create expensive and fashionable jeans.[14] A 2006 report on biopiracy, commissioned by the African Center for Biosafety, shows that Genencor earned $3.4 billion from the exploitation of the Rift Valley bacteria without paying any taxes to the local administration. The government of Nairobi has denounced the situation, asking for compensation, but to no avail.[15]

Biopiracy feeds many industries that supply goods to Western consumers. Procter & Gamble uses a microorganism taken from Lake Nakuteri to produce detergent. Sygenta, a Swiss biotechnology giant, has taken out a patent in Europe and in North America on a plant from Usambala, Tanzania, southeast of Kilimanjaro, known as *Impatiens usambarensis*. A popular plant, impatiens remains the third-bestselling plant in the United States, with annual sales reaching about $148 million.

Often, biopiracy goes unnoticed because it takes place through the complex system of patents. Corporations can patent anything anywhere, and from that moment onward they own the trademark, regardless of the origin of the patented material. In 2004, the Dutch company Soil and Crop Improvements patented teff, a cereal from Ethiopia, and all the derivatives of its flower. Teff is the main staple grain of 80 million Ethiopians.

Cosmetics multinationals have skillfully registered many African enzymes, microorganisms, and fungi as their own new beauty products. The United States company Unigen, for example, patented *Aloe ferox* from South Africa, a plant used by its South Korean subsidiary to produce a whitening cream called Aloewhite.

But biopiracy's most terrifying bounty is our genes. "One fifth of the genes in our bodies are privately owned," wrote Michael Crichton in a 2007 editorial in the *International Herald Tribune*. Pathological genes, those related to major illnesses, which are fundamental to developing treatments, are also privately owned as is the case of influenza and hemophilia. People and companies trademark genes in their name and charge a fee each time that gene is used, including use in medical research. Patent fees, therefore, increase the cost of medical research and inflate the cost of treatment; "a test for breast cancer that could be done for $1,000 now costs $3,000," writes Michael Crichton.[16] Often less expensive tests are blocked by the patent holder, who will not grant permission to use the gene. This surreal situation sprang from a misinterpretation of the Supreme Court ruling by the United States Patent Office. Yet patent holders across the world, such as the owner of the gene for Hepatitis C, continue to receive millions from research labs around the world.

The patenting industry remains very complex and requires special skills. Once again, based on a Western idea, the system appears favorably biased toward Western notions of intellectual and commercial property. In October 2006, the US Patent and Trademark Office rejected two of three varieties of Ethiopian coffee beans that Addis Ababa wanted to trademark in the United States. The decision triggered a dispute between Starbucks, a member of the National Coffee Association of the USA, and Oxfam, a British charity. Oxfam supported the decision to trademark the beans, which would have brought Ethiopian growers an additional $88 million in foreign-exchange earnings. In fact, any company that wanted to use the Ethiopian original would have required a license, thus giving the producers a commercial asset that today they do not have. While Ethiopian beans fetch as little as 5 to 10 cents, specialty brands can get as much as 45 cents per pound. According to Oxfam, "the Ethiopian growers selling to Starbucks earned between 55 cents and $1.60 per pound on beans that Starbucks sold at $26 a pound."[17] To denounce these price discrepancies, the aid organization took out a full-page advertisement on the issue in the *New York Times* and in two newspapers in Seattle, Starbucks's hometown.

AVIATION SAFETY

In the early 1990s, corporations welcomed economic deregulation without fully understanding its wide-ranging implications. Few people foresaw that the very process that would theoretically boost companies' profits weakened legislation that protected trademark, patent, and intellectual properties. Even fewer people predicted that public aviation safety was going to suffer as a result because piracy in aviation spare parts would spread across the world, contaminating an industry, which until then had remained off-limits.

In 1989, Norwegian Convair 589 crashed, killing all fifty-five passengers. The investigation revealed that the low quality of crucial spare parts in the plane caused the tragedy. Plane components are subject to a rigid protocol; their entire life is documented by the manufacturer and by those who purchase them. "They are like people, they have an identity and a life history," explains a Boeing engineer.[18] But the market for bogus and uncertified parts now flourishes, and those who run it, aviation pirates, have become skillful marketeers.

The explosion of a Concorde jet in July 2000, while taking off from Paris, came indirectly from a bogus part, a twenty-centimeter metal strip separated from a US DC10, which had taken off in front of the Concorde. The flimsy strip, much lighter than the required one, flew right into the mechanism of the wheel of the Concorde, causing the tragedy.[19]

The trade in bogus airplane parts is a worrisome development. "More people die in plane crashes caused by faulty parts than perish in terrorist attacks, yet the trade in illegal parts is ignored by politicians," admits an American source on aviation who wants to remain anonymous.[20] The root causes of the racket go back to 1978, when the Carter administration launched the Airline Deregulation Act, shortly thereafter adopted by the Reagan administration. The aviation liberalization, one of the first timid steps of globalization, broke the rigid parameters that had regulated the industry until that time. Plane tickets and prices of parts were lowered, intermediaries appeared on the horizon, and in a very short time, some of them started to trade secondhand equipment at cut-rate prices. Outsourcing became rampant.

Aviation pirates move in a global network similar to the Chinese counterfeit industry. They run sweatshops that produce low-quality, low-cost spare parts, doing business with criminal gangs whenever convenient. On December 20, 1995, an American Airlines flight from Bogotá, Colombia, to Miami crashed against Mount San José. Local gangs immediately seized on the carcass and stripped it bare. A week later, a surge in the supply of plane components appeared on the Miami secondary market. American Airlines had published a list of all stolen parts, in the hope of preventing the resale, clearly to no avail.

Piracy is intertwined with the knockoff industry, which has flourished, thanks to the privatization and deregulation of the early 1990s. Formulated by Western banks and investors, privatization required the lowering of financial and economic barriers to facilitate Western investment. Indeed, Western capital became the main beneficiary, as illustrated, for example, by the sale of Telemex, Mexico's telephone company. In 1992, the World Bank admitted that consumers were the greatest losers in this process, because the privatization of Telemex ended up "taxing" them by making the service much more expensive and by distributing the gains among foreign share-holders, Telemex employees, and the government. By 1992, Mexicans had paid 92 trillion pesos (US$33 billion) more to access and use phone lines. "The government, domestic share-holders, and employees gained 16, 43, and 23.5 trillion pesos, respectively. The biggest winners by far were foreign investors, who gained 67 trillion pesos."[21]

Western corporations fall prey to rogue economics as well. Thanks to the revolutionary privatization and deregulation policies of the 1990s, they continually wage battle with the globalization outlaws that counterfeit their products and sell them globally at rock bottom prices. Against this scenario, the system of patents and trademarks does precious little to curb the industry of fakes. Geographic factors and cultural barriers both pose challenges to enforcement. Globalization outlaws counterfeit Western brands and sell them globally at a fraction of the price of the original. At the same time, that fractional price can be high relative to the cost of manufactures thanks to the aggressive marketing strategies of corporations and cartels as confirmed by the "Chinel No. 5" cargo. Paradoxically, Chanel No. 5 price policing inflates not only the price of the original but also that of the fake.

The counterfeit industry lies at the core of the market matrix, discussed in the following chapter, which carries the virus of rogue economics right into our homes. The market matrix is the offspring of a peculiar union between the fast-growing global economy, with its shadow of illegality and criminality, and weaker and weaker nation-states. The matrix feeds Western-style consumerism, offering consumers comfort, efficiency, lower prices, and readily available goods. At the same time, it hides the true nature of what we consume and what we believe, constantly blurring the boundaries between fact and fiction. Behind this web of commercial illusions there is a different reality shaped by the globalization outlaws. Rogue entrepreneurs feed the matrix, creating economic disorder at the margins of consumer society in the outposts of modern capitalism, where since the beginning of the 1990s, rogue economics has blossomed. But to unveil them and expose the dangers of a world ruled by capitalism's new reality, one must first of all understand the market matrix from which they have hatched.

CHAPTER SIX

THE MARKET MATRIX

"Salt: it probably kills more people
than tobacco."

Dr. James J. Kenney, Director of
Nutrition Research and Educator at
the Pritikin Longevity Center & Spa

At the beginning of July 2005, British authorities removed from the market 120,000 packages of Lipitor, a popular cholesterol-lowering medicine, used daily by millions of British citizens. After a lengthy investigation, it emerged that Pfizer, the pharmaceutical giant that owns the patent for the product, did not manufacture the packages dispensed in Britain; instead, the medicine came from a shipment of bogus Lipitor that had mysteriously reached the United Kingdom.

According to the World Health Organization (WHO), one in every ten pills is counterfeited and sold as the original. Fake medications generate $32 billion in profits and kill about half a million people every year.[1] Projections are that this market will increase exponentially, reaching $75 billion and over 1 million deaths by 2010.[2] Most of the victims come from developing countries, where counterfeit medicines are regularly consumed. In Nigeria, 8 out of 10 pills are fake, admits an employee of the WHO. The list of scandals grows daily and depicts a situation that is even gloomier than that contained in *The Constant Gardener*, John Le Carré's bestseller about the pharmaceutical industry's testing of new products in Africa. In 1995, for example, bogus vaccines against meningitis sold as the authentic GlaxoSmithKline product killed 2,500 African children. Recently, *Lancet*, the authoritative medical magazine, declared that 70 percent of antimalaria treatments in Africa do not have the required components. They serve as useless placebos, which do nothing for malaria patients.

By far the most popular and widely traded counterfeit pills in the West are intended to combat male erection problems: Viagra, Cialis, Levitra, and the like. Many of these are sold over the Internet, free of all regulation and government oversight. This is a highly profitable business. According to Eli Lilly, the producer of Prozac, for every $1,000 invested in criminal organizations, counterfeit currencies generate $3,300, heroin sales $20,000, cigarette smuggling $43,000, pirated software $40 to $100,000, and medications such as Viagra and Cialis $500,000.[3] Counterfeit erection pills net more money than does the heroin trade. This shocking fact explains why, from China to Chile, from South Africa to Iraq, thousands of factories produce bogus Viagra. After the fall of Baghdad, outlets for fake Viagra became among the first to be looted, since Iraq served as one of the largest suppliers in the Middle East. According to several sources, even Western journalists reporting the looting grabbed the odd handful of pills and stuffed them in their pockets.

A SNAPSHOT OF THE MARKET MATRIX

Most governments accuse China, which is considered the number-one supplier of bogus medicine, of being unable and unwilling to regulate the fake pharmaceutical industry within its borders. Indeed, China's drug-enforcement legislation proves ill equipped to deal with the magnitude and depth of the counterfeit industry. The Chinese government has a hard enough time keeping up with the growing international demand for Chinese products. However, in 2006, after several deaths in Panama, Beijing was forced to investigate the supply of diethylene glycol exported to Latin America as pure glycerine and sold as a sweetener for cough medicine and other over-the-counter remedies. Diethylene glycol is an industrial solvent used in antifreeze that tastes exactly like glycerine and costs much less. It is also a deadly poison. After the investigation, it became apparent that no Chinese laws had been broken by the suppliers of fake glycerine. This shocking discovery should not come as a surprise. Tough legislation on pharmaceutical and other potentially deadly products is always triggered by major tragedies. In the United States, for example, the creation of the modern Food and Drug Administration and the very tough regulations on pharmaceutical products were introduced only seventy years ago, ironically, after more than a hundred people died from medicines containing diethylene glycol. In 2006, the Lipitor scandal triggered a more tightly controlled distribution system inside the United Kingdom. The AIDS epidemic in Henan, however, reminds us that, for the time being, the social pressure of a large number of deaths caused by rogue medicine is unlikely to inspire legislation in China similar to that introduced in the United States.

In a global market, however, there are many other controls besides those imposed by an international FDA that could prevent bogus medicines from reaching the shelves of drug stores. The Chinese diethylene glycol shipment, which killed so many people in Panama, for example, had broken several laws while traveling through a commercial pipeline that stretched across three continents. "The *New York Times* traced this pipeline from the Panamanian port of Colon back through trading companies in Barcelona, Beijing, and to its beginning near the Yuntze Delta, in a place local people call 'chemical country.'"[4] Three major trading companies had handled the deadly syrup without testing it. The bills of lading, the commercial passport of goods, which port authorities and customs officers routinely inspect along the way, had been counterfeited several times to disguise the true origins of the shipment. Yet no port or custom authorities noticed or reported the forgery. Had this information become available, the traders who handled the shipment would have discovered that the Chinese manufacturer had no certification to produce pharmaceutical goods.

The case of the Chinese diethylene glycol well illustrates the dangers of the market matrix, which creates a global web of illusion. As in the cult film *The Matrix,* reality changes and is recreated by those living inside it; in other words, we, as producers and consumers of the global market, are the matrix. We point the finger of guilt at China, but that, too, represents an illusion sold by Western politicians and easily bought by consumers. If for a few seconds we could freeze the hectic trade that constitutes the heartbeat of the global market and take a snapshot of what goes on inside the market matrix, we would see the collective responsibilities of those involved in creating and believing in a world of commercial fantasies.

Western governments, which accepted the proposal of the United States to admit China to the World Trade Organization, are at the center of our picture. This decision took place at a time when major human-rights organizations had denounced the appalling human-rights record of the Beijing government. But their responsibility goes well beyond this. Though the media accuses China and Russia of supplying bogus medicine, to date no disciplinary measures or United Nations sanctions have been imposed on either of these nations; thanks to weak patent-protection legislation, Russia supplies about 30 percent of fake medicines worldwide. India and Brazil are also among the biggest global producers of fake medicine, yet no international retaliation has taken place. Industrialized countries remain uninterested in this rogue industry, because death by counterfeit medicine occurs primarily in the developing world. According to the International Medical Products Anti-counterfeiting Taskforce (IMPACT), an organization created by the WHO in 2006, the proportion of fake medicine circulating in the industrial world is rising, but it only amounts to about 1 percent, as compared with 70 percent counterfeit medicine sold in countries like Nigeria. Industrialized countries are more focused on blocking, within their borders, the Internet sales of "lifestyle" fake drugs, i.e. products such as Viagra, than stopping the global trade of bogus medicines.[5]

In the family snapshot of the market matrix, pharmaceutical companies stand next to developed countries. They often remain mute about fake medicines and avoid reporting bogus shipments, for fear of provoking panic and damaging their brand names. In addition, denouncing bogus products can prove very costly. In 2006, Pfizer replaced the fake shipment of Lipitor to the United Kingdom to clear its image. At the same time, many companies define counterfeit too broadly to protect their own products from competition from legal generic products. "Industry reports [show] that many fakes are instead low-priced, high volume, less conspicuous generic drugs."[6] Therefore, the system of patents is used to block the entry of legitimate manufacturers from the developing world. The oligopolistic, price-fixing nature of the global pharmaceutical industry keeps prices artificially high, as does the perfume cartel discussed in the previous chapter. This strategy creates the profit incentives that drive the counterfeit industry. According to a document released in 2007 by Buko Pharma, a German health-promoting group, price cuts and public health intervention could drastically reduce the size of the counterfeit problem.[7]

Trading companies and banks stand at the periphery of our picture. They, too, are part of the market matrix, as proven by the commercial journey of the cargo of bogus glycerine from China. If we look at the four corners of our snapshot, we discover other commercial interdependencies, and if we look more closely and blow up those sections of the photograph, other segments of the market matrix appear. In many cases, the alteration of reality and the construction of commercial illusions go well beyond the negligence or lack of ad hoc legislation; rather, they involve the survival of entire economies. These economic systems are plagued by an epidemic of rogue economics. The Democratic Republic of Congo (DRC) is one of them.

BLOOD GOLD

The phenomenon of blood diamonds from Africa is widely known because it has become the subject of a major Hollywood movie. But the chances that one of us will buy a blood diamond are much lower than the possibility of purchasing the much-less-known blood gold. A tight cartel runs the international diamond industry. This cartel does a good job preventing diamonds from countries ruled by warlords, such as Sierra Leone, from entering the world market. The cartel knows that in Sierra Leone the diamond industry uses children enslaved by armed organizations to mine diamonds, and rogue financiers to trade the gems. The gold industry, on the other hand, is totally unregulated and relies on trading companies scattered around the world. Gold refining rests in the hands of a small group of companies that does not exercise tight control over the origins of the gold they purchase from traders. As is the case of the commerce of blood diamonds, gold trade does not appear on the agenda of any government or international governmental organization.

DRC gold reserves are among the largest in the world, with most of the country's mines located in eastern Congo, a region that, since the official end of the civil war, has fallen into the hands of warlords and criminal gangs. To prevent these from trading the country's rich resources for arms and ammunition, in the 1990s the United Nations imposed one of the toughest arms embargoes in the world. Yet the embargo is regularly circumvented, thanks to the cooperation of foreign trading companies, banks, and gold traders. In 2005, for example,

AngloGold Ashanti, a South African company, part of the mine conglomerate Anglo-American, admitted to paying $9,000 to the warlords to obtain mining concessions from the Congolese government.[8] Since the 1990s, the company has been looking for new mines because South African gold production has begun to decrease. Congolese gold reaches our shores and is sold in jewelry shops thanks to the cooperation of rogue Ugandan trading companies. In 2005, United Nations inspectors discovered that South African, British, and Swiss refineries had purchased blood gold from Congo, sold as Ugandan gold, without verifying its origins.[9]

Those who know the gold trade are aware that until the mid-1990s, the central bank of Uganda did not even produce statistics on gold exports, because Uganda had never previously been an exporter. The entry of the country into the club of major global gold exporters coincided with the liberalization of trading in 1994. The government lifted all export duties, and from that moment on, gold from Congo ceased to be smuggled out of Kenya but found its way to Kampala, Uganda. In 2003, Uganda exported the equivalent of $60 million of gold.

Your wedding ring may be tainted with the blood of child soldiers, kidnapped and enslaved by Eastern Congo's warlords. This fact represents the uncomfortable truth hidden in the market matrix. If we follow the trail of blood gold, we discover a vast economy plagued by rogue economics and at the same time totally dependent on it for its own survival.

"Miners in East Congo sell their gold to *negociants*, small traders who constantly mingle in the mines," explains Rico Carish, a United Nations inspector for Congo. "The *negociants* bring the gold to Ituri, a major gold market controlled by the Congolese war lords. From Ituri, a fleet of smugglers carry the gold to Uganda. Smugglers work for a powerful joint venture. The partners are warlords, which control eastern Congo, Congolese merchants, and a group of trading companies based in Kampala."[10]

Among these trading companies is Manchaga, accused by the United Nations of being at the center of a complex system of rogue trade. Manchaga perpetrates commercial fraud: it exports gold on behalf of the Congolese warlords, but payment does not involve any exchange or transfer of money. Instead, the company receives a line of credit abroad in the form of a letter of credit from the buyer. Officially, the line of credit is used to import products into Uganda on behalf of one of Manchaga's clients. In 2004, for example, Manchaga bought candy and shoes from KenAfric, a company based in Nairobi, in exchange for the sale of Congolese smuggled gold. The purchase took place through a transaction from the banking account of Manchaga in Kampala to the banking account of KenAfric at City Bank in Nairobi. Once the goods arrived, they were smuggled into Congo. KenAfric and City Bank had no idea of either the real importer or the final destination of the sale. They also ignored that the money had been generated by the smuggling of gold from Congo. They had trusted Manchaga because they had done business with the company before.

Kampala trading companies play a pivotal role in breaking the United Nations embargo; they are essential to the illegal trade that enriches warlords. At the same time, however, the rogue economic system they sustain is the lifeline of the economy of an entire region. Smuggled gold provides sustenance for the entire population trapped in eastern Congo, explains Rico Carish. Without such trade, the population could not survive. The warlords act as governments in the region: they levy taxes and custom duties on all products that cross the border, and they provide employment to the population. Without them, millions of people would starve.

Unlike in the film *The Matrix*, the market matrix cannot be reprogrammed or destroyed so easily without affecting the livelihood of millions of people. This circumstance presents us with a serious challenge: how to contain, battle, and eventually defeat the epidemic bearing the lowest possible human cost, both inside the fragile developing economies and inside the industries contaminated by rogue economics.

THE CHALLENGE OF MODERN SLAVERY

Slavery is in our refrigerators. From fruit to beef, from sugar to coffee, slave labor brings food to our tables. "Miguel," a Mexican slave freed by the Coalition of Immokalee Workers, a US human-rights organization, may have harvested the apples we eat at breakfast. Miguel picked fruit under guard in the United States. He had traveled to *el norte* to earn the money to pay for treatment for his six-year-old son who has cancer; instead, his employer enslaved him.[11]

The cocoa we drink while reading the newspaper or watching the morning news shows may come from the Ivory Coast, which supplies half the world market. Children and adolescents from even poorer neighboring countries, such as Mali, trek all the way to the cocoa plantations to earn a subsistence salary. Often, they end up working as slaves in remote farms. "Nineteen-year-old Drissa was one such young man. When he was freed in 2000, he had just gone through a 'breaking-in' period as his master accustomed him to enslavement. His back was laced with scars and wounds from being whipped."[12]

Almost every product we consume has a hidden dark history, from slave labor to piracy, from counterfeit to fraud, from theft to money laundering. We know very little about these economic secrets because modern consumers live inside the market matrix.

The first thought that comes to mind when we discover that our hot chocolate comes directly from slave labor suggests that we boycott Ivory Coast cocoa. But this decision would not help free thousands of young slaves like Drissa. On the contrary, it could make their lives much worse and harm honest farmers as well. "Africa is like a body infested with parasites. One has to be careful not to kill the body to get rid of the parasites," summarized Rico Carish. Millions of people depend for their sustenance on this parasitic rogue economy. The alternative could impoverish them further, if it does not put them at risk of death.

Often, western intervention, even when willing and well intentioned, achieves very little. In the case of many African commodities, Western companies have no direct contact with farmers. Trade occurs through local intermediaries, middlemen, and shippers. The profits of slavery are collected at the farm gate, a practice that effectively incorporates them in the price of the product. Often the intermediaries do not even know or care that slave labor is involved in the production of the goods they trade. This explains why halting imports from the Ivory Coast will not end slavery but force thousands of honest farmers and their families into poverty. To eradicate the problem, one must attack the root causes, a task that only local governments can accomplish. But good governance also proves a rare commodity on the African continent.

Even more shocking is the discovery that in the twenty-first century, slavery is booming on a global scale. According to the United Nations, slavery is growing at an unprecedented rate. Figures put global slavery at 27 million persons, a generation of modern slaves that, according to the International Labor Organization, produces yearly profits of around $31 billion. Population explosion and great migrations coupled with globalization have boosted the slave trade. "The increase in slavery is linked to globalization," concurs Kevin Bales, author of *Ending Slavery: How We Will Free Today's Slaves*. "But this is not about sweat-shop workers existing on misery wages. Slaves are under the complete, violent control of another person; they are economically exploited and get only enough food and shelter to stay alive. For millions of victims, their experience differs little in hardship from that of slaves hundreds of years ago."[13]

Slavery's resurgence exerts a direct effect on its cost, which has now fallen for decades. Bates calculated that, while over the past 3,000 years the average price of a slave has ranged from $20,000 to $80,000 (adjusted to current dollar value) now people can be bought and sold for a tenth of these prices. After World War II, we witnessed a sudden surge in the supply of slave labor, pushing prices down. Ironically, this phenomenon began as a consequence of decolonization, which shifted slave ownership from colonizers to countrymen. Today's slaves are predominantly enslaved by their national peers and not by foreign powers. Like other commodity markets, slavery operates by the law of supply and demand, and today supply proves plentiful among the millions living on a dollar to two dollars a day.

Consumers remain blissfully ignorant of these facts. The market matrix, a complex maze of smoke and mirrors, hides the exploitative nature of trade and commerce. The shelves of Western supermarkets are stacked with items produced by people in developing countries who earn a miniscule fraction of their value. Consumers, if they ever chose to think about it, might be shocked to learn who pockets most of the profits of their daily grocery shopping.

LOST IN THE SUPERMARKET

Bananas are the single most profitable item sold by British supermarkets,[14] and the banana profits are split in the following way: almost half goes to the supermarket (45 percent), importers pocket 18 percent, the plantation company garners 15.5 percent, and the workers receive 2.5 percent.

Since 2002, supermarkets in the United Kingdom have engaged in a fierce banana-price war, slashing prices to gain a larger sector of the market. Tesco and Asda, grocery chains owned by the American giant Wal-Mart, have been at the front lines of this battle. Prices have gone from £1.08 in 2002 to 74 pence per kilo in 2004. Price reductions, however, have not affected the share of profits pocketed by the supermarkets because they have been offset by cuts in plantation workers' wages.

Action Aid,[15] a charity that monitors working conditions in developing countries, suggests that the impact of the banana price war fought in the United Kingdom has halved hourly wages of plantation workers in Costa Rica, which supplies one out of every four bananas consumed in the United Kingdom and Ireland. Workers now earn 33 pence an hour and are under such pressure to produce that they cannot afford to take time off when planes spray pesticides on the crops.

Supermarket shelves are also stocked with products owned by the tobacco industry, which, over the last two decades, has invested its huge revenues in the food industry. A London public-relations agent for this industry, who for obvious reasons asked to remain anonymous, summarizes the extraordinary growth of the industry since the fall of the Berlin Wall:

> Western anti-smoking campaigns have failed to reduce global tobacco consumption. The notion that people today smoke less than twenty years ago is an illusion. On the contrary, since the beginning of the 1990s Western tobacco multinationals have become richer than oil companies, because cigarettes are the ultimate 'consumer' product; while oil consumption is functional, cigarette consumption is determined by need and desire. You cannot beat it!
>
> We run historical comparisons between the growth in global consumption of oil and cigarettes and we have discovered that the latter is growing faster than the former. The extraordinary surge in Western

tobacco manufacturers' sales comes from tobacco multinationals' penetration of the Eastern European and Asian markets. Winston, for example, is the top-selling cigarette in Russia. Now these markets were off limits during the Soviet regime. In recent years growth has been exceptional, mostly because of the younger generation and the Chinese market. From 2003 to 2005, for example, Philip Morris' total sales went from 40 to 70 billion cigarettes, thanks to the Eastern European and Asian market.

In 2005 Philip Morris, whose best selling brand is Marlboro, made $4.6 billion profits in the USA and $7.8 billion internationally, higher than small countries' GDPs. Basic quantitative economic principles explain this phenomenon. The Asian population is so much greater than the Western population that a 30 percent decline in cigarette consumption in the West can be offset by as little as a 2 percent increase in the Asian market. Those who understood this concept have made billions. Japanese Tobacco International, for example, which owns the rights to sell several Western brands of cigarettes outside the West, is one of the fastest growing companies in the world.[16]

Since the dissolution of Communism in Central and Eastern Europe, the tobacco industry has cleverly hidden the extraordinary profits generated by the surge in the global demand for cigarettes from Western consumers. For example, in 2005 the Altria Group, a holding company based in New York, had become the tenth-most-profitable corporation in America. "It used to be called Philip Morris, a name that is still attached to two of its holdings, Philip Morris USA and Philip Morris International. The company also owns Kraft Foods."[17]

Had cigarettes been banned outright in the West, goverments would have outlawed one of the most profitable global industries. "This could have easily happened in the late 1990s in the US, when several lawsuits were launched and pressure from anti-cancer groups and other lobbies was mounting threatening the very survival of the American tobacco industry," notes the London public-relations agent. Dr. James J. Kenney, Director of Nutrition Research and Educator at the Pritikin Longevity Center & Spa in Florida, adds that since the Food and Drug Administration regulates foods and drugs, it should also deal with tobacco, which contains nicotine. "Yet, the FDA does not. Why? Because if the FDA were to regulate tobacco, it would have to ban it!"[18]

The London public-relations agent explains how the tobacco industry survived: "Back in the late 1990s, secret negotiations took place at very high levels to make sure a compromise was reached between the government and the industry. The latter agreed to several conditions, among which [was] to pay over $350 billion in twenty-five years to the American states, some of the money was going to promote anti-smoking campaigns. But the industry knew that such campaigns would not harm its main market: Eastern Europe and Asia. No matter how big the warning 'Smoking Kills,' people will continue to smoke." Today, one in every two long-term smokers will die of lung cancer, heart disease, or other tobacco-related illnesses. The percentage of street-drug users who die from an overdose is much lower, yet tobacco is legal, and street drugs are forbidden.

While tobacco manufacturers profit from our trips to buy Kraft cheese at the grocery store, the maze of smoke and mirrors of the market matrix hide even darker secrets: food that kills.

FOOD ILLUSIONS

When I was a child, my grandmother used to tell me stories about World Wars I and II. Inevitably, her memories all ended with the same conclusion: "We were less hungry during the Great War [World War I], because we lived on a farm." For my grandmother's generation, hunger was a reality and people died from it; illnesses, such as tuberculosis and anemia, destroyed underfed and undernourished bodies. Food was a luxury everywhere, even after World War II ended. In the United Kingdom, for example, sugar rationing was not lifted until the early 1950s. Today, my grandmother's memories seem a thousand years removed from our world, yet they are only a couple of generations in the past. Ironically, today Europeans face the opposite problem: they eat too much and die of food-related problems, such as heart disease and diabetes.

In the United States, the situation looks even worse. A new killer, obesity, has overtaken tobacco as the number-one cause of preventable death. About 400,000 fatalities per year, 16 percent of all United States deaths, are due to obesity. According to the US Surgeon General and the Centers for Disease Control (CDC), about two-thirds of Americans are overweight all their lives. Ironically, the obesity epidemic began in the late 1970s, when Americans became weight-conscious.

From the late 1970s to 2006, the incidence of obesity jumped from 12 percent to 25 percent; today, a quarter of Americans are obese. Two major changes took place during this period: the use of high-fructose corn syrup as the primary caloric sweetener and the "battle of the bulge." Corn sweeteners are cheaper than sucrose and in the United States, corn remains both highly produced and heavily subsidized. The food industry's use of corn sweeteners lowered production costs, which in turn reduced the price of food, encouraging people to consume more.

In the late 1970s, the battle against fat marked the advent of low-fat diets. Fat was systematically removed from food items, and replaced with carbohydrates, which are high in calories and also produce fat. "Farmers have known for thousands of years that you can make animals fat by feeding them grains, as long as you don't let them run around too much. It turns out that applies to humans."[19] Most of the low-fat food found in supermarkets is saturated with carbohydrates, to the extent that the caloric intake of the low-fat version of most food items equals the caloric intake of the replaced product. "The best example is the Snackwell phenomenon," explains Marion Nestle, chair of New York University's Department of Nutrition, Food Studies, and Public Health.[20] "Snackwell cookies were advertised as no-fat cookies, but they had almost the same number of calories. And in fact, if you go to the store today and look at Oreo cookies, they have a reduced-fat Oreo cookie that has, I think, six calories less than the regular Oreo cookie. It's lower in fat, but it's higher in carbohydrates." Next time you shop, compare the number of calories in the non-fat and normal versions of the same product. You will be amazed at the negligible difference, if any, between the numbers.

In the 1980s and 1990s, Americans "mysteriously" grew fatter, even as the percentage of fat in their diets dropped from 40 percent to 34 percent. One can finally debunk this myth. They gained weight because they ate more and their intake of carbohydrates had risen. The consequences of the low-fat market illusion are serious. "In the 1970s, there were 5 million Americans with diabetes. Today, there are over 20 million. The population hasn't quite doubled during that time. But the number of people with diabetes has more than quadrupled," explains Dr. James J. Kenney.

Even more shocking is the fact that Type 2 diabetes, which used to be called adult-onset diabetes, has become prominent in overweight children. Doctors are convinced that this disease is linked to the rise in obesity among children. "In the United States, the prevalence of overweight and obesity among 6- to 19-year-olds was 31 percent and 16 percent, respectively, in 2001–2002. This compares to 5 percent obesity prevalence in 1965," explains Valerio Nobili, pediatrician expert in liver diseases at the Bambin Gesù Hospital in Rome.[21]

Obesity causes what many liver specialists define as the new liver epidemic among children, the extraordinary surge in non-alcoholic fatty liver diseases (NAFLD). "There is a very strong correlation between NAFLD and increased body mass index in very young people. The reported prevalence of NAFLD among children is 2.6 percent, but among obese children it is 53 percent," reveals Nobili. "Over the last four decades, obesity among toddlers has increased dramatically. The rise among preschool children is especially worrying in American children, but the same high prevalence has also been reported in England, Australia, and Europe. Current estimates put the number of obese children at more than 20 million worldwide. Because children are getting fatter and fatter, NAFLD is expected to become one of the most common causes of end-stage liver disease in both children and young adults."

People are also under the illusion that certain foods regarded as low- or no-fat remain good for them. Canned soups are a prime example. "If you are trying to lose weight, soups don't have many calories, nor fat or sugar. But they have a lot of salt. In fact, most canned soups have as much salt as sea water," says a United States doctor, a specialist in nutrition, who asked to remain anonymous.[22] "If you want to get high blood pressure, you eat soups. They are basically salt water with some refined noodles or white rice thrown in and a token amount of meat flavouring, mostly, and smattering of tiny little chunks of vegetables. The percentage of healthy food in it is negligible. There is no way you can justify eating that soup."

According to Doctor Kenney, salt, sugar, and fat are the "matrix agents" of the food industry today. "They are dangerous for your health because they cause high blood pressure, cholesterol, diabetes, etc., but they make things taste good, which is the number one priority for the majority of people. And the food industry has found ways to counterattack research that shows how dangerous these elements are." Campbell's, for example, founded the Salt Institute, which advises people about whether or not salt is really bad.[23] But salt *is* bad, there is no question about it. "Salt kills, around the world, more people than tobacco," says Doctor Kenney. "Almost everyone eats too much salt, and not everyone smokes; 90 percent of the people in Europe and America develop high blood pressure at a certain point. People don't need salt added to their food. If you look at animals or even at those who live a hunter-gatherer lifestyle, they don't eat salt and do not get high blood pressure."

People are also under the wrong impression that modern medicine can protect them from a major killer, such as heart disease. "One example is angioplasty, whereby they keep your arteries from reclogging," says Doctor Kenney. "Everybody thought angioplasty was great, and millions of these operations are performed in the United States every year. But recent research shows that there is no difference between those who have and those who have not had the operation, which means that the former are not less likely to die of heart attack. Yet doctors convince people that after the operation, they are cured, and in doing so they give them a mere illusion. This is the American model: you get people sick with food they love to eat, and then you treat them with drugs and eventually surgery. All of that is very good for the Gross National Product, because a lot of companies are making money."

Illusions are rife in the modern consumer world we inhabit. The market matrix has penetrated our daily lives so deeply that economic fantasies can enslave, rule, and ultimately put an end to our lives. From morning to night we move in a world where little is real and not everything is what we think it is.

Contrary to what many believe, globalization and the rise of corporations are not at the root of the market matrix.

More often then not, companies as well as consumers are trapped inside it, as proven by the bogus Lipitor sold in the United Kingdom. The market matrix is the product of something infinitely more powerful: rogue economics.

At the same time, the matrix is a unique, potent vector of rogue contamination. Never before has such a powerful tool been of service to the sinister forces of economics. As in the film *The Matrix*, cyberspace today is where most of the commercial illusions are manufactured, traded, re-created, and yes, marketed. The cyberuniverse is also where the collective responsibility of consumers in the construction and maintenance of the market matrix becomes apparent. To date, the synthetic worlds remain rogue economics' strongest, most developed economic colonies.

CHAPTER SEVEN

HIGH TECH: A MIXED BLESSING?

> "The first business on the Internet is
> pornography, the second is gambling,
> the third is child pornography. There
> is no doubt about that."
>
> Ivan, an Italian e-gold currency
> exchanger

At the age of fifteen, XXX[1] spends ten to twelve hours in front of a screen, battling the cybermonsters of online video games. He is a Chinese gold farmer, and gold coins are his precious harvest. Gold coins are the means of exchange used in "gamedom," the play currencies of the kingdom of massively multiplayer online games (MMOs), such as EverQuest and World of Warcraft.[2] To access this virtual war zone, would-be players must pay an annual subscription that allows their avatars, virtual warriors, to venture into cyberlandscapes where they fight fantastical battles. Players move from one conflict to the next in increasingly challenging and never-ending higher levels of virtual warfare.

To purchase the equipment that is indispensable to stay in the game—weapons, armor, war machines, and fighting maneuvers—the over 100 million subscribers who every month log on to gamedom need gold coins. Earning play currencies, however, requires ability and time, and most players remain unskilled and have very little time. But because the majority of players have become addicted to the game and will do anything to win, they use the secondary market to purchase gold coins from gold farmers. "When players get stuck in a valley for weeks, battling the same monsters, it can be very frustrating. All they need to move on is a new weapon, a new war trick, so it is understandable that they are willing to pay real money for it," explains XXX. Frustrated players trade everything to get ahead in the game. "Someone emailed me: 'Hey, I don't have any money, but I want to buy a lot of gold from you. I was engaged and I have this awesome ring. It is worth $2,000. Would you like to trade it for gold?' I am like, hmm . . . Let me see . . . The gold [coins] takes me two second to make. I had the ring appraised. It was real," admits another gold farmer.[3]

Addiction often becomes the consequence of the booming secondary market for gold coins, because gamedom's players crave MMOs. Gamedom players share many similarities with compulsive gamblers. "The same reward center in the brain is tapped, the dopamine system. Gambling has all the components that go with these games."[4] Smith & Jones, an addiction consultancy based in the Netherlands, even cures MMO withdrawal with techniques pioneered in the treatment of drug addiction, because game abstinence exhibits many of the characteristics of withdrawal from chemical dependence.

Gold farmers, such as XXX, have become part and parcel of a booming illegal industry. Online video-game companies prohibit the sale of play currencies, as they clearly state in their users' agreements. Gold farmers are professional players, and gamedom means to entertain amateurs. The secondary market inflates the virtual price of gaming equipment and forces online video companies to continually introduce new, more sophisticated virtual warfare landscapes, in other words, to expand the gamedom universe more quickly than anticipated. "We help people to reach the top level, currently level 70," explains XXX. "When they get there, they want something new, more challenging."

Gold farmers don't really want to help gamers as much as they want to make money. Gold farming is a very profitable enterprise because recently the popularity and sales of gamedom have increased exponentially. DFC Intelligence, a San Diego research center of online games, calculated that in 2005 online gaming generated $3.4 billion, with over 12 million players in the United States; by 2011 the company estimates that the business will gross revenues of $13 billion.[5]

In this context, farming gold coins presents great business opportunities. In 2006, for example, Smooth Criminal's game cartel, a network of Chinese and Indonesian online sweatshops owned by a thirty-year-old Chinese programmer, netted $1.5 million by duping (winning battles in) Star Wars Galaxies.[6]

But the secondary market also proves highly exploitative, overrun with people and companies that profit from cheap labor in Asia and Eastern Europe. Once again, China is the epicenter of the black market in play currencies. Sitting in old airport hangars or abandoned warehouses, an army of Chinese spend their lives inside online sweatshops harvesting gold. XXX works in one of them. He earns $200 dollars a month because of his skills, but gold farmers' salaries can often dip as low as 25 cents per hour. Competition is tough, especially in China, where farmers remain professional, cheap, and plentiful, and the industry benefits from the central government's *laissez-faire* policy toward any type of business.

Preventing this illegal trade has become an impossible task. The secondary market operates in the virtual world, an unregulated universe where secrecy comes with the territory. Video-game sweatshops conceal their identities, hire hackers to help them avoid the authorities and "create automatic keys to bolster winnings."[7] Despite harsh penalties and the termination of thousands of accounts by online game companies, the black market continues to boom. In 2006, when Sony decided to launch its own secondary market exchange to curb the growth of the illegal one, it recorded more than 180,000 transactions in less than a month.

Demand for gold coins to purchase new equipment on the secondary market is constantly rising as new players join gamedom. In November 2004, when Blizzard launched World of Warcraft, it sold 250,000 subscriptions, causing the server to collapse; by 2006, the game had 8 million subscribers. Demand for equipment also gets a boost from older players who move on to more challenging levels, often with the help of gold farmers. Sales in video-game equipment, which ranges from armor to war machines, exceeds $1 billion annually, a figure that, according to experts, will soon quadruple as frustrated players spend more and more money on war accessories. "When you have [built] a huge town or castle, it literally requires hundreds of millions in gold coins each week [to keep it going]."[8]

Access to the illegal secondary market is easy; from eBay to underground websites, gold coins and equipment are on offer everywhere. According to Edward Castronova, associate professor of telecommunications at Indiana University, legitimate auction sites, such as eBay, "host $30 million annually in trade for goods that exist only in synthetic worlds—magic wands, play currency, spaceships, armor—making it the biggest foreign exchange market for synthetic money [in the world]."[9] There are even companies, like the Shanghai-based Ucdao.com, that provide customized services for those addicted to gamedom, matching clients' demands to purchase specific war accessories with professional players specializing in such games.

ONLINE PIRACY

China is the single biggest market for online gaming. Recent estimates from the Chinese government set the number of video-game users at 24 million; about one in four Chinese Internet users is a player.[10] China is also the epicenter of online and software piracy. Along Thieves Alley, for example, shops sell cut-rate copies of all types of software, often ahead of announced release dates. Rule of Rose, a Sony PlayStation game, for example, became available in many shops before November 2007, its official release date. The game was not sold in the United States because of "alleged overtones of lesbianism and sadomasochism."[11] The player's avatar is a teenage girl who is repeatedly beaten and humiliated as she tries to break out of an orphanage. "She is bound, gagged, doused with liquids, buried alive and thrown into the 'Filth Room.'"[12] US buyers, however, circumvented Sony's decision and purchased Rule of Rose on the Internet from Chinese suppliers.

Chinese software pirates boast that they have cornered the global software black market. A huge business, computer games' annual revenues now reach higher than online games' earnings; in 2006, they were $17 billion. Market experts expect the US market, which is the world's largest, to double by 2008, reaching $15 billion.

Thieves Alley thrives as the capital of the global kingdom of pirated virtual products. For a few hundred dollars, virtually anything will be duplicated, including serial numbers. Programmers point out that the biggest pirate remains the Chinese government, which not only buys products from Thieves Alley but also copies everything from computer frameworks to warheads.[13]

China's pathological recycling activity, its indifference toward intellectual property, is the cultural foundation of key infrastructures used by Chinese rogue entrepreneurs in synthetic goods. Chinese society welcomes high-tech counterfeit as a major leap forward toward modernization. Laundering dirty electronic profits has become one of these advances. Smooth Criminal, for example, is a master in laundering illegally harvested gold coins. He uses three accounts: a fake account, a filter account, and a delivery account. Each account is created with a different IP (Internet Protocols) address—which is a sort of online identification number, comprising four double-digit numbers—separate credit cards, and computers.[14] Once the operation finishes, the coins are clean, and they appear to have been collected by a legitimate player using a registered account.

Play currencies then get sold to a wholesaler, such as IGE, Internet Gaming Entertainment, which is entitled to trade them in the secondary market.[15] The volume of the illegal business has grown so vast and the laundering techniques are so advanced that wholesalers find it impossible to verify the origin of the coins. They are at the mercy of illegal traders. Wholesalers purchase play currencies with electronic currencies (e-currencies). Without them, cyberspace could not function.

ELECTRONIC CURRENCIES

In the cyberuniverse, though the worlds are synthetic, the economies are real. Money serves as a means of exchange, and its value reflects "the underlying conditions of choice under scarcity that monetary accounting allows us to measure."[16] Cyberspace is ruled by the law of supply and demand, which quantifies prices exactly as happens in the real world, with those prices expressed in electronic currencies. These virtual monies have a real value because traders can exchange them at any given time for real-world currencies.

At the outset of the Internet era, e-currencies sprang from the needs of the pornography and online gambling industries. Essentially, they exploited the principle of "freelosophy," or free access to the Internet, to circumvent the laws of the real world.

"There is a code number that is read by credit cards every time a transaction takes place. The one in restaurants is 321, at petrol stations it's 496. Online casinos have their own code, which is 777. If you try to complete a transaction, let's say in the US, with that code, Visa or MasterCard will automatically block it, alert the authorities, and within minutes a bunch of policemen will be knocking at your door," explains Ivan, an

Italian electronic-currency dealer. "E-currencies were created to avoid this problem because they are untraceable. The way they work is simple. You open an online account and load it with e-currencies using your credit card. The most popular e-currencies are PayPal, Neteller and E-Gold."

Electronic currencies are the product of globalization and new technology. Peter Theil, a former American securities lawyer and options trader, founded PayPal in late 1998. He and a group of friends from Stanford University set up Confinity, PayPal's holding company. Peter Theil then financed Max Levchin, a software developer who saw the need for a secure software system that allowed electronic transfer of payments. Other investors rapidly showed interest, including Nokia Ventures, which put up $3 million, and Deutsche Bank, which contributed another $1.5 million. Following its launch in November 1999, Confinity attracted more backers, including the investment bank Goldman Sachs, which invested $23 million in Confinity's PayPal.com. With the rapid expansion of the Internet, PayPal soon had 1.5 million account holders generating a turnover of $2 million per day. According to several e-currency dealers, PayPal's remarkable growth came mostly from people who used them to purchase pornography and gambling credits.

The rapid success led to eBay's naming PayPal.com its primary online payment service. EBay also attempted to prevent illegal transactions on its site through PayPal. Account holders' credit cards and identity information were required and stored in a secure data bank. Soon PayPal merged with X.com, an online bank founded by Elon Musk, to become the world's largest secure online payment network. The name PayPal remained, although X.com was listed as the parent company. In early 2002, PayPal floated on the stock market for around $900 million. By July 2002, PayPal account holders numbered 16 million, with 295,000 payment transactions taking place every day. In October 2002, eBay acquired PayPal for $1.5 billion.[17] At the end of 2006, PayPal had about 100 million account holders worldwide and was available in 103 countries.[18]

Unlike PayPal, e-gold allows account holders to maintain their anonymity. "You could run your account with any name and address," confirms Ivan. E-gold is a digital gold currency issued by e-gold Ltd, a company incorporated in Nevis, Lesser Antilles, an offshore facility. First created in 1996 by Douglas Jackson, a former medical doctor, and Barry K. Downey, a lawyer, it allows the instant transfer of gold between its users. As the company states: "e-gold is integrated into an account-based payment system that empowers people to use gold as money. The e-gold payment system enables people to send specified weights of gold to other e-gold accounts. Only the ownership changes while the gold in the treasury grade vault stays put."[19]

The difference between PayPal and e-gold is that the latter is attractive to users who want to remain anonymous. "No one verifies your personal details. What you get is a 100 percent anonymous bank account. To load your balance you do not need a credit card, as with PayPal. What you need is to contact one of the ten to fifteen e-gold exchangers," explains Ivan. "I am one of them. So, once you've registered, you contact me and ask me to load your balance. Yet, since I know how many scammers there are out there, I check all their personal details. When Nigerians and Ukrainians contact me, I usually say no. Unfortunately for them, most of the scams come from their countries. Once I have verified the personal details, I have a policy by which I investigate the reason why that person would want to open an e-gold account. If their motivation does not convince me, if they are evasive, I will not load the account. If a German or a Belgian customer contacts me to open an account, I just say no right away. I know from experience that they usually want to access child-pornography websites. Once I've checked your personal details, you can send me the money you want to load via Western Union or bank transfer, and I will take 15 percent of the amount you will deposit each time. Yet, every time you will want to do a transaction, say, to a programmer in Pakistan, it will just take few seconds and only 50 cents."

E-currencies are widely used by online gamblers. Thousands of Americans illegally gamble their savings on 888.com or Intercasino, playing from their homes and offices using electronic accounts. 888.com is the biggest Internet casino in the world, again located offshore, where the bulk of online gambling takes place. "Online gambling in many American states is illegal, but everybody does it because the servers are offshore. Central America and the Caribbean Islands, places such as Costa Rica, Panama, St. Kitts & Nevis, are popular places for online casinos. Taxes are low, as little as $50,000 per year, plus a small percentage of the annual revenues. Online casinos are all operated by local servers that are owned by local companies. Often behind these companies there are big European telecommunications corporations, which use them as screen companies. Internet casinos are also located in several countries of the former Soviet Bloc where you don't even need a license. You can open one with as little as $100,000. It can be a very good business," admitted a Romanian e-currency dealer.[20]

Anurag Dikshit, one of the world's youngest online billionaires, cofounded PartyGaming, which is host to one of the world's most popular online poker sites. In his mid-thirties, Dikshit is worth almost $4 billion. In 1998, Mr. Dikshit went into business with a Californian, Ruth Parasol, who, after selling her online pornography business, decided to invest in online gambling. Dikshit joined her as a partner in PartyGaming. A pioneer of online gambling, Ms. Parasol predicted correctly that this activity would soon be booming. In 2001, PartyGaming successfully floated on the London Stock Exchange. At any given time, more than 70,000 people gamble on its online system.[21]

The virtual universe has no laws because it has no boundaries. PartyGaming and Intercasino, for example, operate from Gibraltar; US authorities cannot go after them when American citizens gamble on these sites. Investing in unregulated gambling also remains illegal in the United States yet both companies are floated on the London Stock Exchange, and investors, including Americans, have bought their stocks. Thus, in cyberspace, rogue entrepreneurs can easily circumvent the laws of one country, such as the US government's prohibition against gambling online, by taking advantage of the legislation in another, such as the permissive gambling legislation in the United Kingdom.

Electronic currencies also gain entry into tax havens. Escapeartist.com, basically a directory on how to avoid taxes in the United States, became very popular among wealthy Americans because, unlike Europeans, Americans are taxed on global income. Offering electronic accounts in e-currencies, the website's motto reads, "Escape from America":

Knowing that an economic haven exists is only part of the equation, one must also know what protection and opportunity that jurisdiction provides. All tax havens are not created equal. As the Internet continues to grow along with the opportunities that eCommerce provide, more and more freethinking individuals will use eCommerce as a path to economic freedom from governmental restraints. If your domain is from Bermuda, your corporation Anguillan, and your website is housed in Panama with a Panamanian merchant service and shipping from the Dominican Republic, who are they going to tax? The essential characteristic of Western civilization is its concern for freedom from the state. As this freedom erodes in America, creative thinkers turn elsewhere.[22]

INTERNET PORNOGRAPHY

Internet pornography has become the single most profitable electronic offshore business. Pornography entrepreneurs pioneered the web by fully exploiting offshore opportunities. Until recently, an oil rig on Havenco Island, in the Channel Islands, hosted one of the biggest servers for online pornography and gambling, reveals Ivan. Servers also operate from countries where organized crime exercises a strong influence, e.g. the former Soviet Bloc. "The biggest pedo-pornographic servers are located in Russia and are managed by the Russian Mafia. They have directories of images and videos which are showed in many porn-sites across the world and are constantly exchanged. Clients are predominantly from Germany and Belgium," adds an Italian e-currency dealer who asked to remain anonymous. "I know it because they come to me to load their electronic currencies."[23]

The porn industry also influenced Internet advertising. Pop-ups were originally introduced by pornography sites to display images to Internet users. Even video technology was pioneered on the Web to promote pornography. Thus, the rogue use of technology, because of its high profit margins, has often become the most innovative driving force in cyberspace. Google and YouTube could be said to have their roots in the online pornography industry, since that is where many of the tools on which they have built their empires originated. Both Internet ads and fast-streaming videos, the mainstays of those two companies, were hallmarks of the Internet porn industry.

Today, Internet pornography boasts one of the fastest-growing industries in the world and by far the biggest electronic rogue business. According to Jerry Ropelato, an analyst for Internet Pornography Statistics, "yearly Internet porn revenue [in 2005] was $57 billion, larger than combined revenues of all professional football, baseball, and basketball franchises [in the United States]. U.S. porn revenue exceeds the combined revenues of ABC, CBS, and NBC ($6.2 billion). Child pornography generates $3 billion annually."[24]

The advent of the Internet opened new commercial avenues for the porn industry. "Those who want to invest in this industry must think in 360 degrees. You need to consider all possible marketing channels from TV to mobile phones. Any production company requires a good Internet site, otherwise you are not competitive," explains Corrado Fumagalli, presenter of the Italian talk show *Sexy Bar*. "Today we have Internet and videophones, marketing channels and many online TVs, the porn demand is enormous and so are the revenues." Traditional media companies cannot afford to ignore such a phenomenon. "My channel Play TV, for example, is distributed by SKY and it is the one with the highest rating. One million people watch my program, which has a monthly turnover of 200,000 euros."[25]

The Internet also serves as a test site for the innovations of the porn industry. According to Oliver Buzz, a porn director, the newest porn products show women enjoying the sex and actively participating in it while they are being gang raped. But the best-selling videos are "reality" movies showing either housewives having sex with porn actors or simply sex between normal couples. "Sometimes reality surpasses fiction. Once I filmed a couple who enjoyed extreme sex; he reached orgasm only when she urinated in his mouth. I filmed it all, and it was a hit," says Buzz, who sells his films only on online TV "because the Internet is where the action takes place."[26]

New technology revolutionized the porn industry, making it more accessible to the masses. "In the old days porno videos were very expensive, people had to shoot them using 16 mm film. Until six years ago the cost of a medium length film was 35–40,000 euros. The advent of the digital era has seriously lowered costs and today the same film can be produced for half the money," explains Silvio Bandinelli, one of the best-known Italian porn directors. "People do not need to have technical knowledge to use digital cameras. This explains why porn actors, who are the working class of the business, are now producing and directing films. Naturally, high tech has damaged directors like me, professionals of the porn industry, but I belong to the extreme left and I am happy that there is more competition. The real problem is amateur videos and sites such as e-Mule where you can exchange and download everything, including homemade porn material. But I should not complain, I also download music from the Internet."[27]

The Internet revolution in pornography took off because the Internet came at a crucial point in time, when pornography had already been liberalized, explains Luciano Mantelli, a pornography historian and editor of the Italian paper *La Mela di Eva*. "The battle to make pornography acceptable was fought in the 1960s and 1970s by porn magazines, mostly in Italy. In 1966, the Italian publisher Saro Balsamo launched the magazine *Men*, which showed women in bikinis. The magazine was very successful and created a buzz. Police confiscated the first seven issues from newstands on the grounds of obscenity. Balsamo circumvented the law by post-dating the next issues, so that by the time the court order was ready, the newstands had sold out of the magazine, and the issue on display carried a different date and required a new court order. Other magazines used the same strategy. In 1971, publishers in the same class as Balsamo launched what became known as the "battle of the tits," because their periodicals featured topless women. Court orders were issued but never really enforced. By 1973, magazines started to show penetration. *OS* was the first truly pornographic magazine in the world. It had photos of copulation between two people, with a black spot to hide the act. Issue after issue, the spot became smaller and smaller, until it disappeared altogether.

"Toward the end of the 1970s *Ora Verità* was launched. It was the first daily porno newspaper and had a circulation of

180,000 copies. In the 1980s celebrities began taking off their clothes and pornography became readily available. Successful porno magazines reached a circulation of 350,000 copies. Sales, however, began to decrease with the advent of the Internet. The porno industry moved to the Internet which can be accessed by everybody, including children. Today we are witnessing another decline in porno magazines' sales due to home videos and piracy."[28]

Because cyberspace operates in lawless space, e-piracy has become widespread. In 2006, for example, movie piracy cost Hollywood's big studios almost $8 billion, twice the amount the industry had previously anticipated. According to a study commissioned by the United States film industry's lobbying group, the Motion Picture Association of America, $3.1 billion of the $8 billion in losses resulted from bootlegging, $1.82 billion was due to illegal copying, and $2.99 billion was lost to Internet piracy.[29] The leading countries for movie piracy are China, Russia, Britain, France, Spain, Brazil, Italy, Poland, and Mexico. As a result of piracy, the movie industry faces a potential loss of 93 percent of its market in China, 62 percent in Thailand, 51 percent in Taiwan, and 29 percent in India.

The laws of the real world do not have any meaning in cyberspace because, first and foremost, they cannot be enforced. Territoriality is paramount for law enforcement. It defines the boundaries of legal jurisdiction, whereas cyberspace's very definition defies borders and boundaries. While servers must exist and operate in the real world, they nonetheless escape the long arm of the law by moving offshore.

Operating at the fringes of legality, rogue Internet entrepreneurs, such as Smooth Criminal, as well as online gambling tycoons, represent the newest breed of globalization outlaw. Yet, attributing their success solely to new technology and offshore servers does not fully explain their path to riches. Just like the pimps of globalization, rogue Internet entrepreneurs have taken advantage of new economic opportunities arising from major transformations. By anticipating and satisfying the demand of their customers, they have constructed new markets. These are the outpost of the market matrix, where consumers have the opportunity to live their darker fantasies, while Slavic women fulfill most men's erotic desires and are just another way to flee the bleakness of everyday life. Equally, rogue economics cybercolonies enable consumers to fantasize and escape reality and the desire to escape grows stronger every day. The willingness to step out of the real world blinds consumers to the dangers of rogue economics.

The popularity of online video games rests on the possibility of stepping into a new reality. They catapult people into a fantasy world, where the players can assume new identities and live different lives. As summarized by Splint, a former online-video-game addict: "When you're a retail jockey, you're nobody. When you're 'Captain Purple' with the best gear around, you're looked up to. People ask you for advice, encourage you to 'keep up the good work,' or just gush at your equipment in comparison to theirs."[30] Thus, rogue entrepreneurs have successfully constructed a market around people's deepest and darkest fantasies: to have a different life, a second life.

SECOND LIFE

I met Chan at the Country Club of Dreamland, a gated community that resembles a fantastical oasis in the Arizona desert. He offered me a drink, and we chatted about his job. Chan had just joined the real-estate team of Dreamland and was excited about his new career. As we talked, I noticed that he was not a native English speaker, so I asked where he came from. "Mainland China," he replied. This surprised me, because he seemed rather European. Chan was pleased at my comment; he wanted to look European, he confessed. Clients relate better to Western-looking real-estate agents; they somehow feel "unsafe" with Asians, he told me.

In the hope of selling me a plot on which to build my ideal home, Chan took me on a tour of Dreamland. We toured the lush, idyllic landscape, stopping by a waterfall to watch the water splash on the stones. I admitted that I liked the whole package and felt tempted to make an offer, but I was concerned that Dreamland seemed just a bit too idyllic for me. "Where are the shops, the restaurants, and the clubs?" I asked. Chan smiled and with a twinkle in his eye replied. "I know what you mean."

Next we visited sophisticated boutiques with the latest fashion, and shopping malls that in size resemble the Mall of America in Minneapolis. Finally, we entered a sex club, and there my cover was blown. Chan introduced me to Hunk, one of his clients who had just purchased a property in Dreamland. Hunk was into bodybuilding and had the physique of a young Arnold Schwarzenegger. He was so proud of his muscles that he kept flexing them in front of us. After a few drinks, Arnold's look-alike asked me if I fancied having sex. Taken aback, I fell silent for a few seconds. Chan immediately came to the rescue. "I bet you forgot to buy genitalia," he whispered. "Most newcomers do it. I know, it is absurd to forget to purchase the most important accessory, but it happens. Do not worry. I can sell you a vagina right away." I declined and said that I was happily married and sexually satisfied. That proved a major mistake! "So why are you here?" asked Hunk. "Yes," echoed Chan, "why are you here?"

The inhabitants of Second Life, the virtual world where Dreamland is located, are predominantly single, young (the average age is thirty-two), and carefree. Marriage, family, and children do not belong to fantasy cyberworlds. Sex does. Almost everybody is into virtual sex, which can assume any form you fancy. "Having sex in Second Life just requires selecting a series of buttons, but it's the instant messaging where the action is."[31] Obviously, if you have no genitalia you cannot do it; instant messaging is unable to translate words into graphic actions without virtual sex organs.

In the near future, online sex is destined to improve tremendously, thanks to "haptic" interfaces. This new technology, presented at Davos during the 2007 World Economic Forum, will soon be launched in cyberspace and will allow sensory feedback from virtual worlds. Today, haptic devices are used in surgery simulations, where they allow doctors "to have a physical sensation almost identical to that they would experience if they were actually wielding a scalpel."[32] According to Laila, a stunning Second Life escort, haptic will revolutionize the art of Internet lovemaking. People will be able to feel cybersexual stimuli and eventually reach "synthetic orgasm."

Second Life is a 3-D virtual world created in 2003 by Philip Rosedale, an Internet entrepreneur whose San Francisco-based company, Linden Lab, owns and operates the site. Second Life is a self-described "world of endless reinvention where you can change your shape, sex, and even your species as easily as you may slip into a pair of shoes back home."[33] New members create avatars, virtual visual personae, which are their Second Life beings. Avatars can be anything you wish: a human being, an animal, or a mix of the two. Chan's avatar is Caucasian, Hunk's is a replica of Schwarzenegger's body, and mine is an athletic young woman. Inspired by Neal Stephenson's science-fiction novel *Snow Crash*, in which people spend most of their time in a "meta-universe," a metaphysical world where they interact with each other through avatars, Second Life has, in only a few years, grown exponentially. Though it is impossible to quantify its population, as it expands daily, in early 2007, the *Financial Times* reported the number of users at 1 million, with about 10,000 people online at any given time.

Second Life is not a video game, it is a virtual world, parallel to our own, with a real economy and a domestic e-currency, Linden dollars. Linden dollars have an official exchange rate of 250 to the US dollar and can be used only inside Second Life. Goods and services are exchanged regularly. At the end of 2006, the GDP of Second Life reached an estimated $60 million, with an annual rate of growth of 15 percent,[34] a rate that rivaled that of emerging economies, such as China and India. Members use credit cards or other electronic currencies such as PayPal to purchase Linden dollars. They can then buy what they like, from body parts to properties. My virtual vagina would have cost the equivalent of $5, or 1,250 Linden dollars.

Members can earn wages, stipends called "dwell," simply by "being popular." "Popularity is determined by the amount of traffic to a resident-owned destination," reads the *Second Life* manual.[35] Wages are meant to facilitate trade and investment. In reality, they are an incentive to spend more time in Second Life. People can produce whatever they want and sell these products at market rate. As in capitalist economies, prices are determined by supply and demand. Profits can be taken out at any given time by exchanging Linden dollars for real money through a currency trader. Linden Lab's LindeX, for example, charges a fee for each transaction, while independent traders make money on the spread between buy and sell. Speculation in Linden dollars is very popular among traders. Members can also open accounts in Second Life banks, risky virtual organizations that offer high interest rates. Banking activity takes place through automated virtual tellers, which can be accessed almost everywhere within Second Life.

Surreal as they seem, virtual worlds such as Second Life simply mirror the real world. "Everything that happens in a synthetic world is the consequence of the interaction of human minds, and our minds have things like Love, Property, Justice, Profit, War and Exploration hard-wired into them."[36] In Second Life, people run businesses, produce goods, provide services, and make real profits. Major corporations, from Microsoft to Intel, also operate in Second Life. During my tour, I could have ordered a Coca Cola, bought a pair of virtual Adidas, and purchased a Toyota cybercar to teleport my avatar (transportation inside Second Life takes place by walking, flying, or teleporting using computer-game graphics, the mouse, and the cursor). As an author, I was tempted to visit Green & Heaton, the London literary agency that at the end of 2006 opened an office for "virtual talents." Pop artists are also venturing into this cyberworld. In the summer of 2006, Duran Duran announced that it was planning a concert on a synthetic island. The media have begun exploring the potential for new business offered by this synthetic world. Reuters opened an office in Second Life staffed with a full-time correspondent who monitors its booming economy.

As cyberworlds grow, the interaction with the real world becomes more frequent and articulated. "Life imitates Second Life" reads the *Second Life* manual. "You may find a real-world job in or through Second Life. It does not have to be in network marketing or something similar, either. For example, a business or a social services organization may look for contractual employees for an online program run in Second Life's virtual world."[37] In 2007, IBM committed to invest $100 million; the company already has a thousand employees spending time in Second Life and three executive directors working exclusively on Second Life projects. In January 2007, IBM announced a joint venture with Circuit Group, a US electronic retailer, to open a store on one of IBM's virtual islands. The idea is aimed at getting people to use cybershopping to buy products for the real world.

Second Life could be regarded as "a virtual incubator for innovation and entrepreneurship,"[38] as evidenced by the business empire of Anshe Chung. By far the most successful entrepreneur of Second Life, Anshe Chung is the owner-developer of Dreamland. Chung is the avatar of Ailin Graef, a

Chinese-born teacher who resides in a wealthy suburb of Frankfurt. At the end of 2006, Mrs. Chung's estimated turnover was $2.5 million. She is a pioneer of Second Life. Having started with an investment of less than ten dollars back in 2003, in 2004 she reinvested profits she had earned by coaching people on the game-playing techniques of Second Life and by designing and selling avatar accessories, such as animation. She then purchased empty cyberspace, which are basically pixels on the screen, from Linden Lab to create an ideal living environment: Dreamland, a place where people can enjoy themselves. With the help of her husband, Ailin Graef built roads, houses, gardens, squares, and beautiful landscapes. "We added value to the land we bought," she told the *Financial Times*.³⁹

Chung advertised in *Second Life* magazine and began selling real estate. By summer 2004, she was the richest person in Second Life. As the business grew, Mrs. Chung outsourced part of it to China. "I decided to move to China because of its affordable labor and because the [Chinese] government welcomed us with a red carpet. [. . .] They were very appreciative of our plans to train people and to create real value from virtual business," said Chung.⁴⁰ Chinese entrepreneurs I met in Second Life confirm that China understands virtual businesses and economies better than any other country. Some estimate that more than half a million Chinese make their livings in virtual economies, ranging from video games to synthetic worlds.⁴¹ The virtual estate agent Chan and XXX are two of them.

CYBERMARKET-STATES

At its outset, the synthetic universe on the Internet had no form of government, something similar to Hobbes's state of nature. Virtual chaos became a "fascinating test bed for ideas about how to govern, just as [it was] for ideas about business management."[42] The long march of cyberworlds away from anarchy has been guided largely by the desire to be entertained. The *Second Life* manual constantly reminds members that their ultimate aim is to have fun. From online video games to pornography, from gambling to movie piracy, the cybermotto remains: "Live it up." Synthetic worlds are constructed to amuse. While escapism permeates this business, its universal principle of targeted marketing is to satisfy the needs to entertain and to be entertained, and these needs alone.

Different universal principles, such as national identity, freedom, and equality, motivated humanity's struggle to emerge from the state of nature described by Hobbes in the *Leviathan*. These principles became the foundation of the nation-state. Today, Western-style democracy is regarded as the best form of government to meet such needs, which, unlike having fun, are priceless and unmarketable.

Democracy does not rule cyberspace. Entertainment does, and amusement requires a variety of accessories that can be easily purchased in synthetic worlds. Therefore, cyberpolity has been guided by utilitarian principles that facilitate the exchange of goods and services to entertain the virtual population. The kingdom of rogue entrepreneurs and marketeers of pleasure fill their accounts with activities ranging from online gambling to pornography, from cyberwars to the construction of synthetic worlds; these businesses carve out the unregulated cybermarkets of today.

But their command of cyberpolitics remains severely limited. "The typical governance model [. . .] consists of isolated moments of oppressive tyranny embedded in widespread anarchy. [. . .] There is a tyrant in place from the beginning, but an extraordinarily inactive one."[43] The "inactivity" of tyrants, or virtual pioneers, refers to the impossibility of controlling the endless synthetic territory and exercising the same authority over all the markets that are in one way or another related to their own. There is simply no authority strong enough. Virtual authority is, by definition, weak because it lacks any type of structures and instruments of enforcement. Online game companies cannot shut down online sweatshops or police the illegal trade in gold coins; equally, they cannot get rid of lurking hackers. Ironically, the ungovernable nature of cyberspace works against its own tyrants.

The surest principle of this universe is loyalty, which is based exclusively on performance. People flock to join World of Warcraft because they believe it represents the best online video game, yet those same subscribers will abandon it if a better game becomes available. Rulers of cyberworlds must constantly provide their members with the best opportunities to guarantee their loyalty in order to stay in power. Synthetic worlds, therefore, share many characteristics of the ultimate market-state, where the individual rules. The task of the government, writes Philip Bobbitt in *The Shield of Achilles,* which brilliantly describes the transition from nation-state to market-state, "is to clear a space for individuals or groups to do their own negotiating, to secure the best deal or the best value for money in pursuing what they want."

To satisfy the needs of the individual, the market-state will stop at nothing. "[It] will [. . .] deregulate the reproduction of our species [. . .] by permitting new reproductive technologies like in vitro fertilization." Avatars can be whatever one fancies: men can become women, as often happens in Second Life; body parts can be assembled from rich catalogs of features. In World of Warcraft, people can choose their war persona. Synthetic worlds are also "classless, indifferent to race and ethnicity as well as to culture"[44] In Second Life, you can change your race, your sex, and your species. Online video games take place in a fantastical world, where race, sex, and species have no meaning.

If the synthetic market-state is a pure vehicle for the individual to amuse himself or herself, then the government is free to maximize access to amusement. Yet, it cannot "take for granted anything much in the way of agreement about common goals or social good."[45] In 2004, the idea of taxing residents of Second Life on the objects they produced was overturned by a mutiny of a group of its first inhabitants. It seems that at the core of the market-state the individual has replaced society.

It was the dismantling of Communism that kick-started the transition from nation-state to market-state. Against this background, rogue economics has allowed globalization outlaws, such as pornography entrepreneurs, to carve out for themselves key outposts of the market matrix. These are commercial strongholds constructed with the use of modern technology around the inner and darkest fantasies of the individual. Unsurprisingly, consumers have welcomed them.

The Internet is rogue economics' most successful colony because it is the terrain where technological innovations introduced by the outlaws, e.g. pop-ups and streaming videos, have been perfected and applied to legitimate businesses. It is also a lawless environment, where rogue contamination is spreading fast. Thus, cyberspace offers us a sneak preview of the impact that the progressive deconstruction of modern politics will have on our daily lives.

The cyberworld that fishes for our fantasies is not the only medium in which we can preview what our world will become if rogue economics prevails. Entire sectors of the real economy have not proven immune to its far-reaching tentacles, including the global fishing industry.

CHAPTER EIGHT

ANARCHY AT SEA

"Once you leave land and you go out
at sea where there's no one watching . . . you are on a different planet
. . . and there is no law."

Hélène Bours, consultant and expert
on illegal fishing

One third of all fish consumed in the United Kingdom is poached from the Baltic and North Seas, a rogue business that is set to expand in the future. At the beginning of 2007, the Norwegian coast guard warned that in those waters illegal fishing will grow at a rate of 30 percent per year. Soon the majority of fish consumed in the United Kingdom will be "black fish." From fish-and-chips shops to sophisticated London restaurants, from organic markets to the frozen-food section of supermarkets, consumers will eat primarily stolen sea stock.

The Baltic and North Sea fishing racket now belongs to the Russian Mafia, which since the dismantling of Soviet Communism has cornered this market. When the Soviet Union collapsed, organized crime took over the Soviet mercantile fleet, and gangs of Russian Mafiosi began raiding the high seas. Today, they supply half the cod purchased as lawful in traditional British fish markets, such as Hull and Grimsby. "The scam involves Russian-owned trawlers, which operate from the northern port of Murmansk, ignoring strict quotas on fishing of cod, red fish and halibut."[1] Ironically, this port was the jewel in the crown of the Soviet mercantile fleet. Murmansk served as part of the Northern Sea Route, a 3,500-mile commercial avenue that stretched all the way to the nickel mines of Norilsk. At its height, in 1987, over 7 million tons of cargo sailed along its icy waters.[2] Today, Murmansk has become the Tortuga, a key pirate's haven, of Russian sea criminals.

From this hideout, fish gangsters poach an estimated 100,000 tons of cod in the North Sea above the annual 480,000-ton quota established by the United Kingdom and Norway. They offload their loot on the high seas into different ships operating under flags of convenience,[3] another rogue business that has expanded with globalization.

The Russian Mafia's fleet avoids easy tracking by renting or leasing vessels for a very short time and reflagging them. This practice known as "flag hopping" confuses surveillance authorities. Even when they are caught, coast guards have trouble identifying the owners of the vessels because they hide behind shell companies and joint ventures incorporated offshore.[4]

According to the Norwegian naval authorities, the Baltic and North Sea's cod scam also involves a multimillion-pound money-laundering racket. Dirty Russian Mafia profits are washed clean through the fishing industry. To stop this traffic, Norway has asked the United Kingdom to supply data on all landings of cod and other fish stock from Russian trawlers or other internationally registered vessels. However, the UK government has not complied, because tracking fishing gangsters is not a high priority. New Labour has bigger fish to fry: Islamist terrorism.

Yet the problem of illegal fishing is real. The Food and Agriculture Organization (FAO) estimates that 75 percent of the world's fish stocks are fully exploited, over-exploited, or depleted.[5] Moreover, it remains impossible to establish the legality of each and every catch. A spokesman for Unilever, which owns the Birds Eye and Igloo frozen-food brands, admitted to the *London Times*: "We can never say with 100 percent security that someone has not circumvented regulations,"[6] that is, exceeded its quota. In 2006, a Swedish TV4 documentary, *Kalla Fakta*, exposed several companies, including Findus, which allegedly bought illegally fished cod from the Barents Sea. The documentary claimed that Findus vessels had deliberately exceeded their legal annual quotas. According to the program, Findus purchased the cod from various fish-trading agents, including the Danish-based company Kangamiut.[7]

Illegally fished cod is a global menace to the fishing industry. Greenpeace warns that "among the companies which buy [rogue] cod from Baltic catches, usually fresh fillets bound for restaurants, are Pickenpack and Frosta (Germany), Fjord Seafood (Netherlands), Västkustfilé (Sweden) and Royal Greenland (Denmark)."[8] Do any of these companies know when they are buying illegally caught fish? The highly elusive nature of rogue fishing makes it impossible to answer this question.

In the absence of any concrete government intervention, NGOs like the World Wildlife Fund International and Greenpeace have attempted to influence major food companies, including Unilever, Young's Blue Fresh, Findus, and supermarket chains in the United Kingdom. They advised them to boycott fish from United Kingdom ports until the legal origin of the catch has been established. But in the anarchic atmosphere of the high seas, the policing of regulations goes well beyond the purview of wholesalers. Patrolling the seas is prohibitively expensive and harms commerce. "The overall cost of monitoring fishing activities in the EU and in its Member States amounts to some 300 million euros, which is about 5 percent of the total value of production (landings). In the specific case of the North Atlantic Fisheries Organization (NAFO), the cost of monitoring EU vessels amounts to some 4 million euros for a total of 55 million euros in landings (in 2002), i.e. over 7 percent of the value of production."[9]

FISHING PIRATES

Illegal fishing is one of the latest offspring of rogue economics. It is also a multibillion-dollar business. The Patagonian toothfish, under threat of extinction, and the bluefin tuna can sell for up to $10,000 and $15,000 per fish, respectively. "Often the catch exceeds the value of the vessel," reveals the deputy secretary of the Indian Ocean Tuna Commission. "Adding all the figures we have, which include cod in the Barents Sea, tuna in the Mediterranean Sea, abalone in South Africa and many more illegal catches, the estimated total volume of illegal fishing ranges from $2 to 15 billion," says David Agnew, Principal Research Fellow at Imperial College in London.[10]

The international hub for rogue fishing is in Europe, specifically in Las Palmas de Gran Canaria in the Canary Islands. "Nearly all the illegally caught fish that passes into Europe comes through Las Palmas. This is at least 400,000 tons per year," admits an FAO expert on illegal fishing who asked to remain anonymous.[11] Las Palmas is an excellent harbor and is very well placed geographically because West Africa is the richest coast for fishing. It is one of the major ports of convenience, providing services and hosting a number of companies that operate illegal vessels.

"Tracking stolen fish which transit through ports such as Las Palmas is almost impossible," says Hélène Bours, expert and international consultant on illegal fishing, "because the catch is offloaded in the high seas and there are simply too many smuggling routes. For instance, there is a huge quantity of what is commonly called pelagic fish, like sardines, etc., which is fished in West Africa but not smuggled to Europe or North America, because they are not a big market for that. European vessels raid pelagic fish off the coast of Mauritania, they bring it to Las Palmas and then they sell to other West African countries, like Nigeria."[12] West African big prawns and some species of flat fish follow a completely different route. They reach Las Palmas for shipment to the Asian market, where they remain in high demand.

Las Palmas resembles a major airline hub, with flights coming and going to and from hundreds of destinations. The only way to track the fish is to follow it all the way to its final market, which is an impossible task. "The fishing vessel never sails to the final destination of the catch. The fish changes vessels at least once before landing in some port, like Las Palmas, where it is sold and loaded on transport vessels," explains Ms. Bours.

Experts concur that the dismantling of Soviet Communism has given an impetus to a new breed of globalization outlaws: fishing pirates. "Fish stocks have always been vulnerable to too much fishing, but wide-scale overexploitation really started with the development of the distant water fishing fleets of the Soviet Union in the 1950s, which in the 1970s was followed by the development of similar fleets in Japan, other Far Eastern states, European states and the USA," reveals the FAO expert on illegal fishing. But while the Cold War lasted, overfishing took place in domestic territorial waters. Illegal fishing at an industrial level started when the Soviet Bloc collapsed, and organized crime took over the Soviet mercantile fleet. China followed suit.[13] Initially, the Baltic Sea was targeted because of its proximity to Murmansk, no longer patrolled by the Soviet Navy. Today, we have witnessed the disastrous consequences of over fifteen years of sea anarchy in that large stretch of water: "overfishing, pollution, eutrophication (nutrient enrichment of the water caused largely by agricultural run-off), climate change, oil spills, bottom trawling and destruction of habitats have made a catastrophic situation, further threatening the survival of cod and other species."[14] The responsibility for such disasters rests with the governments of the Baltic Sea states, which share the indifference of the United Kingdom government to fish piracy in their waters. The maximum average fine recently imposed anywhere in the region for illegal fishing amounts to a mere 538 euros, only slightly more than the fees charged for illegally parked cars towed away in Central London.

Fish piracy attracts little attention. It is not a sexy topic like poverty in Africa, which is supported by celebrities, and neither is it a terrifying menace like Islamist terrorism, which is manipulated by politicians. But the risks to the food supply and the environment are every bit as dire. In addition, patrolling the sea parallels the problems of policing the Internet: it remains expensive, and nobody knows how to do it. Data on piracy are unreliable, and there are no statistics either on the numbers of illegal fishing vessels or on the exact amount of illegally caught fish. Though governments have become well aware of the economic circumstances and of the root causes of piracy, and they are equally conscious of the pernicious consequences of illegal fishing, very little has been done to curb such businesses. The spreading of rogue fishing is a dramatically clear example of the failure of politics to gain control of rogue economics.

The advent of fishing piracy may say less about criminal organizations and more about new economic scenarios created by the advent of the global market. In the Mediterranean, regular fishers exceed their quota simply to make ends meet. "Vessels have to fish double what they are allocated in order to pay back expenses," explains Sebastian Losada, an ocean activist at Greenpeace, Spain.[15] Higher fuel costs and lower fish prices have eroded profits and fishers struggle to support their families. Over the last five years, for example, tuna prices have plummeted from 10 euros per kilogram to as little as half. To get a bigger share of the Japanese tuna market, the largest one in the world, legal and illegal fishing fleets have overfished the Mediterranean, pushing tuna prices down. Data from the Advance Tuna Ranching Technologies show that from 2002 to 2006, to meet the growing and insatiable Asian demand, the tuna catch tripled. Fishers' tales of woe have proliferated along with the growth of sushi bars. These fish stories, however, are true and are spun in many languages, from Arabic to Albanian, along the 46,000-kilometer Mediterranean coastlines.[16]

Global demand feeds into the vicious cycle created by over-fishing, producing extraordinary side effects. "Bluefin tuna, for example, is completely over-fished in the Mediterranean to the extent that it is now very rare and valuable. This is the reason why those who poach it can make a lot of money," reports Losada. Legally and illegally fished bluefin tuna feeds the sashimi market in Japan, which buys 80 percent of the catch. Italian and French pirate vessels control the illegal bluefin tuna fishing market in the Mediterranean Sea.[17] The large profits generated by this business have attracted organized crime. "The authorities claim that the racket is in the hands of a joint venture between the Marseille and Sicilian Mafias. Obviously this is something everybody knows but no one can prove it. The connection, often referred by the police as the Tuna Triangle, is not limited to France and Italy. One of the main markets for illegal fishing is Spain," adds Losada.

The bluefin tuna "triangle" has grown to become a square. Libya has joined the team by purchasing old French commercial vessels at rock-bottom prices. Libyans use these boats to unload the illegal catch from their French fishing fleets on the high seas. The Libyan connection derives directly from a surreal interdependency. "France gets EU subsidies to build new vessels so it sells the old ones at rock bottom prices to Libya, which re-flags them. Both new French and former French vessels, now Libyan flagged, fish illegally offshore Libya, and their fish stock ends up in the port of Marseilles," says Losada.

FISH SWEATSHOPS

Fish piracy has all the characteristics of old-time piracy and bears little resemblance to the modern day fictional image of pirates. Forget blockbusters such as *Pirates of the Caribbean* and think Asian organized crime operating on a global scale in labor conditions reminiscent of the industrial revolution. "Crews often get inhuman treatment. I've spoken with people from mainland China that had been aboard vessels for years in the high seas, without going back home. They are not trained or equipped and they are very poorly paid," says Ms. Bours. Slavery has become commonplace. "Off Guinea we saw a Chinese boat whose crew members didn't have passports. Once on the ship they were trapped and couldn't go anywhere."

Modern fishing pirates have become globalization outlaw's industrialists: they run illegal fishing sweatshops on the high seas. Wages make up a high proportion of running costs, so pirates recruit crews in low-income countries or simply enslave them.[18] Off the coast of West Africa, Greenpeace and Environmental Justice documented the working conditions of these ships, most of which were Chinese:[19]

> The living quarters are extremely dirty, as are the freezing holds, if they even work. There is often not even any safety equipment. [. . .] A Korean ship that was boarded off Sierra Leone during the 2006 expedition, the *Five Star*, had a construction on its deck which was in fact the living quarters of 200 Senegalese fishermen who were on board in addition to the Korean crew. Inside, cardboard mattresses and clothes hanging from strings could be seen. The ceiling was so low that one had to crawl inside the construction. The ship had picked up about 40 canoes and their crew in Saint Louis, in North Senegal, and brought them to the fishing grounds of Sierra Leone for three months. Once there, the canoes were put to sea, each with 5 or 6 fishermen on board. They would fish all day returning to unload their catch in the evening. This practice

is not new, and there are countless testimonies of Senegalese fishermen being abandoned hundreds of miles from home in small wooden canoes once the fish hold is full.

We also came across a group of derelict abandoned ships about sixty nautical miles off the coast of Guinea, such as the *Lian Run 2*. Each had one or two Chinese fishermen on board left stranded in the middle of nowhere, waiting for another crew to take over or for the ship to be repaired. We were told that supply ships bring them food every three months. When they run out they signal to passing boats hoping they will stop. They did not know how long they would be left there. The Chinese trawler *Lian Run 14* had a crew of half a dozen Chinese and one fisherman from Sierra Leone who had fled to Guinea. We were told they had no passports with them and that they work on two-year rotations. These ships stay at sea for many years, never going to port, transferring their cargo to refrigerated cargo vessels. The fish is then landed in ports such as Las Palmas. Meanwhile, the companies which own these ships continue business as usual; some even have offices in Las Palmas.[20]

Fishing sweatshop crews are as expendable to fishing pirates as Slavic prostitutes are to the pimps of globalization. "Once, in 2001, I was on a boat near the coast of West Africa and we got a mayday call from a Chinese fishing vessel sinking three hours away from where we were," recalls Ms. Bours. "We called other Chinese vessels in the area, but all of them said that they were not going to stop fishing for that. By the time we got there we found only two men from the whole ship." During its West African expedition in 2001, Greenpeace witnessed and participated in a rescue mission to search for the survivors of a vessel that had sunk with all its crew.

"Nobody really knew how many people died then or even who they were. Their families probably have no idea what happened to them. It is likely that another ship and crew were simply sent to take their place."[21]

THE DRAGON EATS FISH

The three most important fish importers are Japan, South Korea, and China. But the fastest growing, almost voracious, demand comes from China. Data from the Shanghai International Fisheries and Seafood Exposition show that over the last ten years, the Chinese retail market, not including restaurants and catering sales, has grown by 200 percent. From 2000 to 2006, the volume of fish and seafood retail sales had risen by 70 percent and per capita spending by 75 percent.[22]

"Chinese people in general are becoming richer and able to afford fish. Higher demand from China has an important economic impact upon the fish industry because of the sheer size of the population. One of the recent interesting developments we've seen is that expensive fish, such as toothfish, which used to be taken to China to be processed and then sent to Canada and the United States, today is consumed in China or in other Asian countries, e.g. Singapore and Hong Kong," says David Agnew. Formerly cod from the Baltic went to China for processing to be shipped back to Europe. Today, Poland has become the key processing hub for European cod.

Those attempting to meet the insatiable Asian demand for fish raid West African coasts. Ms. Bours concurs with several sources that illegal fishing in Africa is rampant. "In 2001, an aerial survey of Guinea's territorial waters found that 60 percent of the 2,313 vessels spotted were committing offences. Surveys of Sierra Leone and Guinea Bissau in the same year found levels of illegal fishing at 29 percent (of 947 vessels) and 23 percent (of 946 vessels) respectively. Today it is estimated that some 700 foreign-owned vessels are fully engaged in unlicensed fishing in Somali waters, exploiting high value species such as tuna, shark, lobster and deep-water shrimp."[23]

At any given time, as many as 50 percent of the vessels off the coast of West Africa engage in one form or another of rogue fishing. Greenpeace adds that fishing pirates also operate inside the twelve-mile zone reserved for local fishers. Often, the main victims of illegal fishing are those who depend upon the sea for their sustenance. In West Africa, thousands and thousands of families have no way of supporting themselves other than through fishing. We find it at best difficult to evaluate the economic impact of fish pirates on poor countries, especially in areas where few mechanisms exist for control, monitoring, and surveillance. However, MRAG, a consultancy dedicated to promoting sustainable uses of natural resources through sound integrated management policies and practices, estimates that sub-Saharan Africa loses about $1 billion a year due to illegal fishing. Because Chinese pirates dominate West African waters, they pocket most of the bounty. Fishing analysts, FAO, and United Nations officials concur that the Chinese are among the worst offenders, since they have many vessels and fishers scattered along the African coast; in fact, China owns the second-largest merchant marine in the world, after Panama.[24]

Chinese involvement in West Africa goes back to the early 1990s, when South African authorities unveiled a large racket in shark fins and abalone. Abalone, a delicacy and an aphrodisiac in China, is a shellfish that lives at the bottom of cold oceans. Fisherman can obtain a permit to harvest abalone legally off the shores of the South African coast, but licenses are limited. Illegal fishing became the first major business of Chinese organized crime in South Africa and allowed the Chinese Triad to establish a presence in the country.[25]

Today, abalone piracy is only one of the many activities of Chinese organized crime, which range from drug trafficking and prostitution to money laundering. But abalone traficking remains very profitable. "A conservative estimate by the [South African] police puts the illicit export of abalone, [. . .] at about 500 tons per annum. At a retail price of about $65 per kilogram in Hong Kong, the gross income of illicitly exported abalone is therefore approximately $32.5 million."[26]

Chinese demand for aphrodisiacs has stimulated yet another expedition of Chinese fishing pirates off the coast of Australia to harvest the abundant pot-bellied seahorse. Australia protects all thirteen species of this fish under federal and state law. In China, pot-bellied seahorses get used as sexual stimulants and sell for as much as $1,000 per item. The Hong Kong "seahorse" Mafia has penetrated this $100 million unlawful fishing business and has already smuggled over a quarter of the Australian illegal catches into China.[27]

PIRACY IS BACK IN FASHION

"Piracy is back in fashion," reads one of the many reviews of *Pirates of the Caribbean*. Designers have revived the "pirate look," and Johnny Depp, alias Captain Jack, has "savvied" his way to another blockbuster success. Piracy has come back in fashion on the screen and now thrives on the high seas. Here, the similarities between fact and fiction end. "Water, which covers almost three quarters of the globe is home to roughly 50,000 large ships, carrying 80 percent of the world's traded cargo."[28] Modern pirates target this plentiful bounty.

Over the past decade, sea piracy has risen by 168 percent, and attacks have become more violent, warned the British House of Commons transport committee in July 2006. Ironically, the report on piracy came in the wake of two successful assaults on vessels carrying tsunami relief supplies to Indonesia.

Twenty-first-century pirates now look predominantly Asian, and they sail globally. They mainly operate in the Arabian Sea, Southern China, West Africa, and in the Straits of

Malacca, a 500-mile corridor separating Indonesia and Malaysia, which alone every year suffer 42 percent of global pirate attacks.[29] Modern pirates have the latest technology and use hideouts in the South China Sea. "One pirate ship captured [in 1999] in Indonesia was outfitted with bogus immigration stamps, tools to forge ship documents and sophisticated radar, communications and satellite-tracking equipment."[30]

Above all, modern pirates are businessmen engaged in the global trade of stolen goods, a trade that nets an estimated yearly $16 billion. The bulk of it comes from Asia. The case of the Japanese freighter *Tenyu* illustrates the new, high-tech, high-finance breed of pirates. The 277-foot vessel sailed from Indonesia with a cargo of aluminum ingots worth $3 million. Bound for South Korea, the *Tenyu* never reached its destination; the ship's owners lost radio contact the day after it sailed.

As described in the *Washington Post*, "Three months later, the *Tenyu* turned up at a seedy Chinese port with a new name freshly painted on its bow—its fourth name since it disappeared, a new Indonesian crew and a cargo of palm oil. The 14 original crew members are presumed dead, and investigators say the aluminium ingots were unloaded and sold in Burma, ultimately bound for Chinese buyers. Investigators are confounded by modern pirate syndicates that resemble international business conglomerates, with branches and employees across the region. Maritime experts say the *Tenyu* case involved South Korean planners, Indonesian thugs, Burmese dock-hands and black marketers, and at least some accomplices in China, these people were all part of a network that authorities still have not fully uncovered."[31]

Often pirates work directly with legitimate companies operating in countries where fighting piracy does not receive a high priority. China belongs to this group, but European countries, as discussed above, have remained equally uninterested in punishing overfishing, which is a form of piracy. "The Barents Sea cod is not fished by foreign pirates, but it's all about misreporting and over-catching by legitimate licensed vessels," confirms David Agnew.

Small Chinese ports serve as ideal places for modern pirates: they can easily unload the bounty, sell to plentiful buyers, and buy off local officials. Corruption, in fact, has become rampant and widely accepted. "The pirates know that if they come into a Chinese port, they can get cooperation," said Pottengal Mukundan, director of the International Maritime Bureau, a London-based arm of the International Chamber of Commerce.[32] Ironically, not long ago China had the reputation of being the last place pirates would go to do business.

The Chinese government's *laissez-faire* attitude toward business protects pirates from the long arm of international maritime law, as proven by the incident at Beihai. In 1997, pirates in the South China Sea attacked and hijacked a $5 million sugar cargo. The ship ended up in Beihai, a small port in the region, where a buyer was waiting for its cargo. Beihai, an old fishing port, sees many traditional wooden fishing boats come and go. Pirates find it an easy and inexpensive place to repaint and rename stolen ships. Payment takes place in cash, no questions asked. When the international maritime authorities tracked the cargo down, they ordered it to be returned to the owner and the fourteen pirates to be prosecuted. The local authorities of Beihai simply ignored the order, and Beijing did not intervene.[33] As in the case of the AIDS epidemic in Henan, the geographical distance between the capital and most of the country acts as a buffer when dealing with economic and business matters. Major decisions are left to the local authorities, who are often corrupted by resident outlaws. Had it been a question of the population of Beihai taking a political initiative by staging a mass demonstration against the central government, for example, the long arm of the Party would have crushed them in no time, as happened in Guangdong.

Twenty-first-century piracy does not limit itself to stealing fish, raiding ships, kidnapping oil workers for ransom, and trading stolen cargoes on the high seas. Multinationals and governments often employ pirates to carry away dangerous waste. As much as 47 percent of European rubbish, such as e-waste, is toxic. Electronic litter, ranging from computers to mobile phones, sails from developed to developing countries in suspicious vessels. According to the United Nations Environmental Programme, the watchdog arm of the United Nations, the annual production of e-waste ranges from 20 to 50 million tons. This highly toxic material is split into recyclable and nonrecyclable refuse. The recyclable refuse heads for India and China, while the disposable refuse ends up in Africa, a global dustbin. Basel Action Network (BAN), an organization that tries to prevent a global toxic chemical crisis, revealed that 75 percent of the electronic material that reaches Nigeria cannot be recycled, so it contaminates the environment. Other African countries suffer from "imported contamination." Somalia, for example, regularly receives tons and tons of electronic waste and radioactive junk from Europe. Taking advantage of the absence of central governments, pirates dump their deadly cargoes everywhere, mostly along the seashore. Shockingly, some of this waste resurfaced after the tsunami of December 2005.[34]

ANARCHY UNDER THE SEA

The sea remains the largest dumping ground in the world, and pirates are by no means the only ones using it for that purpose. Consumers, farmers, and corporations pollute seas and rivers on a daily basis.

Water pollution affects us all; in fact, water is a powerful conduit of contamination. The root causes of sea pollution are all in one way or another linked to the rogue nature of the global economy. The first problem has to do with the refuse produced by industry and agriculture entering rivers and seas. This includes phosphorous and nitrogen, which spread macroweeds, notably into the Mediterranean Sea. Macroweeds reduce the oxygen and alter the composition of sea water, with disastrous consequences for fish stocks and sea currents.

Pollution also comes from urban consumption's waste that reaches the sea by way of rivers. Some pollutants include human hormones, for instance estrogens released by women taking birth-control pills, and animal hormones washed downstream with manure. The Potomac River, fed by other rivers in Maryland, Virginia, and West Virginia, is particularly rich in such substances. Studies have shown that these chemicals may prompt male infertility, as well as certain types of cancer, i.e. cancers of the liver, gallbladder, ovaries, and uterus. These claims, however, remain a matter of dispute among scientists and require further study. Though the Potomac supplies most of the drinking water for Washington, DC, the United States Environmental Protection Agency has set no standards for many of these pollutants. They are simply ignored.[35]

Rivers in the United States and Britain now contain high proportions of phthalates and nonylphenols, two groups of chemicals that feminize fish. Research has proved that male fish exposed to effluent containing these chemicals start producing a protein called vitellogenin, usually present only in females. By affecting hormonal systems, the chemicals can cause severe birth defects and sexual abnormalities, not only in fish but also in other species, such as frogs, alligators, and possibly humans. Sources of contaminants include electronic and textile factories, agricultural activities, especially feedlots, as well as municipal and domestic wastewater.

Fish contamination also affects the food chain, so that eventually humans will be harmed. Preservatives, chemicals to make food last longer, are also a worrying source of contamination. Workers at a London morgue confirm that the decomposition of bodies has slowed down because of the high percentage of food preservatives in their bodies. In the West, powerful food lobbies block any attempt to regulate the use of preservatives in foods, while developing countries largely accept preservatives without question.[36] Sea pollution can also stem from the exploitation of submarine soils, caused specifically by the process of deep-sea drilling and petroleum extraction, as well as by accidents in submarine pipelines. Oil companies are the world's worst sea polluters; oil is pumped with sea water, which is then dumped back into the ocean. Oil corporations are not taxed on the damage their industry inflicts on the environment, but they pay reparations only for major harm that causes ecological disasters.[37] Today, however, it is harder to find the culprit when a major sea ecological disaster occurs, as was the case of the *Exxon Valdez*. Because shipping companies are no longer obliged to release the name of the chartering party, the perpetrators of several major oil spills have remained unknown and unpunished.

The pernicious nature of the energy industry becomes apparent when we look at recent major natural disasters. Thanks to Hurricanes Katrina and Rita, oil prices soared, and in 2005 ExxonMobil reported record profits, more than $36 billion, the highest ever earned by a single company in one year. A windfall tax of just 3 percent on such profits earmarked for research and investment in solar-energy technology and development would quadruple the entire United States budget for solar energy.

The sea is also polluted by atmospheric fallout coming from cars, boats, and planes, as well as from fuel consumption in industries and agriculture. Again, oil companies are the biggest villains. While 122 companies are responsible for 90 percent of carbon dioxide emission, five private oil companies—Exxon Mobil, BP, Amoco, Shell, Chevron, and Texaco—contribute 10 percent to the global release of carbon dioxide into the atmosphere.[38] Lastly, certain specific sea-related activities, such as fish farming, locally pollute the sea.

Fish farming is booming everywhere; one in three fish consumed worldwide (55 million tons in 2003) is farmed. Fish farming is also very profitable. In Chile alone, salmon farming generates over $1 billion in foreign exchange per year; in Scotland, it is worth a yearly $1.4 billion. Fish farming is also known as the blue revolution. It is cheap and billed as a sustainable alternative to the consumption of highly depleted wild-caught fish species, such as salmon. Certainly, the incentive for growth is real. Projections from the FAO show that by 2030, global fish production will need to rise by an additional 40 million tons. Such increase can be achieved, not by fishing more efficiently, but by doubling aquaculture production. The collateral effects of fish farming, however, may be more damaging than anticipated.[39]

Fish farming relies on the use of big synthetic net pens, containing between 15,000 and 80,000 fish each. A fish farm generally has around ten nets, each with a base 30 by 30 meters. Many fish farms, therefore, hold up to 700,000 fish, in a very small space. The nets used in the industry allow most of the waste, natural or not, to escape into the sea and therefore to generate several types of pollution. The damage is serious because fish farms are located in fast-flowing waters, such as the mouth of an estuary, thus pollution spreads quickly. Nutrient pollution typically builds up underneath the cages, from the detritus of fecal matter ejected by the fish to waste food (uneaten food pellets, dead fish, and the like). All of these items are carried away by currents.

Chemical pollution arises from antibiotics, antifoulants, and sea-lice treatments given to the fishes. Most farmed species, such as salmon and tuna, are actually carnivorous and therefore must consume many smaller fish in order to grow. To produce a pound of salmon, for example, requires five pounds of oily fishes, such as sand eel, sardines, and herring.

Thus, fish farming relies on industrial fisheries that affect wild-fish stocks by spreading diseases. Because of overconcentration, salmon and other farmed species develop diseases. These diseases spread easily to wild salmon, since farms are generally situated near the wild stock. Over the last twenty years, for example, epidemics have halved wild salmon stocks. Furthermore, the frequent use of antibiotics in farmed stock risks making bacteria more resistant in fish generally.

Fish farming affects ecosystems in different ways. The impact on natural predators, especially in certain regions such as British Columbia and Chile, are huge. Whales, dolphins, seals, and sea lions are repelled and sometimes shot or trapped, so that they do not attack fish farms. Major problems are also frequently caused when fish escape from the nets. Interbreeding with wild salmon causes genetic problems in subsequent generations.[40]

THE ECONOMICS OF CLIMATE CHANGE

Sea pollution has eroded the equilibrium of ocean currents, affecting our global climate. In effect, sea pollution contributes to the warming of the oceans. The melting of global ice reserves is one of the consequences of the chaos that rules the high seas, where state intervention is weak or nonexistent.[41] Anarchy at sea is a sneak preview of the type of watered-down politics that will eventually rule *terra firma*. However, the fast-changing lawless ocean environment also offers a glimpse of the new economic opportunities arising from a world plagued by global warming, with less ice and higher sea levels.

There is a huge propaganda aspect to the issue of global warming, and some countries may actually benefit from this disaster. Such is the hidden message contained in the 2007 Intergovernmental Panel on Climate Change (IPCC)[42] report on climate change. While Africa and Southeast Asia could be hit by drought and floods of biblical proportions, some northern industrialized countries will benefit from global warming. Siberia and the tundra of Northwestern Canada will become fertile land for agriculture. Western Scotland's sandy beaches will turn into a new Riviera. This scenario confirms the conclusions of the previous chapters: economics can blossom outside politics by simply following its rogue nature.

Northern states are actually looking forward to global warming. As ice melts, new lands and new waters will be available for exploitation. The key question is who will own them. "In 2001, Russia made the first move, staking out virtually half the Arctic Ocean, including the North Pole. But after challenges by other nations, including the United States, Russia sought to bolster its claim by sending a research ship north to gather more geographical data. On August 29, it reached the pole without the help of an icebreaker, the first ship ever to do so. The United States, an Arctic nation itself because of Alaska, could also try to expand its territory."[43]

In the summer of 2007, Russia claimed again its portion of the North Pole. But the rush to the Pole involves all Arctic countries. Presently, the United States, Russia, Norway, and Canada are fighting each other in the World Court over the rich undersea territory of the North Polar region, which could be exploited when the ice melts. The dispute could easily become a modern day "Great Game" with the unkown resources of the Arctic at stake. Fishing is only one of them. Commercial transportation, for example, could be extremely profitable. The dream of opening a Northwest and Northeast Passage, the icy shortcut between the Atlantic and Pacific oceans, may soon come true. All Arctic states stand to benefit from navigating it. Russia and Canada, for example, have already signed trade agreements for when the Passage and the Arctic Ocean will be open.[44] Shipping companies would also benefit from the opportunity to considerably shorten their routes. Some routes that presently take seventeen days could be cut to eight.

The melting of the North Pole, therefore, will revolutionize trade flows, and China is well aware of this scenario. Having placed a research station on Spitsbergen, a Norwegian island, China moved its icebreaker *Snow Dragon* from Antarctica, officially to conduct climate research in the region. In reality, the team is looking for oil and new sailing routes to reach the wealthy Western markets. Soon prices of Chinese fakes will be even cheaper thanks to lower freight costs.

Demand for Arctic-hardy vessels has also picked up. In January 2006, Aker Finnyards, a giant shipbuilder based in Helsinki, opened a subsidiary to produce exclusively ice-hardened ships to meet rising demand for this type of vessel. "A Finnish energy company bought two for about $90 million apiece, and after buying one, Russia licensed the design and is building two more."[45] Icebreakers are even used by the booming tourist industry. The now privatized Murmansk Shipping Company offers cruises to the North Pole, ranging from $15,000 to $20,000, on old Soviet icebreakers.

The rush to the frozen lands of the North Pole resembles the beginning of the gold rush in California. Greed motivates it. Visionary entrepreneurs enter extravagant contract betting on the speed of the melting of the icecaps. An example is American Pat Broe, whose company, in 1997, bought the Port of Churchill in Canada for seven dollars. This port, which was little used because it is locked by ice much of the year, could become a major Arctic port if the ice melts. Projections suggest that it could generate $100 million per year. Unfortunately, by that time, Venice may be completely under water.

The chaos on our seas has rogue economics written all over it and mirrors the anarchy of synthetic worlds described in the previous chapter. Surfing the net and sailing the high seas takes place across similar landscapes, because globalization outlaws have turned both cyberspace and our seas into lawless territories. Exploiting exceptional economic opportunities, rogue

Internet entrepreneurs and fishing pirates are blossoming in the shade of progressively weaker state governments. The business of the former pollutes our minds, the activity of the latter contaminates our bodies.

The root causes of the pollution of the sea are many, and all are linked to the changing relationship between politics and economics. Neither individuals nor pressure groups, not NGOs, not even the United Nations have the strength to combat pollution. To save the planet from major climatic change requires a political will and determination that nobody has yet shown. Multinationals and major corporations are not exclusively the villans. Often they, like consumers, are victims of rogue economics as proven by the illegal cod business of the Baltic and North Seas. The inability of the market-state to tackle such major socio-economic issues as the environment is at the root of modern governments' indifference toward the deadly consequences of rogue economics.

However, the rush to the Arctic's icy waters confirms that against this lawless and anarchic background, new, real economic opportunities are taking shape, and some are even beneficial to entire nations. The planet as we have known it may cease to exist, but humankind will not disappear. While floods and desertification will plague the equator and temperate zones, north and south of the tropics of Cancer and Capricorn, new life will blossom. As in the past, the current economic transformation has a rogue nature. And this time it may change the global geography of our world. In doing so, it will wipe out entire populations, redistribute wealth, and create new empires.

Political genocide, slavery, and exploitation have often accompanied the great transformations of the past. The American myth of the frontier was built on the extermination of Native Americans; the wealth of the Southern states was constructed on slavery; the industrial revolution was cemented in ruthless labor exploitation and polluted the planet. However, economic growth eventually and always trickles down and brings progress and modernization to those who survive. If history is our guide, this time rogue economics may literally redesign the map of the world and lead to a new civilization. But before reaching that goal, the world has, once again, to go through biblical chaos, anarchy, floods, and famine. It has to complete the long march through Hannah Arendt's apolitical desert and eventually break through the ultimate illusion: modern politics.

CHAPTER NINE

TWENTIETH-CENTURY GREAT ILLUSIONISTS

"The aim of terrorism is to terrify."

Franz Fanon

In his documentary *An Inconvenient Truth,* Al Gore admits that during the 2000 presidential election campaign his advisors told him not to campaign on environmental issues, even though he clearly believed passionately in the subject, because it would not have brought him votes. This recommendation was based upon nationwide opinion polls. Naturally, today, the situation would be a lot different, as the environmental crisis strongly resonates among millions of people. Increasingly, in the market-state, politicians must perform a task that has nothing to do with traditional politics and all to do with single issues. Instead of putting forward a vision for the future, they essentially tell people what they want to hear.

Opinion polls have become *vox populi* and politics no longer represents a battleground of ideas, but is a confrontation of marketing strategies between successful pollsters. Among the best known is American Mark Penn, who perfected the art of political polling by applying to it commercial principles such as data mining. The British supermarket chain Tesco has pioneered this new technique, described as "gathering of valuable data about customers," by using club cards. These cards are essentially the DNA of shoppers; they contain all the information required to assess their commercial behavior, from social status to tastes in food. Marketing teams work with this information, and focus on customers who change their habits, not on those who always buy the same products.

The rationale is that changes in commercial behavior patterns can be translated into concrete commercial opportunities.

Elections revolve around swing voters because they determine the outcome of any successful campaign. It follows that polling of swing voters is to politicians what club cards are to Tesco; it offers a snapshot of key voters' opinions. Modern political pollsters are essentially data miners and analysts: they collect and study information about swing voters to find important patterns. The controversial New Labour election slogan for the 2005 campaign, "Forward not Back," for example, sprang from this novel type of polling. Ahead of the British election, Penn's company conducted thousands of interviews in the United Kingdom to understand what people wanted to hear from New Labour. That message was passed on to Tony Blair and summarized in the above slogan.[1]

Sociologists have written endlessly about the "undecided" middle class, but only with the advent of the market-state did swing voters become a key factor in politics. Today, issues dear to these minorities, not political parties' ideologies, shape the politics of modern democracies. Stripped of their own intellectual and ideological attributes, politicians are nothing more than political "performers." Their act plays out in a series of great illusions through which they make the masses believe that these policies reflect what the nation needs.

In the market-state, understanding what makes people swing from one party to another is a powerful tool, and whoever masters it can make political propaganda work marvels. Swing voters' fascination with celebrities, for example, plays a critical role in the latter's involvement in politics. This situation has emerged as a new phenomenon. Imagine the all-star cast of Fellini's *La Dolce Vita* campaigning for the Italian Christian Democratic Party! If anything, in the past, the political involvement of distinguished artists proved strictly antiestablishment, as was the case of Charlie Chaplin during the rise of Nazism and later on during McCarthyism. Today, politicians encourage famous people to be part of their team, because their image translates into votes. Celebrities are, by definition, performers, and therefore they have high visibility. For this reason Bob Geldof was appointed a consultant to the British Conservative Party's policy review on global poverty. UNICEF's celebrity supporters include David Beckham, Ricky Martin, and Robbie Williams.[2] Five former Miss Universes are goodwill ambassadors for the United Nations Population Fund.

Status, not knowledge, has become the key factor in celebrities' involvement in world politics. Globalization, of course, tremendously inflated their role, making their faces familiar to the far corners of the earth. But the transition from the nation-state to the market-state then facilitates their entry into mainstream politics. Celebrities belong to the establishment because they owe their stardom and wealth to the obsessive marketization of their image. Their loyalty to the market is unshakable since their existence and continued success depend upon it.

We can compare celebrities, as viewed in the collective imagination, to the Greek gods: capricious people who populate the Mount Olympus of the market-state. Extraordinary wealth and fame has turned them into superhumans, and as such, they can and do conduct their lives outside normal parameters. Brad Pitt driving a hybrid car becomes a statement about saving the planet. However, he regularly travels by private jet,[3] as when he went with Angelina Jolie to Namibia, burning an estimated 11,000 gallons in jet fuel, enough to take his hybrid car to the moon.[4] Bono's crusades to save Africa from poverty won him a nomination for the Nobel Peace Prize; at the same time, his band, U2, avoids taxation in the United Kingdom by using Dutch tax havens.[5] Such contradictory behavior would be equivalent to Charlie Chaplin having dinner at the height of McCarthyism with Senator McCarthy himself, or perhaps with the Dulles brothers. In the past, these hypocritical performances were not tolerated the way they are today.

Why are celebrities allowed to behave in such ways? The answer rests on their superhuman condition, a status the masses do not want to destroy. People have become addicted to celebrities and they would find themselves lost without their daily intake of real-life soap operas. Celebrities' love affairs distract from everyday life and, at the same time, the tabloid intimacy created by the media helps the readers daydream. Like Mr. and Mrs. Jones, what many people want has nothing to do with creating a better world, but everything to do with joining the celebrity's world. They have a consuming desire to escape the day-to-day, bleak reality for a world of fantasy.

Even with their superhuman status, however, celebrities are manipulated by politicians to perform their illusory political magic acts. Politicians, not pop singers, international footballers, or Hollywood megastars, are the great illusionists. As discussed in the following section, though George W. Bush and Tony Blair endorsed Bono and Geldof's Live 8 campaign to end poverty in Africa, the two politicians' real motivation had everything to do with safeguarding their own interests and those of their own electorate and little or nothing to do with lifting Africa out of poverty. The involvement of celebrities in politics and the use of megamedia events constructed by their publicity apparatuses prove crucial in presenting the initiative as the altruistic gesture of Western masses toward Africa. In reality, the implementation of the agenda ended up perpetuating the African continent's subjugation to the economics of Western powers.

AFRICAN FOOD FOR THOUGHT

The dilemma of Africa has plagued more than one generation of economists and politicians. Since the 1960s, this continent has received over half a trillion dollars in aid, yet today it remains poorer than when the loans began. Why? For such celebrities as Bono, the answer is simple. A shortage of cash and the inability of Africans to repay their countries' debt have crippled African economic growth. The solution rings even simpler: donors should scrap the existing outstanding debt and double financial aid. At the G8 summit of 2005, Tony Blair embraced this message, while Bono and Bob Geldof played a key role in mobilizing fans to put pressure on the G8 members to back such an initiative.

However, distinguished economists, diplomats, and people who have dedicated their lives to ending poverty in developing countries strongly disagree. What turns a developing into a developed nation is not the amount of foreign aid it attracts, "but how the money is spent," as Carlo Cibó, an Italian diplomat who lived for decades in Africa, reminds us.[6] What really matters is how the African political elite disposes of foreign aid. Most of the half-trillion dollars received by Africa since the 1960s has funded military coups and civil wars, not economic development. During the 1980s alone, at least ninety-two attempted military takeovers took place in sub-Saharan Africa, affecting twenty-nine countries. Between 1982 and 1985, Zimbabwe spent $1.3 out of $1.5 billion of foreign assistance on arms and ammunitions.

Historically, foreign aid to Africa has served as a rogue force, notably as an important form of terrorist financing. In war-torn countries such as Ethiopia, Somalia, and Sudan, foreign-asset transfers, defined as the redistribution of external assistance and assets, has provided the most lucrative source of revenue for local armed groups. During the civil war in Sudan, the bulk of food aid intended for famine-stricken regions was spent by local armed groups and warlords, who bought Iraqi weapons to use against the Sudanese army and the population. African governments participate equally in such robberies. The Sudanese government used its share of foreign aid to buy Iraqi oil to keep the war machinery running and to pay military advisers from Iran. Asset transfer is so widespread that donor countries even accept a built-in 5-percent standard diversion of any aid, in cash or kind. For certain African countries, this percentage goes as high as 20 percent. When foreign aid is not stolen at the source, i.e. before cash or products reach those in need, people will be robbed of their share of aid in or near their homes. This popular form of terrorist financing involves domestic asset transfers in which armed organizations "confiscate" goods at roadblocks scattered around the territory they control or through raids against villages. This straightforward robbery often leads to famine, as happened in Sudan. During the civil war, the Bagara militia from the north pillaged villages in the south, regarded as the stronghold of the Sudanese People's Liberation Army (SPLA), the local armed group. Among other atrocities, the militia conducted widespread cattle raids, which destroyed the livelihoods of the local population and led to widespread famine in south Sudan.

Aid initiatives, such as Live Aid for Ethiopia in the mid-1980s and the Live 8 concert in 2005, although well intentioned, end up perpetuating civil wars, not mitigating the economic problems of Africa. In the early 1980s, two years of drought did not bring on famine in Ethiopia; rather, it came as a direct result of the massive dislocation of populations forced to flee from decades of civil wars involving the government, Addis Ababa, the Eritrean guerrillas, and the Tigrean People's Liberation Front. Between 1982 and 1985, Ethiopia received $1.8 billion in foreign aid, including the Live Aid contribution. Far from feeding the starving population, the bulk of the money, a total of $1.6 billion, went to purchase military equipment. Without being aware of conditions, Live Aid and foreign donors endorsed the politics of war, unleashing a ruthless fight between armed and criminal groups and the government over the dividing up of foreign aid. Live Aid and Western aid sealed the tragic destiny of Ethiopia, a country that today is poorer than it was in the early 1980s.[7]

Pop, "feel good" initiatives easily fall prey to rogue economics, especially in African countries. Yet they are popular because they give people the false impression of helping. Carlo Cibó adds that often pop concerts' message is "give more," and thus they offer people a clear conscience even while remaining at a comfortable distance from the real, complex problems on the ground. Moreover, what remains after concert expenses are covered is quickly and badly spent, to avoid the image that the money raised does not end up in the organizers' pockets. This isn't the type of aid Africa needs.[8]

Even the World Bank remains adamant that abolishing the debt and increasing aid would further impoverish Africa. Ending agricultural tariffs and the $300-million subsidies that rich countries distribute among their farmers would help much more. Such a strategy could increase African agricultural profits by $100 billion, i.e. $20 billion more than the $80 billion that industrialized countries sent to Africa in aid in 2006. Ending subsidies and tariffs in the developed world would allow African products to freely compete with Western products and generate an inflow of $500 billion, enough to lift 150 million Africans from poverty by 2015. But campaigning for this type of change would alienate Western farmers, the backbone of President Bush's electorate and a very important pressure group in Europe. This is the reason why both Bush and Blair welcomed Bono's suggestion, to hide commercial protectionism behind Western generosity.

The truth behind the "End Poverty" campaign remains that foreign aid is mostly beneficial to those who give it, as proven by the Marshall Plan, which created a novel market for American products. According to Mumo Kisau, an economist who has worked for several humanitarian organizations in Africa, for each dollar in aid that reaches Africa, three go back to the country giving the aid, mostly because labor and products come from industrialized countries. Thus, aid creates a market for Western products. According to several World Bank sources with whom I spoke, 70 percent of loans go to purchasing goods and services from Western corporations.[9]

Many African leaders who have spoken out against additional foreign aid have instead demanded technology transfer and development of key infrastructures. Africa lacks the structures and personnel to help itself rise from poverty, as shown by the construction of a dam along the river Niger. The $15-million project went to an American engineering company because the government of Niger proved unable to handle a project of that magnitude.

While the Marshall Plan aimed at kick-starting the reconstruction of war-torn Europe, so that consumers could purchase American products, the financial aid to Africa has opposite goals. To protect its farmers, for example, the European Union, which is a generous donor, still vetoes the sale to Africa of genetically modified seeds that produce crops requiring less irrigation. Aid serves as a sort of insurance that donors pay to protect their own industries from the competition of African products.

Against this background, it becomes clear why foreign aid is the true cause of the malaise of Africa: foreign aid is an economic virus as infectious and deadly as AIDS. The Swedish economist Fredrik Erixon has shown that, since the 1970s, the volume of aid received by African countries has proven inversely proportional to economic growth. Far from being the cure, foreign aid has caused the disease. The more money a country receives, the more it sinks into poverty. Tanzania and Kenya, two countries that in the 1960s, after independence, enjoyed a vigorous rate of growth, began to stagnate in the mid-1970s. Economic decline coincided with the advent of foreign aid. From the 1970s to 1996, Tanzania and Kenya each received about $16 billion in aid. These monies helped implement disastrous economic policies. Tanzania pursued a form of African socialism and Kenya a policy of import substitution. Foreign aid did not bring political stability either. In the summer of 1998, members of al Qaeda attacked the United States embassies in Kenya and Tanzania, causing hundreds of deaths. In sharp contrast, Botswana, a country that over the last thirty years has attracted very modest amounts in foreign aid, has grown at a faster rate than China (GDP per capita rose from $1,600 in 1975 to $8,000 in 2004) and, politically, Botswana remains one of the most stable countries in Africa.

To back Erixon's thesis, Thomas Sheehy, the author of the comparative study *Beyond Dependence and Poverty: Rethinking U.S. Aid to Africa*,[10] shows that Africa has received on average four times the aid of Asia. Yet today, Africa has a per-capita GDP close to the poverty line, with fifteen countries among the poorest in the world, while Asian GDP booms. A 2007 World Bank report states that world poverty, i.e., the number of people living on less than a dollar a day, is decreasing, thanks to China and India's economic growth.

The problem of Africa is not economic but political. Good governance, not money, will solve it. John Reader's book, *Africa: A Biography of the Continent*, describes the success story of Ukara, a small Tanzanian island in Lake Victoria. A densely populated island with poor sandy soil and no natural vegetation or resources, Ukara has never suffered food shortages or famine. Reader attributes Ukara's success to its system of private ownership of property and absence of chiefs or dictators. African economists remain adamant that Africa does not need more foreign aid, but a bourgeois revolution: the emergence of an entrepreneurial middle class to create local jobs by making and selling products other people want to buy.

Two years from the historic decision to scrap the African debt, the continent has become poorer than ever. None of the new initiatives have helped, including RED, the pool of companies gathered by Bono, which dedicates a percentage of their sales to help Africa. All they have achieved is free publicity for their own brands. The "End Poverty" fiasco outlines the limitations of celebrities, even when they are well intentioned, when they enter the political arena. They are ill-informed and often lack the scientific and professional background to understand complex issues, such as poverty in Africa, but above all they fall easy prey to the greater performers, politicians, and their Machiavellian marketing machines.

Political illusions complement the market matrix because they contribute to blurring the divide between reality and fantasy. Political illusions lie at the core of the market-state's propaganda engine; politicians manufacture and the media endorse them. The most powerful illusion to date is the fear of terrorism, carefully constructed to fill the ideological vacuum created by the disintegration of Communism.

THE POLITICS OF FEAR

On a foggy Monday morning, on December 11, 2006, I arrived at Heathrow Airport Terminal 2 at 5:30 in the morning, two hours before I was due to catch an Alitalia flight to Rome. After standing in line for forty-five minutes, I successfully checked in my luggage and went upstairs to discover that the line for security stretched to outside the terminal. To protect unlucky travelers from the freezing fog, the airport authorities had erected heated tents along the terminal's perimeter. I took my place in the tent at the tail end of the line of passengers, fearing that I would not make my flight. As time passed, travelers grew nervous, old people fell ill, babies started to cry, businessmen looked increasingly annoyed.

When I finally reentered the terminal, I was forced into another winding line, which doubled back several times across the width of the terminal. On the flight-departure screen the dreaded words "last call" flashed next to five of the seven flights listed. I noticed that several passengers looked at each other in disbelief as they nervously checked their watches and calculated the time it would take them to get through security. Others tried to attract the attention of the officers wearing bright yellow vests, camping in front of the departure entrance. Finally, a tall security guy approached my section of the queue. "My flight is about to depart. Can you let me skip the queue?" a middle-aged businessman asked politely. The man shook his head and explained that he had no instructions to let anybody go through. "What are we supposed to do?" asked a woman next to me. Wait and hope that the plane would not take off on time, was the phlegmatic reply. I pointed out that I, like most of the other passengers, had already checked in my luggage. Removing the luggage from the plane would cost time and money, and surely it would be easier to get me on the plane. At this point the man turned and walked away.

The lack of concern about the cost of delayed departures generated by securities bottlenecks is striking. In 2002, the economist Roger Congleton calculated that every additional thirty minutes spent by passengers in airports costs the economy $15 billion per year, almost three times the yearly profits of the entire airline industry in the 1990s.[11] These astronomic additional costs should be added to the salaries of thousands of people (including those camping at the departure gate that Monday morning) employed since 9/11 by security firms to inspect air passengers.

By the time I reached security, it was 7:30 am. Along with several other people, I began removing all my accessories: belts, boots, hairpins, and so on. I then extracted from the single piece of hand luggage I was permitted to carry on my laptop, makeup, toiletries, and liquid medicine carefully packed in several plastic bags of 20 by 20 centimeters. Suddenly, a young couple rushed in front of me and jumped the queue. They deposited their hand luggage on the belt and ran through the metal detector, which immediately started beeping. A security guard stopped the couple and told them to go back to follow the undressing procedure performed by all the other passengers. The man and woman looked at each other and in Italian cried: "We are late, we must run or we will miss our flight."

As this scene unfolded, Italian passengers stuck in the queue behind me started to protest. They were also going to miss their flight, so why was the couple allowed to jump the line? A shouting match developed. Insults were traded in English and Italian among people clearly stressed to the limit by the whole situation. Behind me an old lady fainted. Security rushed to rescue her and collided with a couple with two screaming infants in a stroller, all being whisked through by a security woman. It was a scene of utter chaos. This is the legacy of 9/11: the additional, often unbearable and unnecessary degree of stress imposed on all of us when we are traveling by the cleverly manufactured "fear of terror."

TERRORISM BY THE NUMBERS

The belief that today Western air transportation is more likely to fall victim to hijacking than in the past remains one of the many myths of the politics of fear. This is a well-crafted political illusion because boarding a plane from or to Western Europe or North America reached the apex of danger in the 1970s. During that decade, both regions fell victim to thirty-one hijackings, which resulted in twenty-nine deaths. In the 1980s, there were only thirteen hijackings and sixty-one deaths. In the 1990s, the number plummeted to six, with no casualties, and so far in the 2000s, there have been only seven hijackings, four of which took place on 9/11.[12]

Joe Sulmona, an aviation consultant, concurs that since the

1970s, hijackings have significantly decreased, thanks to major improvements in aviation security introduced since the 1980s. New policies and strategies have successfully addressed the threats of that decade. "The aviation industry does not see any longer these fears as confined to particular continents, such as Europe and the Middle East," explains Sulmona.[13] "As for suicide missions, until 9/11 they were regarded as a local means of drawing attention to causes and not as part of the perils of hijacking. Prior to 9/11, the protocol was to gain time and to establish a dialogue with the hijackers; this is exactly what aviation authorities did on 9/11. Today the procedure would be very different." Sulmona confirms that the International Civic Aviation Organization (ICAO) has ad hoc protocols on this matter, and he stresses that replicating 9/11 is not going to be so simple. Today it is much easier to target urban transit systems than to focus on high-security airports and airlines, as shown by the Madrid and London bombings. Psychologically, the impact may even be greater since the average Westerner does not fly everyday but does move about cities constantly. Yet political propaganda remains primarily focused on airport security.[14]

Even the probability of Americans or Europeans falling victim to an international terrorist attack was higher in the past.[15] Official statistics from RAND show that in the 1970s, there were 920 international terrorist attacks; in the 1980s, the number rose to 1,219, only to fall to 626 in the 1990s. So far, in the 2000s, the number is only 188 excluding 9/11, which is considered by terrorist experts an exceptional event in which approximately 3,000 people died.[16] Data show that the risk of dying in an international terrorist attack in Western Europe and North America was higher in the 1980s than ever before or since. While 287 people lost their lives in the 1970s, 990 perished in the 1980s. The death toll declined to 367 in the 1990s, and with the exception of 9/11, only 330 people have been killed by international terrorism in the current decade.[17]

Statistics on international terrorism do not include domestic terrorist attacks, defined as attacks that do not involve foreign victims. The incidence of international versus national terrorism has increased over the last twenty years because people tend to travel more. A quick analysis of statistics in Europe confirms that even the risk of perishing in a domestic terrorist attack in Europe was much greater in the 1970s than today. In 1972, 467 people, including 103 army officers and soldiers, died because of the IRA conflict. So far, in the 2000s, only fifty-two people have died in the United Kingdom—during the July 7 London bombing.

This trend is apparent all over Europe. Since 1968, Italy has witnessed more than 14,000 terrorist attacks, carried out both by left- and right-wing groups. Most of these took place in the 1970s and early 1980s. In 1973, forty people died, the year after twenty-four fell victim of terrorism, and in 1980, 120 lost their lives in violent action carried out by local groups.[18] In the 2000s, so far, only two people have died because of terrorism in Italy.[19] In 1976, 100 people were assassinated for political reasons in Turkey; by 1978 and 1979, the number had risen to 2,400.[20] Right-wing local groups were responsible for the bulk of the assassinations. Terrorist experts across the world concur that both domestic and international terrorism in the Western world peaked in the 1980s and have been declining ever since.

Many people would argue that the reason why we are "more secure" today is because since 9/11 security has been tighter. This is a false impression, which is quickly entering the realms of modern political myths. When I was a student at the University of Rome in the late 1970s, there were road blocks to check people's identities and inspect their cars all over the city. Yet terrorist activity in the capital was booming. Even the belief that to prevent terrorism it is sufficient to carry less than 100 milliliters of shampoo on board a plane, to take off your boots at departure, and have your fingerprints and eyes checked upon arrival is nothing more than a comforting illusion for travelers terrorized by their own governments.[21] Israeli security has proven that the only effective way to screen travelers is by profiling or interviewing them one by one.[22]

In 2006, an Italian long-haul pilot told me that far easier and deadlier than making a plane explode in mid-air would be to drive a car bomb straight into one of the terminals of Heathrow Airport at peak time, when the interval between planes taking off and landing is at a minimum. The air surrounding the terminals is saturated with fuel fumes. The detonation would be extremely powerful because of the jet-fuel vapors, and potentially could destroy an entire terminal and kill thousands of people. This was the scenario of the failed attack at Glasgow Airport in the summer of 2007. In the United States, this type of attack is considered the number one aviation threat.[23] However, only a few airports in the world, such as Narita in Tokyo, have facilities to screen cars, because to do so is prohibitively expensive. A proposal to address this threat at Los Angeles airport put the cost of upgrading security at $9 billion dollars.

Next time you take off your shoes and show your toiletries at airport security during peak time, it might be useful to reflect on the following: with a bit of imagination, a replica of the July 7 suicide mission on the London tube could target the entrance of the terminal. A car driven by a young British Muslim indoctrinated in less than twelve months could drive straight into the entrance. Remember also that constructing a bomb is not going to be a serious impediment, nor is the procurement of ingredients. Type the words, "how to make a bomb" into Google and you will get over 200,000 results, some of which require only substances that can be bought in any drugstore.

Though politicians want us to believe that new security measures at airports are necessary to save lives, the hunt for terrorists inside terminals has been meager. In 2003, former US Attorney General John Ashcroft told the Senate Judiciary Committee that since 9/11, 478 individuals had been deported (most of them arrested while traveling), yet he failed to specify that they were not terrorists but people guilty of visa violations. The fact that they were repatriated is proof that they were not terrorists (the FBI must affirmatively clear someone of being a terrorism suspect before deportation).[24]

Politicians have always skillfully manipulated numbers to support their policies, to raise money for their pet projects, and to project more positive scenarios. Robert McNamara inflated enemy body counts to give politicians in Washington the possibility of bragging about the progress the United States was making in Vietnam. However, never before have politicians "cooked the books" to project a dangerous and terrifying future as they are doing today. This trend began before 9/11. In 2001 Andrew Bacevich, a professor of international relations at Boston University, wrote in *Foreign Policy* that the State Department's 2001 Patterns of Global Terrorism report "not only exaggerates and distorts reality but also obscures the political context in which specific episodes of terrorism actually occur." According to Bacevich, 170 of the 200 attacks considered international terrorism were bombings of a United States-owned oil pipeline in Colombia.[25]

Data manipulation and political propaganda have contributed to develop what professor Leif Wenar of the University of Sheffield has labeled "a false sense of insecurity" about terrorism in the "free world." The motto has been: "Be scared. Be very, very scared. But go on with your lives."[26] This mantra is reinforced by security rituals performed each time we board a plane. In reality, "we need to be far more concerned with the spread of diseases, narcotics, human smuggling, and other criminal acts through aviation and transportation," points out Joe Sulmona. "On a day-to-day basis, these threats represent a higher risk of human calamity." Yet such fears are not publicized by celebrities and cannot be visualized or illustrated with shocking photos. Above all, they do not inflate politicians' ratings on a wide spectrum. In the aftermath of 9/11, the false sense of insecurity projected by the Bush administration boosted the popularity of an unpopular president and, three years later, provided the electoral platform of his reelection campaign, as anticipated in 2003 by his chief political adviser, Karl Rove.[27]

The plain truth, carefully hidden behind a web of illusions, is that terrorism is an inefficient killing machine. "Many academic terrorism analyses," wrote Bruce Hoffman, a leading expert on terrorism at the RAND Corporation, "are self-limited to mostly lurid hypotheses of worst-case scenarios, almost exclusively involving CBRN (chemical, biological, radiological, or nuclear) weapons, as opposed to trying to understand why—with the exception of September 11—terrorists have only rarely realized their true killing potential."[28] Moreover, terrorism is an infrequent activity in the West. "The number of lives lost at the hands of terrorists over the past 30 years is relatively few compared to the thousands who die from drug abuse, or cancer or automobile accidents in any given year," adds Sulmona. Terrorism is not a major global killer; on the contrary, for a Westerner, the chances of dying in a terrorist attack are a fraction of those of winning the lottery. As US Senator John McCain put it: "Calculate the odds of being harmed by a terrorist! It's still about as likely as being swept out to sea by a tidal wave."[29]

The law of the big numbers seems to contradict the nightmare scenario projected by the political illusionists. Americans are more likely to be killed in their own home than fall victims to a terrorist attack. In the United States, each year, 16,000 people lose their lives to homicide. As I write, deaths resulting from car accidents since 9/11 in America total more than 200,000. The chance that an American will die in a plane crash is about 1 in 13 million (even taking 9/11 into account), while to reach that same level of risk when driving on America's safest roads, i.e. rural interstate highways, one would have to travel a mere 11.2 miles.[30] People are more likely to die while driving to the airport than to be blown up by a terrorist inside the terminal or in midair.

Even taking the highest terrorist casualties, which occurred in 1995, when over 6,000 people died worldwide, this figure is a fraction of the 50,000 to 100,000 people who die every year from snake bites, never mind the 10 million children who perish from preventable causes, such as malnutrition and malaria. So why are we so scared? The answer must be sought in the mythology that politicians constructed to legitimize the market-state.

CHAPTER TEN

THE MYTHOLOGY OF THE MARKET-STATE

"Berlusconi is Ulysses."

Alessandro Meluzzi, member of
Forza Italia

The market-state's great political illusionists foster a culture replete with mythology. The politics of fear, for example, rests on the cleverly engineered modern version of an old myth: political violence. Celebrities have acquired a superhuman status reminiscent of the Greek gods, and their soap-opera lives and shallow political involvement are chapters of the market-state's mythological annals.

The politics of fear test out a well-known postulate: when people become vulnerable, especially in times of great transition, they want to believe that their leaders can protect them. Myths provide comforting tales that strengthen this conviction. At the same time, myths legitimize the new state. All modern politicians draw on the memories, practices, and symbols that populate the collective imagination to find legitimacy. For example, the Cultural Revolution allowed Mao to become the new emperor of Communist China. Today, leaders of the market-state fervently search for comforting myths because of the turmoil and uncertainty that surround modern politics. As Ernst Cassirer, the German philosopher, wrote in 1946, after another great transformation called World War II:

In politics we are always living on volcanic soil. We must be prepared for abrupt convulsions and eruptions. In all critical moments of man's social life, the rational forces that resist the rise of the old mythical conceptions are no longer sure of themselves. In these moments the time for myth has come again. For myth has not been really vanquished and subjugated. It is always there, lurking in the dark and waiting for its hour and opportunity. This hour comes as soon as the other binding forces of man's social life, for one reason, or another, lose their strength and are no longer able to combat the demonic mythical powers.[1]

THE DISINTEGRATION OF THE LEFT AND RIGHT

The fall of the Berlin Wall marked the beginning of a period of great convulsions and eruptions in world politics. The Wall's volcanic ash prompted the disintegration of the historical political division between left and right. The dissolution of the Soviet Union, in fact, caused the intellectual retreat from socialism. Francis Fukuyama's influential thesis about the end of history clearly illustrates this phenomenon. Fukuyama associates the dismantling of Communism with the final point of "mankind's ideological evolution." History, as the outcome of ideological battles, crumbled along with the bricks of the Berlin Wall. What made the intellectual conflicts of the past obsolete was the global convergence toward liberal democratic institutions, a force which paved the way for a new era of world politics.

"Today the traditional Left . . . is getting more and more conservative in trying to hold on to the established welfare state, whereas the traditional conservatives, the Right, to a large extent have turned into neo-liberals arguing in favor of the free market and thereby contributing to the erosion of tradition."[2] The parameters of politics ostensibly have shifted from the historical spectrum of Left/Right to a complex of single-issue politics, mechanically moving towards convergence.

What Fukuyama could not have predicted was that the epicenter of the new system would become the market-state, a state disembodied from politics.[3]

If the end of Communism damaged the historical dichotomy between left and right, globalization struck the mortal blow. Globalization has redrawn the relationship between workers and industry. While capital moves freely and industry can enjoy the advantages of outsourcing and offshoring, Western labor remains intrinsically immobile. Even inside the European Union, language constitutes a real barrier to the relocation of skilled labor. Class relationships, therefore, have changed. "The fact that a transnational company can move its plant while a worker cannot move to another country has robbed labor unions in industrialized countries of their power...."[4] Consequently, trade unions now find themselves arguing for status-quo industrial formations, often at the expense of their own traditional values. For instance, the British unions AMICUS, TGWU, and the GMB lobbied their government to maintain the heavy subsidies to the United Kingdom military industry in Britain,[5] the products of which have been used for internal repression and external aggression in many conflict areas around the world, including Iraq.[6]

"The stresses and strains of globalization have created a new schism in our society. On one side are those who are at ease, or relatively so, with technological advance and the cosmopolitan interchange of cultures, and who possess the qualifications to do well in the new economy. On the other side, much farther down the socio-economic scale, are those, often lacking in skills or qualifications, who feel that their jobs or even their way of life are threatened."[7]

Outside the traditional left and right political paradigm, the market-state faces a double crisis: a crisis of rationality and a crisis of legitimacy. How can it manage outsourcing when it benefits industry but harms domestic labor? How can it contain globalization when it becomes a requirement for economic growth? How can it make certain that the deleterious ecological effects of industries are properly controlled? These crises of governance derive directly from the weakening of the nation-state. A weak state cannot protect its own citizens; consequently, a weak state cannot rely on their loyalty. Thus, citizens vote for those who offer better personal conditions. The personalization of politics has broken down the old, traditional patterns of voting.[8]

In this context, fear becomes a powerful political tool to legitimize politicians and their policies. Fear is irrational and easily manipulated. But to feed fear the modern propaganda machine needs to create terrifying images and myths as powerful conduits. In the aftermath of 9/11, Bush's reference to the Crusades aimed at reviving the false, mythical images of the Arabs as the medieval bloodthirsty enemies of the West. Ironically, Islamist terrorists legitimize their actions using equally terrifying memories and myths from the past. Abu Musab al Zarqawi and his followers called the American soldiers who had invaded Iraq the New Mongols. Comparing the United States invasion to the arrival of the Mongols in Iraq during the thirteenth century stirred deeply rooted fears among the Iraqi population.

In the absence of an ideological dichotomy, therefore, political loyalties have been reorganized along mythical lines, which in turn provide the key ingredients for populism. "Much more consequential for social democracy are the conditions that lead to right-wing populism. [Disenfranchised] groups blame the "establishment," "outsiders," or both for what is going on, and are easily attracted to racist or xenophobic sentiments. Many are erstwhile social-democratic voters who feel let down or disenfranchised by the mainstream parties."[9] The great illusionists repackage old myths to fill the vacuum of politics created by the dismantling of Communism, and in so doing, they trivialize politics. The political involvement of celebrities and the revival of old prejudices represent just two aspects of this trivialization. The ultimate effect of such illusions often proves detrimental for large segments of the population. In the United States over the past thirty years, the Republicans have, bit by bit, exploited an array of biblical discourses to encourage the poorest sections of the American electorate to vote against their own economic interests.[10]

Against this background, the quest for suitable myths becomes fundamental, and it has to have a wide radius that includes historical, cultural, and even tribal traditions. To succeed, these myths do not need to be related to politics but they must be deeply rooted in society, as proven by Silvio Berlusconi, Italy's outstanding myths manipulator.[11] A self-made man with dubious connections with the world of politics and crime, he rose to power exploiting the tribalism of Italian football. In the aftermath of one of the darkest hours of post–World War II Italian history, he revamped and repackaged the mythical symbolism of the game Italians love to bits and sold it to the electorate as the new formula of politics.

BERLUSCONI, CHAVEZ, AND THE POPULISM OF THE MARKET-STATE

Italy is an outstanding example of market-state populism. The Italian First Republic, along with many other nation-states, was built on the ideological dichotomy between left and right. These doctrines embodied opposite visions with regard to equality and class loyalties, as well as in relation to the role of the state versus private ownership and of public versus private spending. In the market-state these fundamental issues have not totally disappeared,[12] but they have been diluted by the rising power of swing voters. The blurring of the boundaries between left and right has also confused traditional voters, those who are driven by ideology, often forcing them to cast their vote on single issues rather than expressing their preference on the basis of a comprehensive socio-economic political platform.[13] In 2006, La Margherita, a party in the Italian left coalition headed by Romano Prodi, campaigned against abortion and stem-cell research. Forza Italia, Berlusconi's own party, by contrast, has always given its members a free vote on stem-cell research.

Amid this troubled and contradictory political landscape, Silvio Berlusconi constructed his populist agenda around the game of football. He bypassed traditional politics and stimulated the tribal instinct of the nation, using football as the base for his legitimacy and appeal to the electorate.[14] Berlusconi's political strategy, therefore, tapped into the unity and communal devotion of football communities, whose souls are deeply tribal.

In 1986, Berlusconi bought AC Milan, one of two A teams in Milan, and led it to several domestic and European titles. In 1994, when he entered the political arena, he used Milan fans, forever grateful to him for all those victories, as the basis of his electorate. He named his party Forza Italia, "Go Italy," a well-known football slogan; he converted football clubs into local party headquarters and members of Forza Italia were referred to as "Azzurri," the nickname for the Italian national football team.[15] Berlusconi's rhetoric swam in football slang, his style was colloquial and direct as if he were talking to fans, not voters, and Italians found this formula refreshing and fell in love with it and him.

As his team gained championship after championship, Berlusconi told Italians that he would run the country like a football club and offered the successes of AC Milan as proof that he could do so. He cleverly manipulated the football mythology to gain the support of voters. Using his powerful media network, he boosted Italian football's sense of pride and transmuted it into politics. "Italy will be a great country because it always had great football teams" became the not-so-hidden message of his political campaign. This incredible slogan not only was heard by the electorate, it became a powerful myth. In 1992, in the midst of the collapse of the First Republic, Berlusconi's football politics comforted the Italians, who had very little to be proud of beyond football. It also provided them with the arrogance needed to overcome the fall of the First Republic, the disintegration of the Left, and the widespread fallout from the anticorruption crusade known as "Mani Pulite" (literally, "clean hands," the name of a judicial investigation that uncovered widespread corruption and led to the end of the First Republic).

The tribalism of football supplied the mythological elements needed to legitimize the Italian dream of a better future. Many in the country still cling to such illusion, too scared to admit they have been duped by one of the great political illusionists of our time or too afraid to venture outside the football pitch of Forza Italia's mythical society. Fear of the unknown, therefore, remains at the root of the 22 percent of voters gathered by Berlusconi during the 2006 elections, the largest share of any Italian political party.

On the other side of the world, Venezuela has experienced a different, yet equally colossal, political rupture. Hugo Chavez's anti-corporate, anti-imperialist libertarian revolution took place under the banner of Bolivarianism. But while Simon Bolivar professed a love of classical liberalism and free-market economics, Chavez built his populism around music, the undisputed deep passion of Venezuelans.

To charm the under-thirties who live in the *barrios* of Caracas and the shanty towns, *ranchitos,* of Venezuela, Chavez has used rappers as a political channel. "We get in touch with the local rappers," explains Piki Figueroa, one of the producers of Chavez's rap politics. "We suggest that they play in the streets, in the *barrio's* toughest place. They talk with the gang leaders, whom they know because they are born and raised in the *barrio.* The rappers ask for a truce during the concert, to promote their music. The *malandros* [gang members] end up in charge of security, so peace and tranquillity is guaranteed. For one day, instead of gang fighting, the residents of the *barrio* listen to music."[16]

In Chavez's Venezuela, rap, ska, salsa, anti-imperialist populism, and extreme left-wing politics go hand in hand. In the 23 de Enero, a ranchito between Caracas and Catia, a massive shantytown that stretches like a long snake along the hillsides west of the capital, supporters of Chavez live next door to the Tupamaros, a gang of hooded kids that takes its inspiration from the Uruguayan armed organization Tupamaros.[17] Music provides the mythical terrain upon which Chavez's populism appeals to the instinctive tribalism of his compatriots. Through such processes, music becomes a powerful political and anti-imperialist symbol.

The successful construction of this myth is linked to Venezuela's deep roots in the musical tradition. Rap, ska, and salsa are for Venezuelans what football is for Italians, they represent a national cultural passion. In Caracas alone, hundreds of music groups enjoy immense popularity. Some of the leaders, like Bambino of Santos Negros, have huge followings. "These guys are bigger then Madonna," says a sixteen-year-old *rappero* from Caracas.[18] Gang music is the mythology of Chavez the political rapper, the anti-Bush crusader, the ultimate left-winger.

Chavez's left-wing populism, however, is part actuality and part mirage. Venezuela represents America's second largest exporter of oil,[19] and many analysts question whether Chavez's policies really improve living conditions among the population. "When I was in Caracas in 2002," writes Dennis MacShane, a former British Foreign Office minister in charge of Latin America, in the *Guardian*. "Hugo announced he was fed up with the unions running the state-owned oil company and wanted to Thatcherize the workforce. They went on strike which he denounced as a plot against him using the 'enemy within' language dear to populist leaders. He won, the union leaders were busted and now Hugo does handsome capitalist business with his favorite enemy, the United States. He insults them in the morning and makes a fortune selling oil in the afternoon."[20] Yet his rhetoric comforts the masses because it places Venezuelans into the powerful tribal dichotomy of us versus them, the *gringos*.

In Venezuela, as in the rest of the world, rappers represent the ultimate revolutionaries whose keyword is "antiestablishment." But when Chavez lashes out at the globalization of American multinationals, appropriating politics charged with the rebellion of the *rapperos*, the message becomes part of his establishment. Thus, *rap salsero* underground has become a government propaganda tool, as Chavez's supporters fight to establish a state apparatus capable of fulfilling the false ideals of the Bolivarian revolution.

Outside Venezuela however, gang culture, rap and hip-hop music have maintained their antiestablishment connotation and spread their messages on the wings of modern tribalism. Hip-hoppers and rappers sing *la vida loca,* the extraordinary, artistic cry of clusters of disenfranchised youngsters plunged into a world ruled by rogue economics and globalization. These very people have broken through the illusion of modern politics, these are people who do not vote and live at the margins of traditional societies. For them, as for those who choose to believe in the myths of politicians like Berlusconi and Chavez, tribalism remains an equally comforting sociopolitical and economic cocoon, protecting them from the perils of the global village.

Modern tribalism, in the form of Maoist tribalism, also prepared China for its great leap forward into rogue economics and globalization. In the global village, a pattern seems to emerge: tribalism, clans, clusters of ethnic and religious groups, i.e. modern tribes, have become the socio-economic vehicles to cope with and to prosper from rogue economics and globalization.

CHAPTER ELEVEN

THE EXTRAVAGANT FORCE OF GLOBALIZATION

> Salvatrucho yo nacì, Salvatrucho yo
> crecì, Salvatrucho yo seré, y Salva-
> trucho moriré
>
> That's the way it's gonna be. . . .
>
> Rap lyrics from the Mara Salvatrucha

On Christmas Eve of 2004, a crowded bus cruised along a busy road in the barrios of San Pedro Sula, Honduras. Inside, late commuters were anxious to reach home to enjoy their Christmas celebrations. Suddenly, a black pickup truck jerked forward from a side alley and blocked the road. The bus driver managed to stop, avoiding a collision. A group of hooded men carrying machine guns and machetes jumped out of the truck and, moving quickly toward the bus, broke down the door and stormed inside. Passengers screamed in panic, but their cries went unheard, drowned out by the sound of gunfire and the hacking of machetes. The massacre was over in a few minutes: twenty-eight dead, including four children, and fourteen injured.

Before leaving, the killers attached a long communiqué to the front of the bus, criticizing the government of Honduras for its anticrime campaign. The assailants' message to the government ended with a warning: do not dare challenge us!

A government investigation revealed that Mara Salvatrucha, or MS 13, one of the gangs plaguing Central American cities, had carried out the attack whose aim was twofold: to send a "hands off" message to politicians in the capital and to challenge the rival gang, Mara 18, or M 18, on whose local turf the massacre had taken place.

LA VIDA LOCA

Though *maras*, or *pandillas*, are known for their bloody deeds in Central America, few people know that they hatched in the 1950s in Southern California. Their raison d'être then involved protecting Hispanic immigrants, mostly Mexicans, from the members of other ethnic gangs, primarily African Americans and Asians. One of the earliest pandillas to be formed was Maras 18, also known as Calle 18, after Eighteenth Street in Los Angeles, the neighborhood where its exclusively Mexican members lived.[1]

Mara Salvatrucha appeared much later, in the 1980s, as the offspring of one the bloodiest wars by proxy of the Cold War, between the Marxist group Frente Farabundo Marti de Liberacion National (FMLN) and the right-wing government of El Salvador, which was backed financially and militarily by the Reagan administration. The vicious civil war displaced thousands, and many left the country for Southern California. Former *guerrilleros* and local criminals also took the road to *el norte*. Refugees from El Salvador ended up living in poor neighborhoods among Mexicans, Asians, and Afro-Americans in the Thirteenth District of California, which gave M 13 its name. Here, they became ostracized by everybody, including local Mexican gangs, predominantly M 18. Thus, Mara Salvatrucha, which means "gang of street-smart Salvadorans," was born to protect Salvadoran immigrants from their new neighbors.

Throughout the 1980s, the pandillas maintained a strong nationalist identity. In the streets of Southern California, gangs fought each other to conquer and maintain their territory, often as small as a section of a street, where people of the same nationality could live in relative safety. Nationalism, therefore, served as the transplanted root cause of the violent antagonism among the gangs as well as of their defense. During the Cold War, nationalism also played a pivotal role in the armed struggle. From the Palestine Liberation Organization (PLO) to the Basque separatists Euskadi Ta Askatasuna (ETA), armed organizations fought under the banner of national identity.[2] Thus, throughout the Cold War, gangs and armed groups, who sought to forge new nations, shared the same motivations. With the fall of the Berlin Wall and the advent of globalization, this situation changed dramatically and inside the global village nationalism lost its meaning.

The end of the Cold War eventually brought a halt to wars by proxy, which had for decades plagued the periphery of the two superpowers' spheres of influence. Against this fast-changing, political backdrop, in the early 1990s, the US government decided to repatriate thousands of Hispanic immigrants and refugees. While many were petty criminals, others were simply illegal immigrants; some had spent most of their lives in Southern California and hardly knew their country of origin. Upon deportation, they ended up unemployed and dispossessed, in war-torn countries.

The exodus to Central America from United States cities such as Los Angeles and San Diego provided a powerful source of manpower for the drug lords of Medellin, Cali, and Tijuana, who sought to spread their wings on the wake of globalization. As with the Mutras in Bulgaria, it became apparent that the social network of the *maras* complemented the new transnational criminal activity of the cartels. Soon the maras took over all the drug lords' dirty jobs, including contract killing. Exploiting contacts developed "back home" in Southern California, MS 13 and M 18 also monopolized the delivery of drugs from Colombia to the United States.

Their departure from America's ethnically divided poor neighborhoods, coupled with their involvement with the Colombian and Mexican drug cartels, further diluted the nationalistic identity of the *maras*, which soon evolved into transnational criminal gangs.[3] Instead of recruiting from single areas, the reconstituted gangs drew their membership and their territorial boundaries from across the slums ringing the outskirts of Latin American cities. Membership was no longer linked to nationality, but it was dictated by the *barrios* of birth of the *mareros* or *pandilleros*. M 18 and MS 13 blossomed in shantytowns all across Central America. As early as 1992, gang fighting started to plague the *barrios*, which became rich breeding grounds for violence and crime. Once the nationalist motivation began fading, gang hostility took on a more acute economic and territorial tenor. It became tribal. When asked why she hates M 18 *pandilleros*, Flor de Maria, a member of Mara Salvatrucha from San Salvador replied, "Why do I hate them? Because they want to kill us. They want to control our barrios. But we will not let them do it."[4] Territory, not nationality, defines the *mareros*.

While as nationalist organizations the *maras* had the task of protecting their *paisanos* (countrymen) from other gangs, as criminal organizations with an overwhelming tribal identity, they began preying on the inhabitants of their own territory, the *barrios*. This behavior is shared by members of the *n'drangheta* and the Bulgarian Mafia. "My boyfriend and I get protection money from local truck drivers and small traders," admits Flor de Maria. Thus, at the local level, the war among the gangs aims at gaining control of the informal economy of the lower classes of the population, those who are forced to live in the *barrios*. As with the *n'drangheta* and the Mutras, territorial economic subjugation dictates how the *maras* construct their power.

Across the Atlantic, in the slums of Nigeria, we find similar trends. Tribal gangs entrench their dominance in the control of their own terroritory. There, "Area Boys," criminal gangs that live in the urban areas, especially Lagos, a metropolis of thirteen million people, prey on the local population. In the streets and sections of towns controlled by the gangs, taxi, bus, and truck drivers, as well as shopkeepers, street vendors, and passersby, all must pay a road tax.

"In the unbearable heat of the early afternoon, I was driving in Obalende, a working-class section of Lagos," remembers an *okada* (motorbike taxi) driver. "Suddenly, at an intersection, a group of boys blocked the road. 'Okada man, you must pay the road tax,' they shouted at me. 'Why should I pay you? I have already paid some other kids just a few blocks away. If I also pay you I will have no money left,' I replied and that was a mistake. One of the boys got closer to me and aimed a pen at my eyes. 'Give me the money or I will take your eyes.' I just managed to avoid the tip of the pen and to extract 100 naira [about 50 cents]. They beat me up a bit and then they let me go."[5]

The criminal colonization of urban enclaves is by no means a phenomenon of the developing world. Since the early 1990s, the proliferation of gangs has also affected inner enclaves in many Western cities. As discussed earlier, the dismantling of Communism and the advent of rogue economics has helped organized crime colonize urban enclaves in the West. The economy surrounding illegal drugs has woven a tangled web that allows such colonization to spread globally. Thus, today the socio-economic landscape of inner-city slums resembles, if not replicates, the lawless and violent barrios of El Salvador and Nigeria.

Despite renewed multilateral efforts at seizure and treatment, increase in the production of cannabis resin, heroin, and ATS stimulants (synthetic drugs) has boosted the abuse of these substances in an overwhelming majority of countries.[6] The rising prevalence of cocaine abuse in England and Wales, for example, has seen the proportion of the general population using the drug rise eightfold from 1992 to 2004,[7] fueling further criminality and spreading violence, the primary ingredients of gang culture. A recent survey by the British government shows that in 2005 drug abuse among eleven- to fifteen-year-olds in the United Kingdom reached its highest level since surveys began twenty years ago. Sam, a thirteen-year-old boy from East London, admitted that he does not use the school toilet because "it's a well known fact that you only go to the toilet if you want to take drugs."[8]

Illegal possession of firearms has also skyrocketed. In 2005, 35,000 Britons owned firearms, up from 10,000 in 1999. This figure seems particularly shocking when we consider that the 1997 National Firearms Amendment Act sought to ban handguns altogether and develop a national firearms registry. The latter is still not in place, and no firearms database has been developed.[9] The Dunblane massacre in 1996, where a former scout leader shot dead sixteen young schoolchildren and their teacher in their primary school gymnasium, prompted the legislation. Ten years after the tragedy, buying guns in the United Kingdom remains very easy and fairly straightforward. "I know people who can easily get me a gun," admits John, a gang member from Hackney, East London.[10]

The successful criminal colonization of Western urban enclaves is primed by the indifference of the market-state toward these areas. Poor economic opportunity, coupled with the electoral irrelevance of the population, most of whom do not even vote, is at the root of the market-state's lack of interest. Ironically, globalization has opened new avenues at a geographical distance from the market-state, while closing others at the heart of such state.[11] The so-called ghetto tax symbolizes the roadblocks erected between the new state and its poorest neighborhoods. A Brookings Institution study, *From Poverty, Opportunity*,[12] published in 2006, shows that being poor in America costs more than being middle class. Every year, low-income households end up paying thousands of dollars more than high-income ones for everyday necessities, simply because they are poor and live in poor areas.[13]

Banks and building societies often blacklist these neighborhoods, contributing to the lack of social capital and severing links to the "outer" world. In Los Angeles, high-income areas like Manhattan Beach have roughly one bank for every 4,000 residents; Compton, a poor Los Angeles neighborhood, has one for every 25,000. "Instead, it has hundreds of alternative financial services, mostly absent from wealthy areas of Los Angeles, that charge jaw-dropping fees. Cashing checks, for instance, costs 3 percent or more of the check's value." And "in poor areas, cashing a $500 check in storefront check-cashing services can range from $5 to $50 more than it would cost in a bank. Customers who take out a short-term loan can be hit with an annual percentage rate of 400 percent or more, a rate estimated to be more than 35 times higher than the average credit card rate in California."[14]

FEAR OF GLOBALIZATION

The first victims of the criminal colonization of urban enclaves are the younger generation. "There is a lot of crime, a lot of underground drug dealing and people getting shot because of that in the area [Forest Gate]," explains Plan B, a London rapper.[15] Forest Gate belongs to one of a number of inner-city and suburban areas in British cities where multiethnic communities find themselves living amid the spats and strikes of gangs battling to control tiny territories. However, while many of the criminals involved are portrayed as the new "folk devils" of the modern age, the typically understated British government euphemism of "anti-social behavior" belies the atmosphere of mutual mistrust gripping these neighborhoods.

Fear of their own environment forces millions of young people and children to seek emotional refuge in the haven of modern tribal enclaves, i.e. the territory controlled by their gang. "*Mara* for us is like a big family. As long as you are inside and you stay in your *barrio* you are safe, nobody can touch you. When you are outside you must be very careful," explains Skid, a thirty-three-year-old who has been a member of Mara Salvatrucha in El Salvador since he was seventeen. "When you are in a gang, no one messes with you," echoes Sam, a seventeen-year-old boy from East London.[16] Thus, the world outside the territory controlled by one's own gang, the global village we live in, can become intimidating and, above all, unwelcoming. This is the landscape drawn by rogue economics and globalization under the indifferent gaze of the market-state.

Gangs find themselves constantly engaged in territorial warfare to defend their enclaves and maintain a lifestyle enclosed within walled and impenetrable barrios. "This is our area, we were born and raised here, it is where we operate" explains Ikechukwu, an Area Boy in the market of Idumota, Lagos. He is a big boy with several scars on his face. When I meet him, he is high on drugs and his eyes are red. On his right hand he wears a big ring, which he uses like a set of brass knuckles. "Whoever passes here must pay a toll to move around. If he goes to another area he must pay someone else. That is the rule." While we are talking, a boy on a motorbike tries to bypass him without paying the toll. Ikechukwu turns around, grabs him by the arm, and pummels the trespasser, leaving him in the mud. Turning back to me, he hardly misses a beat: "Sorry, what were we talking about?"[17] For the gangs, control of territory remains as important today as it was a thousand years ago for the starving peasants of Western Europe, because it is still the sole lifeline of the tribe. "The territory is the only real space we have, it is where we are safe," confirms a London gang member.[18]

While the social disintegration caused by globalization spurred the growth of gangs, their structure and proliferation is a reaction to the phenomenon of globalization, at the core of which stands the notion of enclosed territory. Confined space, not history or tradition, is the new tribal identity; such a space can be filled with new, artificially created memories, myths and folk stories. The past, therefore, is reshaped to fit a harsh present. Here the parallel with pre- and post-Cultural Revolution China is striking.

Never larger than the neighborhood of a member's birth, the *barrio* represents the geographic and emotional universe of the gang. Any attempt to step outside will fail. "Once you are in, you cannot get out, at least not alive," confirms Edwin, a member of Mara Salatrucha from Villa Mariona, a *barrio* on the outskirts of San Salvador. History is narrowed, trapped, and constantly recycled inside such boundaries, and therefore the *maras* have no memory of their national origins—just as the Chinese are oblivious of what happened before Mao. Culture becomes a spatial cage without any chance of escape, explained Plan B. After two years at the University of Essex, less than twenty kilometers from Forest Gate, he dropped out of school. "I could not find myself living in the suburbs, I find it too small-minded. That's one thing I love about the city. Although there's a lot of crime, and all of that shit, there's a lot of people with brains in their head who know what's going on. The people in the suburbs are kinda shielded from that."[19]

Modern gangs fight fear with violence, and violence has become a way of life. As in China, violence is encoded in people's emotional DNA. In the British documentary *Gang Wars,* Taba, a London gang leader, tells the interviewer that violence "is gonna go on forever, because it's the way people are, it is the way people are and not just gangs." Here, violence emerges as a badge of honor, marking acceptance or rejection by the tribe. To join any gang requires a harsh rite of passage. Future *mareros* submit to a complex and painful ordeal, reminiscent of those imposed by medieval satanic sects. They must kill a member of a rival gang or witness an execution. "The first time I saw a beheading I was ten years old. For a month I dreamt of the dead man who came toward me with his head in his hands. Then, with time, you get used to the killing and when you see one of your friends kill someone from another gang, you actually enjoy it. You tease the guy while he dies,"[20] says Necio, a member of Mara Salvatrucha. Would-be members also have to survive a thirteen-second beating by the gang, while women must have sex with each male member of the gang, but nobody dares complain.

Across the world, gang life redraws social rules from scratch. New sexual codes and a fascination with death are innovative components, absent in preglobalization gang culture. "The best thing about this life is that you live it to the extreme," explains Necio, who has a tombstone tattoo on his chest with the names of all the friends who have died. "This is the life of the gangster, *la vida loca*. You stay with your gang and you are protected. But, at the same time, you know that you cannot think about the future, you have no future, there is only the present." The daily interaction with death brings gang members to life day-to-day, in and for the moment. Western political modeling remains foreign to them; they look at life in a fashion similar to Chinese culture: nothing is permanent and everything is immediate, the present is the only existential dimension of the individual.

"Tomorrow you may be dead. Who cares? After death there is hell and it is in hell that I will find all my friends," continues Necio. Death becomes an event, nothing more than that, and as such cannot break the tribe. Tribalism continues after life. Suicide bombers and early Christian martyrs, joyfully entering the Coliseum and facing their death by wild animals, share a similar belief. For them and their modern-day equivalents, life after death is better than the horrors of life on earth. For Necio, he will be reunited with his friends in hell; for a suicide bomber, martyrdom means paradise and enjoying the pleasures of seventy-two virgins; for the Christian martyrs, paradise provided the opportunity to reunite with Christ. These myths assumed the power of reality only through fear of everyday life.

Fear dominates modern tribalism, and young artists like Plan B rap about stories of ordinary fright. The world they depict in their songs is dark and hopeless. "I am affected by the stuff I read in the paper. When I've read about an honor killing or something like that, and knowing that it is happening so close to my doorstep, that's kinda why I write about the darker stuff. I'm a bit of a pessimist when it comes to life, you know. I only expect the worst, or think the worst."[21]

Up-and-coming rappers like Akala are at the forefront of new forms of urban bricolage. His record label, Illa State, uses the Union Jack as a logo but takes its colors from the black, green, and gold of the Jamaican flag. The culture of acute fear is addressed by young British hip-hop artists; as Bristol-based rapper Dynamite MC explains in his elaborate and heartening vision of a better world: "It was a vision of precision, but I knew it would melt."

Early American hip-hop, especially on the West Coast, was almost exclusively gang-related. Artists such as Compton's Most Wanted made music for gang bangers, producing albums with titles like *Music to Driveby* and *Music to Gang Bang*. Today, rap music provides the vehicle through which the antiestablishment's new tribalism of gangs has globalized. "Who killed Saro-Wiwa for oil money? Soldier!! Who killed my nation for oil money?? Soldier!!" raps a song sung in a creole English by the Ogoni people protesting against the exploitation of their territory in the Niger River delta in Nigeria. A prominent vehicle of much popular present-day critical reflection across the world, rap music is also the latest cultural manifestation of the long-standing tribal dynamics of anti-globalization societies.

Rappers have become the poets and philosophers of the new culture. "I sing street life, the death of my friends, I sing for the children, so that they will know that also poetry is a weapon," says a lyric of the Santos Negros, a naïf group from Caracas, Venezuela. "A young nigga got it bad cause I'm brown," raps Ice Cube from the group N.W.A. United States rappers often incorporate the notion of police brutality and racial profiling in their lyrics. Rappers live in the *barrios* of Central America and the slums of Africa, as well as the inner cities of the West, and hip-hop has, from its roots in the African griots, scat singing and beatbox, seen itself coopted by gang culture. Therefore, confrontation among tribes is paramount in its artistic manifestation. MCs "battle" with each other when they make their music. In the film *8 Mile*, Eminem—Marshal Mathers—fights the rappers from the rival gangs using sharp words in front of a deeply hostile audience. Rap is competitive and confrontational when it is performed. As one young London rapper, Max, summarizes: "Rap is not about being together, rap is about your group being the best."

FROM PLATO TO HOOLIGANISM, THE DISCREET CHARM OF TRIBALISM

The late philosopher Karl Popper would describe the correlation between globalization and the spreading of tribalism among modern gangs as one of the "strains of civilization." Historically, major transitions toward what Popper called "open society" often boost tribalism.

The first example of what Popper defines as the move to an open society took place in Greece in the sixth and fifth centuries BC. Economic necessity triggered the transition. Overpopulation among the Athenian ruling elites had put tremendous economic pressure on landowners because available land had become scarce. Colonization then presented a clever solution to the problem. Yet, Greek colonization proved very different from modern colonization in that it fostered the birth of daughter societies, replicas of the Athenian socio-economic and political establishment. Along the northern shores of the Mediterranean basin, this policy created a cluster of new *poleis*, city-states founded by wealthy Athenians and run as democracies. Colonies blossomed in southern Italy, which was renamed Magna Graeca.

At the time, the dissemination of democracy and spreading of Greek culture gave birth to the concept of cosmopolitanism, the idea that free people were citizens of the world, a world ruled by democracy under the banner of Greek civilization. Cosmopolitanism became the essence of Greek colonization. Conceptually, the cosmopolitan man came very close to personifying the globalized individual, someone at ease in every corner of the global village. The British sociologist Anthony Giddens even describes globalization as global cosmopolitanism.[22]

Ironically, both cosmopolitanism and globalization rest on the homogenization of civilizations. Greek "daughter societies," for example, were replicas of Athens. More than a modicum of arrogance surrounded this idea that the leading civilization of Greece proved far superior to all others. As seen in Chapter One, the West never doubted that Russia's forced entry into global capitalism was a great improvement for the local population as well as for Western investors, because Western-style capitalism stood tall as the best possible economic model. In this context, any type of indigenous diversity can be shunned. The cosmopolitan or globalized world is a "world where there are many others; but also where there are no others," writes Giddens.[23]

In the fifth and sixth centuries, Greek culture, armed with the wealth of the colonizing Athenians, had simply taken over the known world. In the Mediterranean world, poetry, music, and scientific discovery came largely from Greek civilization, even when they originated in daughter societies. While the universal language of the cosmopolitan man then was Greek, today's globalized individuals express themselves in English. Anglo-Saxon culture has created the driving force of globalization as well as of antiestablishment movements such as hip-hop. Though its roots are African and Creole, hip-hop has spread globally through the English version of its songs. Around the world, hip-hop groups have disseminated an enormous range of orchestral, rhythmic, and sampling techniques that have grown into the biggest-selling genre worldwide in music today. This cultural development uses English as its lingua franca but expresses in many other tongues. Today, rappers sing stories from *la vida loca* in many different languages.

Athens' colonialism brought great prosperity to the colonies and soon threatened Sparta, a city still deeply tribal. At the beginning of the sixth century, Sparta began its revolt against Athens, motivated by the fear of being forced into the Athenian model of colonization, as well as by economic pressure from the colonies. Spartan oligarchs feared cosmopolitanism; they understood that the Athenian colonization model had altered trade flows and that the colonies had begun to grow faster than Athens. They sensed that soon the daughter societies would take over the economy of the colonizer and damage Sparta economically.

After the fall of the Berlin Wall, Western powers proved unable to keep the globalization of the Russian economy under control. In a similar fashion, the transition of Athens from a closed to an open society had opened a Pandora's box. The ruling elite and the formerly privileged classes of Athens eventually came to share Sparta's concerns. Fear motivated their decision to turn their backs on what they "saw as one complex democracy, a monetary commercialism and naval policy."[24] In an unexpected twist of alliances, they called for the tribal armies of Sparta to end the rule of Athens. This betrayal marked the beginning of the Peloponnesian War. Athens eventually fell, and Sparta installed a puppet regime in the city, the government of the Thirty Tyrants. This so-called reign of terror lasted eight months and cost more lives than had been lost in ten years of war.

Thus, this major leap in civilization, the spreading of Athenian democracy through Athens' colonies, brought with it the unknown and altered the Athenian identity. It confused the masses. People panicked. And so they reverted to tribalism, to a closed society, a society they knew how to deal with, away from the uncertainty of transition. Tribalism offered certainty and gave them security.

A closed society is essentially a tribe. It is a society "whose members hold together, caring nothing for the rest of humanity, on the alert for attack and defense, bound, in fact, to a perpetual readiness for battle. Such is human society fresh from the hands of nature. Man was made for this society," writes Henry Bergson.[25] Tribalism is essentially a system of stereotypes with which we are familiar. In the sixth century, Athenians were comfortable with a closed society, and it was that type of society that they believed could save them from the perils of cosmopolitanism. Stereotyping as a form of defense has long existed as a social impulse for all human beings. Indeed, such categorizing of other people is necessary not only in maintaining a system of differences and distinctions as a tested formula for affirming membership of a community. Tribalism, in this respect, is encoded in human nature. Without it people could not understand the world. In fact, the inability to identify and read such social codes is medically defined as a disorder, in the form of autism.[26]

The difficulty of moving from a tribal to an open society, as analyzed by Popper, prefigured the difficult process of modern globalization. "The primitive mentality of the closed society survives in Western man and surfaces again in times of stress," he writes. Consider George W. Bush's famous speech after the September 11, 2001, attack. He divided the world into two groups: "those who are with us or against us." This is perhaps the "poorest expression of tribal politics ever conceived," writes Decca Aitkenhead in *The Guardian*.[27] How can we define *them* and *us* if, for example, the London suicide bombers were British citizens? Nationality, therefore, no longer serves as the sole determinant or as a valid category. Tribalism seems to fit much better into the new scenario.

Fifteen centuries before Bush reverted to tribal politics, Plato fell victim to the discreet charm of tribalism. After the reign of terror, he sought a closed society where tribal values prevailed, gained acceptance, and were promoted. Popper's criticism of Plato centers on the Greek philosopher's fear of moving forward toward an open society. He presents Plato "as a totalitarian party-politician, unsuccessful in his immediate and practical undertakings, but, in the long run, only too successful in his propaganda for the arrest and overthrow of a civilization he hated."[28] Plato's *Republic* became a model for an authoritarian and immobile closed society, identical to Mao's China. This same criticism could easily apply to the politics of American neoconservatives. The cosmopolitan revolution the Greeks began still lives on through globalization, its latest version. Yet history and civilization find themselves constantly threatened by the "perennial revolt against freedom." "This struggle touches our feelings, for it is still going on within ourselves. Plato was the child of a time that is still our own," writes Popper.[29]

The strain of civilization "is still felt even in our own day, especially in times of social change. It is the strain created by the effort which life in an open and partially abstract society continually demands from us. . . . It is the price we have to pay for being human." Yet, we do not have to go through the reign of terror of the Athenians to experience the same primitive emotions, to relive "the birth trauma of our civilization";[30] it remains enough to be conscious of present-day political manipulation. The market matrix and the web of political illusions that engulf modern humanity have the scope to hide the strains of civilization from the citizens of the global village. But if these manipulations force us to be ignorant about the world we live in, they do not shield us from the impact of rogue economics.

Thus, violence, war, and fear plague the globalized world and during times like these, human ideals vanish while the values of closed societies remain. "Murder and pillage and perfidy, cheating and lying become not only lawful," writes Bergson, "they are praiseworthy. The warring nations espouse the values of *Macbeth*'s witches: 'Fair is foul, and foul is fair.'"[31] In the fifth and sixth centuries BC, cosmopolitanism did not pacify the known world; it led to a decade of bloody wars. Equally, globalization not only fails to bring about peace and stability to a planet in deep political turmoil, it unwittingly fosters modern tribalism.

FOOTBALL, A WINDOW INTO OUR WORLD

Never before has the witches' chant seemed so relevant. In Scotland, Macbeth's land, hooligans from the Glasgow Ranger Football Club march to the football ground, where the derby with Celtic Rangers takes place, singing "Rule Britannia." The song embodies their willingness to walk the path of their ancestors, to fight and subdue the rival's fans, the Celtic stock of Catholics. During the derby, Glasgow becomes a gigantic *barrio*, where two rival gangs fight each other. "These rivalries generate the game's horror stories: jobs denied because of allegiance to the foe; fans murdered for wearing the wrong jersey in the wrong neighborhood."[32] Unsurprisingly, during the derby, the death toll rises as the result of football-related crimes. With eight murders per match, it sounds as if the *maras* have come to town.

Football hooliganism is one of the surreal outcomes of globalization. Fan violence in Britain, exacerbated by the tensions brought about by political and industrial unrest in the 1970s and early 1980s, has become a truly globalized phenomenon. In the 1980s, Margaret Thatcher, one of the pioneers of privatization, described hooligans as "a disgrace to civilized society." Yet, with the liberalization of the player transfer market and the market expansion of large clubs, football was re-exported worldwide, complete with its accompanying baggage of mythology, messianic passions, and off-field violence. As Roger Milla, the talismanic Cameroon captain at the 1990 World Cup has reflected, "I'll tell you something: if we had beaten England, Africa would have exploded. Ex-plo-ded. There would even have been deaths. The Good Lord knows what He does. Me, I thank Him for stopping us in the quarter-finals. That permitted a little pliancy."[33]

Globalization radicalized football fans and spread hooliganism, which in the 1990s became a universal phenomenon. The fine line between football providing "an arena in which social relations are realized and social groups come into being"[34] and acting as a trigger for contagious violence became ever tighter to walk. Throughout the 1990s, regional and international football authorities alike gave greater prominence to football antiracism messages, yet hooligans stained the stadiums of the world with their blood. Ironically, this violence exploded globally while in the United Kingdom hooliganism began declining. Following the 1985 Heysel Stadium disaster, the European competition ban for British clubs, the 1989 Hillsbrough disaster, and the implementation of the Taylor report to segregate fans in the stadiums, Thatcher's "disgrace to civilized society" was contained and polititcians could sweep the problem under the carpet. Yet the problem persists outside the stadiums and when fans travel abroad.

Beyond Britain, the global boom in football violence brought about unpredictable local outcomes. "Wandering among lunatic fans, gangster owners, and crazed Bulgarian strikers, I kept noticing the ways globalization had failed to diminish the game's local cultures, local blood feuds, and even local corruption. In fact, I began to suspect that globalization had actually increased the power of these local entities—and not always in such good ways," wrote Franklin Foer in the prologue to his book, *How Soccer Explains the World.*

Thus, football became a window into our society as society is a window into football. While the move toward an open society gives greater rein to cosmopolitanism, it intensifies competition well beyond the simple game. Never before has a sport been so distant from the universal Olympic motto of De Coubertin: "the important thing is to be part of the game." As with rap music, what matters is winning, being the best.

In the globalized world of football, hooligans use the game as a vehicle toward tribalism, and violence and victory dictate the way forward. As described by Popper and Bergson, this retrenchment is a response both to the threat posed by the big, globalized teams, which could swallow local teams, and to globalization's message of a homogenized society, where everything local, including football teams, vanishes. Football fans do not want to live in a "world where there are many others; but also where there are no others."[35] Like the honest fans of football, hooligans feel entitled to their own identity and diversity. And their football team becomes a vehicle to express such difference.

Just like the *maras*, hooligans carry on their bodies the symbols of their gang. Many Rangers fans wear orange shirts and hold orange banners, orange being the color of William of Orange, the leader of the Protestant revolution that ousted the Catholic monarchy in 1688. During the derby in Glasgow, other banners display with pride the symbols of the Ulster Volunteer Force and Ulster Defence Association, the Protestant paramilitaries of Northern Ireland, just a short way across the Irish Sea from Glasgow. The end of the armed conflict in Northern Ireland, the official pacification of the IRA and of the Ulster Paramilitaries, has not eliminated the roots of the conflict, which go far back in history to "the unfinished fight over the Protestant Reformation."[36] Religious and ethnic tribalism begat the Reformation and its closed society that Glasgow's hooligans cling to as the game proceeds.

Culture and history are once again recycled to fit the new tribe that centers on a sport, football. Modern tribalism seems to be able to emerge from whatever brings people together, from music to sport, from religion to crime. The requisite accessories are rogue economics, globalization, and strong myths around which to embroider the identity of the tribe. Although modern tribalism draws from old myths, which are comforting tales for those who are intimidated by globalization, modern tribalism is defensive and apolitical. But it doesn't have to be that way. On the contrary: it can constitute the platform of a challenging and creative response to rogue economics. The construction of Islamic finance around sharia law illustrates an outstanding example of economic tribalism. To date, this experiment remains the sole real challenge to rogue economics, and as such, it could become the blueprint for the postglobalization economic system.

CHAPTER TWELVE

ECONOMIC TRIBALISM

"A friend in need is a friend indeed."

Egyptian-born entrepreneur
Mohamad al-Fayed

Islamic finance has become the fastest-growing, most dynamic sector of global finance. Every Western-style financial product has its sharia, i.e. Islamic law, compliant instrument: microfinance, mortgages, oil and gas exploration, bridge building, even sponsorship of sporting events. Islamic finance is innovative, flexible, and potentially very profitable. "Operating in 70 countries with about $500bn in assets, it is poised to expand geometrically."[1] With more than one billion Muslims eager to support it, analysts project that this system will soon manage approximately 4 percent of the world economy, equivalent to $1 trillion in assets. Such figures explain the eagerness of Western banks to tap into sharia financial services. Citigroup, along with many other Western banking retailers, have opened Islamic branches in Muslim countries. At the end of 2004, the Islamic Bank of Britain, the first bank catering to a European Muslim client base, floated its shares on the London Stock Exchange. Ironically, Western capitalism's three major global economic crises—the 1970s oil shocks, the late 1990s Asian crisis, and 9/11—paved the way to the ascent of Islamic finance.

Unlike market economics, Islamic finance centers on the religious tenets of Islam and operates in a way to keep Muslims compliant with sharia, the religious law that comes directly from the Koran. Islamic activists, intellectuals, writers, and religious leaders have always upheld the prohibition of *riba*, the interest charged by moneylenders, and denounced

237

gharar, which refers to any type of speculation. Under this belief, money must not become a commodity in itself to create more money. Islamic finance thus shuns hedge funds and private equities, because they simply multiply cash by stripping assets. Money serves as a means or instrument of productivity as originally envisioned by Adam Smith and David Ricardo. This principle is embodied in the *sukuks,* Islamic bonds. *Sukuks* always link to real investments—for example, to pay for the construction of a toll highway—and never for speculative purposes. This principle springs from the sharia's ban on gambling as well as on the prohibition of any forms of debt and activities that trade risk.

At the end of the nineteenth century, supporters and promoters of Islamic finance repeatedly expressed discontent with the Western-style banks that had penetrated Muslim countries. Several fatwas, or religious decrees, were issued to reiterate the tenet that the interest-based activities of the colonizers' banks proved incompatible with the sharia. Yet, because Western financial institutions were the only banks active in the Muslim world, the faithful had to use them even if they performed poisonous practices based on prohibited activities.

From the mid-1950s to the mid-1970s, economists, financiers, sharia scholars, and intellectuals studied the possibility of scrapping interest rates and of creating financial institutions centered on a sharia-compatible alternative to the *riba.* In their mind the Islamic economic system would incorporate the *zakat*—obligatory almsgiving to help the poor—and other fundamental elements of the Muslim religion, such as the funding of the *haj,* i.e. the pilgrimage to Mecca.

The first projects of applied Islamic economics came into existence concurrently in the 1950s in the countryside of Lower Egypt and in Kuala Lumpur, Malaysia. The Egyptian project, located in Meet Ghamr, Egypt, supported a housing plan for the less wealthy. The Malaysian government-sponsored experiment, was promoted by the Pilgrims' Administration and Fund of Malaysia. It supervised financial institutions that collected savings and invested them in accordance with the sharia. It aimed to finance the *haj*, which, together with the *zakat*, is one of the five pillars of Islam.

Until the early 1970s, Islamic economics was essentially embryonic and regarded with deep skepticism. "Back then, no one really thought Islamic banking would ever become big," recalls Sheik Hussein Hamid Hassan, an Egyptian scholar involved in the creation of one of the first Islamic banks. "People thought it was a strange idea—as strange as talking about Islamic whiskey!"[2] Western skepticism compounded daily because of the Muslim countries' chronic lack of capital. They had no money to start an alternative banking system, many thought they never would, therefore people dismissed the idea of Islamic finance as merely utopian. This scenario changed with the 1973–1974 oil shock, which generated a massive capital inflow into Arab oil-producing countries from Western importers. The quadrupled price of oil generated the capital needed to put into practice what had remained only an idea debated for decades.

That idea materialized with the establishment of an international developmental bank for the Islamic region. Such a bank would enhance the Organization of the Islamic Conference, considered a potential power base for some of the newly enriched countries, especially Saudi Arabia and Algeria. At the same time, the bank would serve as the instrument for distributing financial help from oil-rich Muslim countries to their brethren in Africa and Asia. The first call for the establishment of the Islamic Development Bank (IDB) came from the heads of state of Saudi Arabia, Algeria, and Somalia. In 1974, when the articles of agreement of the IDB were drafted, it formally stated that the bank's activities had to be conducted in accordance with the sharia.

At the core of sharia-compliant economics there is an

exceptional joint venture. Indeed, this alliance emerged in the 1970s when rich Muslims and sharia scholars began working together. This unusual partnership is a phenomenon unique in modern economics, but one that cemented the foundation of a new economic system. A few visionary personalities, like Prince Mohammad al Faisal (son of the late Saudi King Faisal bin Abdul-Aziz), Saleh Kamel of Saudi Arabia, Ahmed al Yaseen of Kuwait, and Sami Hamoud of Jordan, channeled some of the new wealth produced by the first oil shock into the formation of a new breed of Islamic banks. Sharia scholars and clerics drew up the monetary structure of the new banks.[3]

Partnership between leaders and clerics, therefore, serves as the root of Islamic finance. This concept springs from the essence of the *Umma*, the body or community of believers, central to the spirit of Islam. For Muslims, the *Umma* represents a single and unified entity; it breathes, thinks, and prays in unison. It exudes the soul of Islam. Individualism within Islam does not make sense because Islam, based on tribal culture, does not recognize it. Traditional tribal values, such as the strong sense of belonging, the obligation to help friends in need, and the acceptance of religious leaders' authority are the pillars of Muslim culture. Sharia scholars transplanted these values into Islamic economics; these same principles allowed Arab Bedouins to withstand the harshness of the desert for centuries. Cooperation was essential in such a hostile environment and is still a must in modern times.

Partnership is the heartbeat of Islamic economics. "Underlying the system is the philosophy of *risk sharing*: the lender must share the borrower's risk, making the two in effect partners, injecting a strong social component into the financial system. This concept separates Islamic Finance from Western Finance, which seeks to maximize profits and minimize loss through diversification and risk transfer."[4] Also, money must be put to work. Because Islamic finance prohibits interest, it seeks revenues from rents, royalties, business profits, or commodity trading; a mortgage, for example, represents a "rent to buy" arrangement. Thus, conceptually, Islamic economics is the opposite of Western finance, which revolves around the individual's self-interest.

Above all, Islamic finance represents the sole global economic force that conceptually challenges rogue economics. It does not allow investment in pornography, prostitution, narcotics, tobacco, or gambling. As discussed above, since the fall of the Berlin Wall, all these areas have blossomed thanks to globalization outlaws under the indifferent eyes of the market-state.

THE MAGIC OF THE MARKET

In his masterpiece, *An Inquiry into the Nature and Causes of the Wealth of Nations*,[5] Adam Smith claims that an invisible hand regulates the market. This hidden hand directs market forces according to people's need to maximize gains or benefits to their own advantage. Such behavior, he adds, proves rational and perfectly in line with human nature. Smith's compelling argument tells us that while each individual seeks exclusively personal interest, the sum of these egotistical behaviors ends up enriching and benefiting the nation. How can such a process happen? For Smith, the collective selfish behavior ensures that capital's scarce resources are always directed into investments that provide the highest returns for the lowest risk.[6] In other words, by seeking to maximize profits and minimize losses, people contribute to the wealth of their nation. This phenomenon, in short, is the magic of the market.

To market economists, Smith's invisible hand represents a quasi-religious icon that no one in their right minds would dream of challenging. Many believe that this icon remains at work in the globalized economy. "The vast majority of economic decisions today fit those earlier presumptions of individuals acting more or less in their rational self-interest," said Alan Greenspan, former chairman of the United States Federal Reserve Bank, in 2005. "Indeed, without the presumption of rational self-interest, the supply and demand curves of classical economics might not intersect, eliminating the possibility of market-determined prices. For example, one could hardly imagine that today's awesome array of international transactions would produce the relative economic stability that we experience daily if they were not led by some international version of Smith's invisible hand."[7]

Adam Smith would agree that outsourcing, i.e. the relocation of business abroad according to low costs of production, comes as the direct result of the globalized market's invisible hand. In the late 1990s, for example, Japanese and American industrialists relocated some of their factories to China (the low cost of labor offset the transportation costs of finished products to domestic and foreign outlets). In a globalized world, populated by multinationals and transnational industrialists, however, Smith's invisible hand no longer just works in single countries but can inflence market forces everywhere. Rational self-interest, therefore, can enrich and impoverish large sections of the world's population well away from national boundaries. In the 1990s, the relocation of foreign industries to China, for example, altered the direct capital flows to Southeast Asia. At the beginning of the 1990s, the bulk of Asia's foreign direct investment from Japan and the United States went to this region while China received the remainder. By the end of the decade the situation reversed. Highly competitive production and labor costs transformed China's factories into workshops for the world, shutting down industries elsewhere and affecting the economic performance of distant regions, such as Mexico. In 2002, Royal Philips Electronics closed two-thirds of its television production lines in Mexico and relocated them to China.[8]

If Smith's invisible hand guides the globalization revolution, one could argue that in the long run, Western capitalism will take over the world economy and that people and nations will be enriched thanks to a better, more efficient distribution of resources. Yet, a closer look at the growth of Islamic finance seems to contradict such an argument. By facilitating transnational tribalism, globalization generated the ideal conditions for Islamic finance to blossom, as illustrated by the Islamization of the Malaysian economy. This represents a new and potentially rival economic system to Western capitalism regulated by principles foreign to market economics. Adam Smith would agree that Malaysia's remarkable adventure into Islamic finance did not have the guiding invisible hand of the market, but rather religious factors, such as Muslim tribal solidarity.

SHARIA ECONOMICS

Two of globalization's major crises boosted the nascent Islamic finance: the 1997 Asian market crash and 9/11. The first triggered a retrenchment, the second a closure from Western-style economics. Malaysia, a committed Muslim country, paved the way to such dramatic changes.

The Asian crisis emerges as a textbook reversal of fortune written by the schizophrenic, globalized capital markets. It came from the sudden and unexpected withdrawal of capital from five Asian countries (South Korea, Indonesia, Thailand, Malaysia, and the Philippines). Almost overnight, $100 billion capital inflow—equivalent, in 1996, to one-third of worldwide flows into emerging markets—turned into $12 billion capital outflow. The magnitude of the crisis was unprecedented, the consequences disastrous. As much as 10 percent of the GDP of the five Asian countries simply vanished. A decade after the crash, investors still debate what really happened. Was the exceptional pre-crisis GDP growth of those countries a mirage? Many believe that the crisis was a by-product of globalization euphoria: the money-intoxicated collective hallucination described by Tom Wolfe in *The Bonfire of the Vanities,* experienced by the "Wall Street masters of the universe."

Though distinguished economists have tried to find a rational explanation for the crisis, the best interpretations center on the bipolar behavior of globalized markets, what Stiglitz calls the "instability in beliefs" and Keynes defined as "animal spirits."[9] Though capitalism had seen similar reversals of confidence before, for example, in October 1987, when the equity market unexpectedly crashed, "there was a touch of the absurd in the unfolding Asian drama. International money managers harshly castigated the very same Asian governments they were praising just months before."[10]

Post-crisis disillusionment spread across the world at a speed and intensity rivaling that which had characterized the rampant enthusiasm of the boom years. The euphoria of the early 1990s turned into mass hysteria, which soon degenerated into chronic phobia. Irrational emotions simply took over the markets. "You can't trust the companies, you can't trust the governments, you can't trust the analysts, and you can't trust the mutual funds managers. Watch out,"[11] was the mantra repeated by Western financial operators regarding their former Asian partners.

The reversal of confidence hit the Asian economies with the intensity of a financial tsunami and seriously crippled them. "The Thai currency dropped 40 percent in value; the Indonesian rupiah dropped 80 percent; the Malaysian ringgit [fell] by 30 percent; the Singapore dollar fell by 15 percent; the Philippine peso [dropped] by 50 percent. Stock markets contracted by similar percentages."[12] As panic spread across the dealing rooms of globalized finance, the International Monetary Fund came to the rescue. In cooperation with the World Bank and the Asian Development Bank, it put together a $112 million foreign-exchange loan. They aimed to defend the currencies of Indonesia, Korea, and Thailand, which had accepted the rescue package. The initiative proved a disaster; it failed to reinstate investors' confidence and did not prevent a further deterioration of the Asian economies.[13]

While the IMF desperately tried to avoid the inevitable, i.e. the financial meltdown of emerging Asian markets, the Malaysian prime minister, Dr Mohamad Mahathir took the international finance community by surprise. He publicly attacked foreign-currency speculators, accusing them of running down a prosperous and fast-growing Muslim country. He played an unexpected trump card: the *gharar*, the Islamic prohibition of speculation. Malaysia had become a victim of greedy Western traders, he asserted in his message to the Muslim world. Spurning intervention from the IMF and the World Bank, icons of Western finance, Mathahir turned to his fellow Muslims to sustain the Malaysian economy. Muslim investors and the Islamic Development Bank put together an alternative rescue package with loans and investments. Unexpectedly, Muslim solidarity rebuffed the standard of Western finance, challenging Western capitalism's traditional rescue packages. While Thailand's GDP took another dive after the failure of the IMF aid plan, Malaysia hosted a string of rich Muslim investors, all eager to start business ventures in the country—among them was Mohamed al Fayed, the Egyptian-born owner of Harrods in London. "At the end of his trip, al Fayed announced that the upmarket department store would open an outlet at the new Kuala Lumpur International Airport and his 25 stores around the world would carry the line of electrical appliances made by the Malaysian Electric Company. Mr. Ong Eian Siew, the company's chief operating officer, said it hoped to export $2.5 million worth of goods to Yemen [in 1998]."[14]

Mahathir's decision to seek help from fellow Muslims shocked the IMF. His justification for such a radical departure proved even more shocking. In a speech delivered when he accepted an award from the Islamic financial company LARIBA, in the United States, he said:

> About 90 per cent of the Bumiputeras [Malays] are Muslims. In terms of wealth and income, the Bumiputeras had always lagged behind the non-Bumiputeras. In 1970, we embarked on a New Economic Policy (NEP) to ensure that the Bumiputeras enjoy their fair share of the economic pie. As 90 per cent of the Bumiputeras are Muslim, the NEP is almost synonymous with enhancing the economic status of the *Umma* in Malaysia. Many expected us to go to the IMF for loans to tide over our crisis. But we did not do that. Calling in the IMF would have been a disaster for the Malaysian *Umma*, as the NEP policies are not in keeping with the IMF's idea of free unfettered competition in which the strongest would take all. Equity is not of concern to the IMF.[15]

Perhaps Mahathir had learned a lesson from the Russians—when the 1990s IMF rescue packages enriched the oligarchs—and did not want to replicate such a scenario.

The cocktail of religion, economics, and politics mixed by Prime Minister Mahathir symbolizes the complexity and uniqueness of Malaysian society where, on a daily basis, sharia edicts shape economic life, and religious and economic tribalism intersect. The secret of the success of this remarkable mix becomes apparent when one examines the self-definition of the society. At the end of 2005, a telephone survey of over 1,000 randomly selected Muslims reported that "in terms of identity, when asked to choose which defined them most, i.e. being Malay, Muslim or Malaysian, 72.7 per cent chose being Muslim as their primary identity. As their second choice of identity, more respondents chose being

Malaysian (14.4 per cent) than being Malay (12.5 per cent). [. . .] The results of the survey indicate that the majority of Muslims in Peninsular Malaysia are defined primarily by Islam rather than by their national identity as Malaysians, but are comfortable with living alongside people of other faiths."[16]

Malaysia's revolutionary decision appealed to fellow Muslims, so much so that they rallied around it. This is an outstanding example of economic tribalism. By putting the interests of the Muslim community and the wellbeing of the *Umma* above the principles of market economics, Mahathir reminded Muslim investors that the strength of Islamic economics is partnership. Indeed, money from the Gulf continued flowing even while the economic crisis peaked, and in quick succession came capital controls: the removal of the Malaysian currency from international markets because it was no longer tradable, the sacking of the governor of the Central Bank, and the sacking and subsequent jailing of the then-finance minister and deputy prime minister, Anwar Ibrahim. By the end of 1998, when Bank Negara issued new projections for 1999 GDP, Malaysian economic growth was negative (-2.8 percent). Against this tragic economic scenario, Adam Smith supporters would have jumped boat and left the country to sink into depression.

In sharp contrast, Muslim investors came to the rescue. Against all odds and with the disapproval of international financial institutions, such as the IMF and the World Bank, Malaysia weathered the financial storm by retrenching and moving away from Western-style economics. It did so because it had an alternative that other countries, such as Thailand, did not have: the embryo of an Islamic financial system. Thus, the country's ability to follow such a radical policy rested, in fact, on Malaysia's long-term efforts to become part of a team of nations eager to create an Islamic banking system. In 1997, no other country could offer Muslim investors a sufficiently sophisticated financial system into which to channel their funds. As explained by Mahmoud Amin el Gamal, professor of Economics and Statistics at Rice University in Houston, "Malaysia has always been at the forefront of innovation of Islamic finance—at least 10 years ahead of Bahrain, the United Arab Emirates, and so on. Very early on, Malaysia developed an inter-bank money system for Islamic bonds certified by the powers that be. And the size of the Malaysian economy is a huge attraction."[17]

Throughout the 1990s, Malaysia, a recipient of vast capital inflow, had worked hard to develop a domestic Islamic banking system. As early as 1992, Finance Minister Anwar Ibrahim had encouraged bankers to provide alternative financial services in line with sharia. "Let your officers identify and come up with new instruments that can compete with other financial instruments," he reiterated in 1996, just months before the Asian crisis began. "They must not be too constrained by the nature of Islamic products, but must be innovative within the requirements of the Islamic Sharia."[18] By 1994, encouraged by the success of sharia financial products among resident and foreign Muslim investors, Ibrahim suggested that Western and Islamic banking could not coexist without producing serious contradictions. He therefore suggested that Malaysia's finances should be totally Islamized.

Malaysia soon emerged as the leading country in Islamic finance; it became a magnet for direct investments. Two factors seem to have boosted capital inflow: the gravitation of Muslim funds from abroad and the migration of conventional investments away from Western finance in favor of Islamic financial instruments. The first was a consequence of the Asian financial crisis, the second the result of 9/11.

The attack on the World Trade Center was followed by a rush of Muslim investors to Islamize their portfolios. Until 9/11, the bulk of Muslim finance had come from conventional investments held in the West. America's response to the attack served as the key factor in the quest for alternative investments. Fearing tougher controls introduced under the Patriot Act, visa restrictions, and possible asset freezing as a consequence of new antiterrorism financial policies, Muslim investors turned to such countries as Malaysia, which had a well-developed Islamic financial system. The forced migration of conventional investments away from Western finance awakened dormant feelings of religious identity. "Many Muslim professionals have looked for ways to express their identity," says Qudeer Latif, a Dubai-based partner at Clifford Chance, the British law firm, which has a sizable Islamic finance business. "Choosing sharia-compliant products is one way to do that."[19]

Countries like Malaysia, at the forefront of Islamic economics, led the way, as proven by the growth of the Malaysian Islamic bond market. According to Moody's, the international rating agency, as of 2004, $41bn in Islamic bonds had been issued globally, and of that total $30bn or 75 percent in Malaysia and only $11bn in the Gulf.[20]

Sharia-compliant products became key accessories of transnational economic tribalism, and its roots are intertwined with the religious pride of being Muslim. To be sold, a sharia-compliant product requires a fatwa, or religious edict, from a recognized Islamic scholar. This gives Islamic finance a greater degree of flexibility than traditional Western finance,[21] while at the same time it offers investors a degree of security unknown to Westerners. The ethical issue, central to modern finance, does not arise in Islamic finance because the fatwa clears investment from any notion of wrongdoing.

Paradoxically, Islamic finance blossomed under the dark shadow of the neoconservative's "clash of civilizations." In the midst of the War on Terror, which many Muslims perceived as a witchhunt against them, Muslim investors greatly reduced their Western portfolios and turned to Islamic finance. This closure went hand in hand with the revisitation of their traditional values, which had allowed their Arab ancestors to conquer hostile environments; once again, partnership represented the most important value. On a new terrain, economics, the old and the new finally met. Islamic bankers and investors, with the blessing of religious scholars, forged alliances to conquer another, deeply hostile environment: global finance.

The success story of Islamic finance is still unfolding, and it affects a growing number of sectors of the world. Tim Harrison, associate director of Asda's Financial Practice, a consultancy, believes that soon Islamic finance will sponsor "big ticket items," such as concerts and major sporting events. Since these events produce revenues from concessions and ticket sales, they are a natural fit with the growing degree of sophistication now developing in the field.[22] Many believe that the bounty is much bigger than we could possibly anticipate: a new Islamic monetary system.

THE GOLDEN CALIPHATE

Malaysia's perceived bullying by the IMF during the Asian crisis reopened another debate that had engaged Islamic economists, politicians, and religious scholars for decades: the push toward the gold dinar. Until the collapse of the Ottoman Empire in 1923, the gold-dinar standard represented a means of exchange for thirteen centuries.[23] It lasted much longer than has our current monetary system, (the dollar standard was born only in 1971, after the collapse of the Bretton Woods agreement, signed in the aftermath of World War II.) In the collective imagination, the gold dinar "holds historical, cultural and theological appeal for many Muslims. Many Islamic economists advocate a rejection of paper money— since it can be created out of thin air—and a return to gold," writes Ann Berg, a former commodities trader turned artist.[24] Politicians, intellectuals, religious scholars, and even terror-

ists—Osama bin Laden is reportedly among the strongest supporters of the gold dinar—share this view.

In 2001, Malaysia attempted to reintroduce the gold dinar
as a reserve currency to be held in the central banks of Muslim countries. Prime Minister Mahathir hoped that by 2003,
at least a dozen of the 57 countries in the Organization of the
Islamic Conference would join the system. For several reasons,
the attempt never came to fruition; these reasons included
Washington's opposition to the plan, to the extent that the
White House convinced the IMF to prohibit any member state
from pegging its currency to gold. The failure turned the gold
dinar into something of a joke, identical to the analogy
between Islamic finance and Islamic whiskey. Yet, technically
speaking, no major impediments stand in the way of intro-
ducing the gold dinar. Malaysia, and any other Muslim
country willing to use the currency, does not need gold bullion
to fully back the value of the dinar. In reality, all they need is to
peg the currency to the price of gold and to use the fluctuations
of the metal as a regulator of the value of the currency. Inci-
dentally, this technique was used by the United States when it
introduced the bimetallic monetary system linking the dollar
to silver and gold.[25] At that time, the newly formed United
States republic lacked gold reserves.[26]

The introduction of the gold standard in Islamic economics therefore remains feasible even if the IMF prohibits debtor
countries from linking their currency to gold. Since Malaysia
took its revolutionary stand against the IMF, the power of this
organization has eroded. At the same time, many countries
question the soundness of the current monetary system in the
light of America's new protectionism. In her article, "The
Golden Caliphate," Ann Berg summarized such changes:

> As the world gets richer, it is starting to reject dollar-
> based loans. Argentina, Brazil, and Russia have
> decided to pay off their IMF loans, and Turkey—

which suffered economic collapse in 2001—has asserted it will no longer need IMF assistance by 2008. Also, the dramatic oil price increase has made most Islamic countries much wealthier in a short time span. What's more, the global easing of interest rates has made access to capital in domestic currency far easier and, at the same time, the major fiat currencies—a technical term for the fiduciary currencies that are traded internationally—are quickly depreciating against gold.

Additionally, the United States is becoming increasingly protectionist. By saying no to foreign investment, particularly Middle East investment, it is throwing down the gauntlet to foreigners, daring them to jettison their dollar-based investments. Also, since the floating-currency system has proved clumsy at regulating trade balances, it has forfeited some of this macroeconomic function to lawmakers bearing spare economic know-how and blunt instruments such as tariffs, quotas, sanctions, and engineered revaluations. Therefore, several conditions—both economic and political—are in place to cause a shift in global finance.[27]

Today, the real obstacle to a gold-dinar standard is confidence. The essence of a monetary system is fiduciary—people must believe in the value of paper money. With Islamic finance growing at the speed of light and the dollar losing its shine, the gold dinar standard may soon become a possibility. Once established, it will work as a potent magnet. "With an Islamic gold dinar," wrote Jude Wanniski, President Ronald Reagan's economic advisor and one of the original supply-side economists, "the Islamic world would have the best money in the world. The US would be forced to again fix the dollar to gold and the euro and the yuan/yen bloc would join as well. The reason is that the best money becomes a magnet for international finance, because exporters and importers of every country in the world can save the many hundreds of billions of dollars a year now spent hedging against currency losses in the global trade."[28]

International finance will, therefore, adjust to the new standard, as it always does. Politics may not have the strength to do the same. Because monetary systems must be fiduciary, based on trust between governments and people who use the currencies, it is imperative that the gold-dinar standard is coupled with a better distribution of wealth in Muslim countries. Unless partnership in economics goes hand in hand with partnership in politics, it could trigger a political meltdown. The true danger of a gold-dinar standard is the destabilization of Muslim countries, in the event of inequalities of wealth that are not addressed and that a gold-dinar standard might aggravate, leading to civil unrest.

This destabilization scenario becomes particularly real when we consider that one of al Qaeda's central goals remains the creation of the Golden Caliphate as a long-term strategy to destroy the West. In a letter that surfaced in 2005, Saif al Adl, al Qaeda's former security chief, outlined the various stages of the formation of the Caliphate, which included the destruction of the US economy. "Islamists will promote the idea of using gold as the international medium of exchange, leading to the collapse of the dollar. Then an Islamic Caliphate can be declared, inaugurating the fifth stage of al Qaeda's grand plan, which will last until 2016."[29] The world experienced a similar apocalyptic scenario at the end of another globalization. It was triggered by Fascist economics.

STATE TRIBALISM

Fascist economics involved a global reach that stretched from Tokyo to Buenos Aires. It hatched as the offspring of two major global crises: the post–World War I economic meltdown and the crash of 1929. The former produced a retrenchment from economic liberalism, the doctrine that had characterized the exceptional economic growth of the nineteenth century, while the latter buried market economics. One country, Italy, paved the way in the attempt to create a new economic order. The rascal nature of such a system sprang from the failure to promote the economic interest of the masses and from its degeneration into a tool in the hands of ruthless dictators.

In the aftermath of World War I, the transition from wartime to peacetime economics was characterized by the desire to go back to the prewar economic system. Its economic pillars had been the gold standard and the self-regulating market. Politically, the hundred years of relative peace that ended in 1914 rested on the liberal state and the balance of power, which prevented long-lasting wars between the Great Powers.[30] Against this background, the civilization of the nineteenth century produced what A. G. Hopkins described as modern globalization.[31] Centered on the nation-state, this globalization was marked by the spread of industrialization and cosmopolitanism. Labor shifted from farms to towns, with wage labor becoming the norm. Land was given over to property, which became the key source of ownership in the era. Strategies of control over local populations also emerged, through assimilation and association with the global power.

Any postwar attempts to recapture such a unique scenario were doomed to fail. For a start, the collapse of the exceptional political equilibrium of the previous hundred years' peace had triggered World War I. For almost a century, three competing power blocs had kept major war at bay. Unusual circumstances, therefore, had made economic liberalism possible. For the essence of the nineteenth-century globalization was faith in the magic of the self-regulating market, guided exclusively by Adam Smith's invisible hand. Yet, such self-guiding magic could only happen in peacetime.

The world that emerged after World War I proved deeply different from the one before it. "The war had changed the global political landscape forever. Battle and famine had claimed fifteen million people. Empires and dynasties imploded into multiple states throughout eastern and central Europe."[32] The past could not be recreated. As with the Asian crisis of the late 1990s, neither Western finance nor world powers could prevent the economic meltdown.

At the end of World War I, the gold standard lay in ruins. That standard, unlike the current floating-currency system, involved a fixed system of sovereign currencies backed by gold bullion; technically, paper money could be exchanged for its value in gold. All international trade rested upon that concept. At the end of the war, the United Kingdom, until then the world's largest overseas investor, became one of the largest debtors, with 40 percent of its government spending absorbed by the repayment of war debt. Russia, which under the tsarist regime had enjoyed a great deal of foreign investment, suffered a chronic capital outflow as the Bolsheviks took over the economy. France and Belgium, devastated by the German invasion, began stockpiling gold to pay for reconstruction. Payment for war reparations drained Germany's gold reserves and absorbed revenues from the sale of natural resources, such as coal and steel.

Without the restraints of the gold standard, hyperinflation ravaged the economies of Germany, Hungary, Austria, Bulgaria, and Russia. Between 1919 and 1923 these countries printed money to keep their economies alive, and thus, they fueled inflation. Against this scenario, every nation sought the restoration of the gold standard. Yet, starting with Russia in 1923 and ending with Britain, France, Belgium, and Italy, by 1926 it was apparent that the gold parity was short-lived. With the *laissez-faire* economy forever altered, countries needing money creation for debt repayment found the gold standard a straitjacket onto their political aspirations, and its collapse became inevitable. When the hyperinflation of the 1920s was followed by the deflationary spiral spurred by the 1929 stock market crash and a collapse of world trade, the meltdown began.

Against this apocalyptic scenario, Italy retrenched from liberal economic ideals and took refuge in Fascist economics. From the ashes of the hundred-years' peace rose Fascism, and from the debris of the market economy, Mussolini's autarchic regime shaped a new kind of state tribalism. The state became the expression of a collective identity, the essence and soul of the people inside its political and geographical boundaries. "Twenty million people: one single heart-beat, one single mind, one single decision. This event shows and will show the world that Italy and Fascism have one, absolute, unchangeable identity," said Mussolini in 1935 to 20 million Italians who had taken to the streets to listen to his speech.[33] Reverence for the individual similarly vanished into the Fascist state.

State tribalism is alien to nationalism where the state is constructed around the national identity of its people; that is, the state is the expression of such identity. Fascism's state tribalism is exactly the opposite: the national identity becomes the expression of the Fascist state that is the core of the nation. This concept is summarized in Mussolini's definition of fascism: "The Fascist State organizes the nation, but leaves a sufficient margin of liberty to the individual; the latter is deprived of all useless and possibly harmful freedom, but retains what is essential: the deciding power in this question cannot be individual, but the state alone."[34]

It took Mussolini ten years to fully develop the tenets of the Fascist economy. By the time the disastrous consequences of 1929 hit the world, Italy's state tribalism was ripe for global export to countries suffering from similar economic diseases. Yet, its design was visible from the beginning. Having been handed the premiership by King Vittorio Emanuele III in 1922, after the March on Rome, Mussolini began a series of economic reforms that slowly allowed the state to take over the role of the nation. Like modern politicians, he was a master illusionist, hiding the true elitist nature of Fascism under a populist rhetoric. While advocating liberal economic reforms—tax cuts, corporate vitality, and a return to the gold standard (all three achieved)—Il Duce subordinated economic institutions to the firm grip of the state. In 1923, he established the Istituto Nazionale delle Assicurazioni (INA), the national life insurance institute, to compete in the private sector, a decision that gave the state the necessary instruments to influence the market. This innovation proved to be the first step in the creation, in the 1930s, of partecipazioni statali, the partnership between the state and the productive sectors of the economy through massive state holdings. Economic reforms became the long arm of Fascism, paving the way to its authoritarian political expression. At the micro level, the restructuring of the economy was carried out with the help of the infamous *camicie nere*, the black-shirted Fascist militia that used violence, torture, and murder to silence all opposition.

The degeneration of state tribalism into a repressive police state was the inevitable consequence of the totalitarian nature of Fascism. Far from being a movement, an idea that implies the participation of large numbers of people, Fascism was an elitist phenomenon. As summarized by the late Hungarian thinker Karl Polanyi, its strength rested in the "influence of the persons in high position whose good will the fascist leaders possessed, and whose influence in the community could be counted upon to shelter them from the consequences of an abortive revolt, thus taking the risk of revolution."[35] Creating the modern market-state, Mussolini did not care about the nation as much as about preserving the privileges of select groups of individuals who controlled Italian finance and the economy.

Sharia economics centers on the concept of partnership and springs from a religious vision of the world, which is embraced by the over one billion Muslims. Its final aim is to honor the values of the community, the *Umma,* it serves. Fascist economics centered on the repressive and corrupt nature of the state, whose sole expression was the Fascist Party and whose final aim was securing the interests of the Fascist elite.

While Fascist economics disregarded the needs of the masses, its rhetoric took them into consideration. Il Duce's populist speeches, his celebration of *italianitá,* the outstanding qualities of the Italian people, were skillful marketing illusions thrown at people exhausted by a long war and impoverished by the economic crisis. Those carefully crafted words hid the real goal of fascism: to safeguard an elitist class that had found in Mussolini a valuable buffer against revolutionary movements.

Against this ideological backdrop, it comes as no surprise that under the banner of syndicalism, the state began to intervene in every sector of Italian life. Fascist economics pulverized all democratic institutions, which had been achieved through economic liberalism, and ended up impoverishing people. The de facto introduction of Fascist corporations abolished the class struggle; unions and strikes were banned, as well as any other association or body that did not come under the banner of the Fascist Party. The secret fascist police, OVRA, made sure to implement these restrictions.

Democracy was derided as the cause of all evil suffered by postwar Italy. "After Socialism," wrote Mussolini in his definition of Fascism, "Fascism combats the whole complex system of democratic ideology, and repudiates it, whether in its theoretical premises or in its practical application."[36] The dismantling of the liberal state went hand in hand with the reeducation of the people. Stripped of their individuality, Italians were indoctrinated by the "tenets of a political religion that denied the idea of the brotherhood of man in all forms," wrote Polanyi.[37]

The transformation of the nation into a Fascist entity went hand in hand with the replacement of the nation with the state; both came about through forced mass conversions, as messianic as it was celebrative. State tribalism was built on the myth of the resurgence of Italy as an imperial power—its genes Roman, its soul fascist. Thus the illusory projected final aim of Fascist economics involved resurrecting the greatness of Italians, to revitalize *italianitá*. Mussolini used this masterfully marketed mirage even if Italy had no chance or strength to recapture its greatness. Its economy represented a form of "capitalism without capital" in which, thanks to a peculiarly incestuous relationship, banks and industries shared the same scarce capital. Known as *banca mista,* this system allowed banks to participate in the management of industries, while industries, controlling large shares of banks, used banks' savings to fund themselves.

In sharp contrast, Deng's modern China builds on and complements Maoist tribalism through a careful recycling of history. Mao's resurrected pride for China's imperial stardom remained intact and channeled into economic growth instead of democratization. If Mussolini's Italy was "capitalism without capital," Deng's China is "Communism with capital." This surreal phenomenon is the product of Deng's great intuition in the aftermath of Mao's death. A clear agreement honored by both political and economic parties has so far guaranteed China's stability. While the party maintains a firm grip on politics, the people can reap the benefits of economic growth. Between politics and economics there is a division of labor, with each of them entitled to its own exclusive domain. And both partners have prospered from this situation.

Protectionism was Mussolini's economic answer to the post–World War I attempts to recapture the tenets of economic liberalism. In 1926, he launched the Battle of Wheat, an ambitious program to make Italy self-sufficient, backing the policy with prohibitive customs duties on imports.[38] Such measures took the world's leaders by surprise, as did Il Duce's confrontational style. When the United States slapped a big tariff on olive oil, he openly accused the United States of hoarding gold and plotting to ruin the whole world.[39]

The great crash of 1929 propelled economic state tribalism into a higher gear. The crisis hit the world economy, already suffering from hyperinflation, and plunged it into a deflationary spiral. The invisible hand of Adam Smith became the curse of the world economy, slashing commodity prices, ending economic growth, and bankrupting banks. Market hysteria spread like the influenza that killed millions of people at the end of World War I. Fascist Italy was not spared; banks, in particular, were hard hit by the crisis. Abandoning the last vestiges of economic liberalism, Mussolini introduced tight foreign-exchange controls, ended the *banca mista,* and through a gigantic state holding company, Istituto per la Ricostruzione Industriale (IRI), the fascist state took control of the economy. Italians were told that the state had come to the rescue of the private sector, which in turn, according to Mussolini, "threw itself into the arms of the state."[40]

In reality, state tribalism had successfully mutated into a ruthless dictatorship that cleverly hid the fundamental weakness of the economy and used the world crisis to enslave all productive sectors. The disastrous consequences of such deceit would soon arise. "No government, whatever its political complexion, [can] escape from Italy's fundamental dilemma: the disproportion . . . between the country's limited resources and the needs and aspirations of a prolific race," wrote Vera Michaels Dean in *Foreign Policy Reports,* a journal of international affairs in 1935. "Should international stabilization fail to materialize, Italy under fascism might come to regard territorial expansion as the only escape from its economic problems."[41] That same year, Italy started its imperial adventure by invading Ethiopia.

Yet, the Fascist economic model remained useful to countries in the grip of the depression. State tribalism replaced economic liberalism, so that the state could have a free hand in the economy. From Japan to Hungary, from Argentina to Spain, from Germany to Brazil, fascist dictators rose to power under the banner of state tribalism. None escaped its political degeneration. Retrenching from the values of nineteenth-century globalization, authoritarian governments blamed the economic crisis on democratic values and smashed them one by one.

State intervention was essential to help economies to rise again from the depths of the Depression, as was the case with America's New Deal and the Soviet Union's Bolshevik economic planning after World War I. However, the excessive power that accumulated in the hands of the state ended up pulverizing the individual, while the bureaucracy of corrupted states further stripped citizens of their own power. The degeneration of the roles and obligations of the state vis-à-vis its citizens paved the way to the tragedy of World War II. Against this background, a class of outlaws went to work, Fascist elites guided by ruthless dictators like Hitler and Mussolini, people who were able to create a web of illusions that trapped the masses in a surreal reality. The forms of statehood and the types of leadership our society embraces have not yet changed from what emerged at the end of World War II.

Today, economic tribalism could help to overcome the crisis of modern globalization, as we saw happen during the Asian crisis, when it came to the rescue of hard-hit countries within a certain tribal sphere. Economic tribalism gave birth to Islamic finance, a new economic system that is growing rapidly and that may come to challenge the fundamentals of rogue economics. Thus far, Islamic finance has been beneficial for those who have promoted and used it. Its ultimate success will depend on the ability of its proponents to keep the outlaws of globalization as well as populist dictators like Mussolini at bay. The success of economic tribalism in moderating the hard transition into a truly global economy, therefore, will depend on the ability of modern society to silence the propaganda of the outlaws of globalization. As long as Osama bin Laden and his Islamist fundamentalist followers and warmongering American neoconservatives are kept under control, there is no reason why Islamic finance could not contribute to helping to define a new world order, one free from the anarchy of rogue economics. But to reach this goal, a new social contract will need to be forged between the leaders and the people of the future leading nations.

THE NEW SOCIAL CONTRACT

The genesis of the nation-state is the stipulation of a social contract by which people form nations to maintain social order within them. The basis of that contract depends on the willingness of citizens to relinquish some rights to their government in exchange for peace and stability. Every politician's legitimacy springs from the consent of the electorate to ratify this social contract.

At the root of the contract is a belief in the state of nature, synonymous with anarchy and chaos. In this state, an individual's action is bound only by his or her conscience, as life takes place outside the rule of positive law. Rogue economics resembles such a state of nature—chaotic, anarchic, and lawless. Inside it, globalization outlaws act to their exclusive personal advantage.

Though occurring now for the first time on a global scale, this anarchic state of the economy has existed before. The Industrial Revolution witnessed a massive economic upheaval guided by lawless greed and rampant exploitation. It embodied many of the rogue characteristics of the present economic turmoil: slavery, income inequality, piracy, prostitution, pollution, criminality, and fraud. It also shared with the current situation many positive outcomes: rapid economic growth and technological advancement. When the dust eventually settled, the world saw itself redesigned by the ruthless, invisible hand of capitalism. China and India no longer held the first rung as the largest contributors to world GDP; England had surpassed them.

Yet, during the Industrial Revolution, the privileged classes were largely unaware that the great transformation that was improving their lives came directly from a brutal and exploitative economy. The concept of human equality had just arrived, and many people remained skeptical and suspicious of it, associated as it was with violent upheavals and revolutions.

Today, Western consumers, too, are largely blind to the dark forces that fuel the current economic changes. The market matrix and the illusionist theater of modern politicians prevent them from seeing the economic anarchy that is sweeping across our planet. Trapped in a web of fantasies and commercial illusions, they do not see the spread of rogue economics at the fringes of their world. Yet, day by day, its corrosive force increasingly penetrates our sheltered, fantastical world. The pressure of the outlaws, the spreading of corruption and greed, has become apparent in Western society and is eroding the very foundation of the nation-state, which becomes weaker and weaker. As the transition to the market-state proceeds, the state progressively risks becoming a powerful instrument controlled by globalization outlaws.

Myths and illusions have replaced ideology as the source of the legitimacy of politicians. But the populism of the new myth manipulators can and will fail as people inevitably break through the tangled web of lies and illusions that imprisons them.

Those on the front lines of the battle that is reshaping our world are the masses of the developing world, the exploited men, women, and children, the middle classes of the Western world, the young disenfranchised inhabitants of the *barrios* of the global village—all must fend for themselves. They live in constant fear because they rightly sense that the state can no longer protect them. Fear of the environment they live in, fear of globalization, fear of the future prompt them to retrench to ancient forms of community. Modern tribalism has emerged as the natural response of the residents of the global village to rogue economics.

Modern tribalism seems to be the winning formula for coping with the economic strains of globalization and providing the socioeconomic structure to prosper inside the anarchy of rogue economics. The economic miracle of China and the exceptional success of Islamic finance stand as testimony to this new type of socioeconomic tribalism. As this formula spreads across the vast impoverished Chinese and Muslim populations, its economic benefits are likely to trickle down, and with economic growth, people will enjoy prosperity and feel entitled to social order and stability. At that point, they will want to negotiate a new social contract. It will not look like Jean-Jacques Rousseau's version to end the state of nature described by Thomas Hobbes in the *Leviathan*, because the new social contract will be drafted in China and the Middle East.

The Industrial Revolution did end up benefiting the poorest sections of society, the grandchildren of the starving peasants forced into the Dickensian work houses. Economic exploitation paved the way for workers' associations and trade unions that sought to protect the rights of their members against industrial capitalists. Trade unions became a type of economic tribe by sheltering workers from the abuses of industrialization. Fear of their working environment mixed with a sense of having been abandoned during the turmoil of the Industrial Revolution prompted workers to form unions. Eventually, economic growth brought prosperity, and trade unions negotiated better labor contracts. Socialism and Communism, as political ideologies, were born out of the workers' unions' early struggles. Left-wing parties waged battles for equality, and these included the renegotiation of the social contract.

A similar scenario is likely to emerge when the dust created by rogue economics eventually settles. The winners may be the populations of China and Islam, who have so much to gain. Though it is too early to predict, we can imagine some of the main provisions and stipulations of the new social contract. For a start, the post-globalization social contract will define a clear separation between the state and the individual. While the latter will have a free hand in commerce and economics, the former will maintain the monopoly of politics, which will include foreign policy and monetary policy. Islamic finance will provide the structure of the new monetary standard, which will once again be pegged to gold, as we saw after the Industrial Revolution. The gold dinar will become the benchmark of monetary stability and receive a global endorsement. The fiduciary nature of money will require the involvement of the state to guarantee that paper money maintains its value in gold. People will willingly delegate such responsibility to the politicians, and in return, they will have stable exchange rates.

Politicians will refrain from intervening directly in commerce and economics. Islamic finance, with its encoded value system, will reduce and eventually crush the power of the outlaws. The rogue nature of the economy will be trimmed by sharia economics. The outlaws will be shunned through a code of ethics that prohibits such businesses as gambling, prostitution, pornography, and trade in illegal drugs. Hedge funds and private equities will be regulated by a financial system that rejects the concept that money can create money.

Patents and trademarks will disappear, reducing capitalism's ancient privileges, giving impetus to hard-working individuals, who will flourish thanks to this form of liberalization. History will lose its shine and be recycled to fit the needs of the moment. The quality of fake goods will improve until it becomes all but impossible to distinguish the original from its replica. Western brands' commercial edge will vanish. This simple fact will trigger a massive redistribution of wealth at global levels.

Central governments will delegate key responsibilities to local authorities. Taxation, for example, will be levied locally. Central governments will, however, retain the monopoly on defense. In exchange for physical protection, communities will pass along a share of their wealth to the central governments.

The media will see their power reduced by the proliferation of information on the Internet. As long as the contractual parties stick to the new social contract, political issues will be debated but will not lead to great upheavals.

The new world order will be ruled by an invisible axis stretching from Beijing to Cape Town. Europe and America will lose out. Africa and the Middle East will provide the necessary resources for new global economic leadership. Eventually, nanotechnology will consolidate this scenario, but that is a topic for another book.

NOTES

INTRODUCTION

1. Though the student cry for democracy was brutally silenced in Tiananmen Square, the message did not remain unheard; it became the foundation of Deng Xiaoping's new course.

CHAPTER ONE—IN BED WITH THE ENEMY

1. The Marshall Plan was a US-sponsored program to provide economic aid to European countries after World War II. In 1947, George Marshall, then Secretary of State, developed the idea of a European self-help plan financed by the United States, and that same year Congress authorized it as the European Recovery Program. Providing almost $13 billion in grants and loans to seventeen countries, it was a key factor in reviving their economies and stabilizing their political structures. The Soviet Union refused to accept the plan.
2. John Maynard Keynes, member of the Bloomsbury group and quintessential British gentleman, was one of the most important economists of the postwar era.
3. For a full discussion of pre–World War II trade, see Chapter 12, "Economic Tribalism."
4. Anna Nowak, "Political Transformation in Poland: The Rise in Sex Work," *Research for Sex Work 2*, Volume Two, 9–11 (Amsterdam: Vrije Universiteit,1999), www.researchforsexwork.org.
5. Victor Malarek, *The Natashas: Inside the New Global Sex Trade* (New York: Arcade Publishing, 2004), 37.
6. Interview with a former Ukrainian prostitute, October 2006.
7. Juliette Engel, "Direct Intervention With Highest Risk Girls and Young Women of the Russian Federation to Avert Unwitting Recruitment into International Sex Alavery and Economic Imprisonment" (Moscow: MiraMed Institute, 1998).
8. Donna M. Hughes, "Supplying Women for the Sex Industry: Trafficking from the Russian Federation (Kingston: University of Rhode Island, 2002), http://www.uri.edu/artsci/wms/hughes/supplying_women.pdf.
9. Interview with Stephen, German pimp, September 2006. All subsequent quotes from Stephen are taken from this interview.
10. Michael started working in the sex industry when he was about sixteen. He was a pimp who initially had a few girls, but in the early 1990s, with the influx of Slavic women and the liberalization of prostitution, he switched to sex bars.
11. Interview with Michael, German pimp, September 2006. All subsequent quotes from Michael are taken from this interview.
12. Laurie Garrett, "Crumbled Empire, Shatters Health: Expanding Sex Industry Spreads Disease," *Newsday*, November 4, 1997, http://www.aegis.com/news/NEWSDAY/1997/ND971105.html.

13. Ibid.
14. Trading in Slavic sex slaves has proved to be equally profitable as the prostitution business. In 2001, global profits of sex slaves were estimated at $7 billion; by 2004, they had reached $12 billion, of which $3 billion was exclusively generated by trafficking in women from the former Soviet Bloc.
15. Malarek, *Natashas*, 75.
16. See http://www.ynetnews.com/articles/o,7340,L-3062297,00.html.
17. Menachem Amir, "Organized Crime in Israel," *Organized Crime, Uncertainties and Dilemmas*, edited by Stanley Einstein and Menachem Amir (Chicago: Office of International Criminal Justice, 1999), 231–248.
18. Malarek, *Natashas,* xvi.
19. Ibid., 77.
20. Interview with Ildiko, Hungarian prostitute, March 2006.
21. Danny Bobman, "Insider's View: The Bombs, the Babies and the Southern Border," http://www.jewishtucson.org/page.html?ArticleID=65912.
22. Richard Woods, "Selling Sex the Middle Class Way," *Sunday Times* (London), January 22, 2006.
23. Roger Scruton, "Shameless and Loveless," *The Spectator* (April 16, 2005), Catholic Education Resource Center, http://www.catholiceducation.org/articles/sexuality/seo121.htm.
24. Woods, "Selling Sex."
25. The Russian film industry has not been immune to the new culture. "In Russia prostitution was glamorized by popular films such as *Interdevochka*, in which a woman works as a 'hard currency prostitute.'" Mikhailina Karina, "The Myth of *Pretty Woman*—Russian Women are Victims of Illegal Trafficking," March 23, 1999, http://veracity.univpubs.american.edu/weeklypast/032399/story_1.html.
26. See http://www.bbc.co.uk/worldservice/programmes.
27. Garrett, "Crumbled Empire."
28. These statistics come from the World Health Organization (WHO) Statistics; see World Health Organization, *Highlights in Health in Estonia*, December 2001,19, http://www.euro.who.int/document/e74339.pdf; Pan American Health Organization, http://www.paho.org/English/DD/AIS/cp_840.htm.
29. WHO, "3 by 5," (Fact Sheet, June 2005).
30. In 2005, the rate in Russia was 1.62 lifetime births per woman.
31. Karina, "Myth of *Pretty Woman*."
32. Viktor Erofeyev, "More Little Russians, Please," *International Herald Tribune*, May 20–21, 2006.
33. Mogilevich helped to smuggle the money out of Russia to avoid the loses stemming from the collapse of the ruble. Some of the money belonged to the nomenklatura, the former Communist political elites who took over the ruling of Russia after the disintegration of the Soviet regime. Jaroslav Koshiw, "A Native Son of the Bank of New York Scandal," *Kyiv Post*, August 26, 1999. See also "Le Nouvelle Mafia d'Europe de l'Est," Marianne en ligne.fr, December 5, 1997.
34. Chrystia Freeland, *Sale of the Century: Russia's Wild Ride from Communism to Capitalism* (New York: Crown Publishers, 2000), 122.
35. David E. Hoffman, *The Oligarchs: Wealth and Power in the New Russia* (New York: Public Affairs, 2002), 113.
36. Interview with the former Russian banker, September 2006.

37. Interview with Bart Stevens, September 2006. By January 1990, about 2,000 small private businesses, wrongly described as Kooperativs (co-ops), were operational in Russia. See Amy Chua, *World on Fire* (New York: Doubleday, 2003), 83.

38. Life expectancy for men fell from sixty-five in 1987 to fifty-nine in 1993. The number of suicides rose by 65 percent, second only to the rate in Lithuania globally.

39. Interview with Miklos Marshal, Regional Director of Transparency International (TI) for Europe and Central Asia, September 2006. All subsequent quotes from Miklos Marshal are taken from this interview.

40. Mancur Olson, *Power and Prosperity: Outgrowing Communist and Capitalist Dictatorships*, Reviewed by David M. Woodruff, East European *Constitutional Review*, Winter 2001, Volume 10 n.1, http://personal.lse.ac.uk/woodruff/_private/materials/olson_review.htm. See also Mancur Olson, *Power and Prosperity: Outgrowing Communist and Capitalist Dictatorships* (New York: Basic Books, 2000).

41. Joseph Stiglitz, "Russian People Paid the Price for Shock Therapy," *New York Times*, June 22, 2002.

42. Raymond Baker, "The Biggest Loophole in the Free-Market System," Center for Strategic and International Studies and the Massachusetts Institute of Technology, *Washington Quarterly*, Autumn 1999. According to Baker, throughout the 1990s, Russia suffered a serious capital outflow, totalling $15 to 25 billion per year.

43. Stiglitz, "Russian People Paid the Price."

44. Adam Smith, *The Wealth of Nations*, Book V, Chapter III.

45. Olson, *Power and Prosperity*.

CHAPTER TWO—NOBODY CONTROLS ROGUE ECONOMICS

1. Gerald J. Swansin, *America the Broke* (New York: Doubleday, 2004), 15; see also "Reality Check, Life and Death: Why American Families Are Borrowing to the Hilt; A Century Foundation Guide to the Issue" (New York: The Century Foundation), http://www.tcf.org/Publications/EconomicsInequality/baker_debt.pdf.

2. "Our Financial Failings," *Washington Post*, March 5, 2006; see also Federal Reserve Consumer Survey Statistics.

3. Scheherazade Daneshkhu and Krishna Guha, "Home Truths? How America's Housing Boom May Be Coming to a Tricky End," *Financial Times*, October 24, 2006.

4. The global labor supply went from 1.46 to 2.93 billion. Richard Freeman, "The Great Doubling: The Challenge of the New Global Labor Market" (Boston: Federal Reserve Bank of Boston, 2006).

5. Jeff Faux, *The Global Class War* (Hoboken, New Jersey: Wiley, 2006).

6. Richard Tomkins, "Profits of Doom," *Financial Times*, October 14–15, 2006.

7. Ibid.; see also Freeman, "Great Doubling."

8. Paul Craig Roberts, "Forget Iran, Americans Should Be Hysterical About This," http://www.rense.com/general69/nucon.htm, February 2006.

9. Alan Blinder, "Offshoring: The Next Industrial Revolution?" *Foreign Affairs*, March/April 2006, http://www.foreignaffairs.org/20060301faessay85209/alan-s-blinder/offshoring-the-next-industrial-revolution.html.

10. Paul Craig Roberts, "How Safe is Your Job?" *Counterpunch*, April 18, 2006, http://www.counterpunch.org/roberts04182006.html.

11. In 2006, the consensus was that China had $1 trillion in foreign reserves—the largest on the globe; most experts believed that about three-quarters of that reserve was in dollars.

12. Peter Navarro, "Dollar, Yuan, and Wary Euro," *International Herald Tribune*, December 8, 2006.

13. From 1989 to the mid-1990s, three-month interest rates in the United States fell from over 10 percent to below 4 percent.

14. Interview with John, a London builder, June 2006.

15. Introduced in the United States in 1987, revolving credit cards took off in the early 1990s.

16. In 2006, mortgage debt was equivalent to 80 percent of household disposable income; in the 1980s, it had been less than 50 percent. Middle-class earners were primarily responsible for the surge; from 1989 to 2001; their mortgage debt nearly tripled. This trend continued after 2001; in 2003 and 2004, for example, mortgage debt rose by 12 percent each year. There is no question that the decline in interest rates in 2001–04 reflects the Federal Reserve's fears of a corporate investment bust after the Internet bubble burst in 2001. This wasn't the first time Greenspan switched on the monetary taps. He did it in 1995 during the Mexican crisis, in 1997–98 during the Asia crisis, in the 2000–01 stock market burst, after 9/11, obviously, and in the deflation scare of 2002–03.

17. Interview with George Magnus, October 2006. All subsequent quotes by Magnus are taken from this interview.

18. Jim Pickard, Rebecca Knight, and Sheila McNulty, "A Nation Starts to Shiver as the Chill Sets In," *Financial Times*, October 24, 2006.

19. According to Elizabeth Warren and Amelia Warren Tyagi, *The Two Income Trap: Why Middle-Class Mothers and Fathers Are Going Broke* (New York: Basic Books, 2004), 90 percent of people in bankruptcy qualify as middle class.

20. United Kingdom figures from the Insolvency Service: "Statistics Release: Insolvencies in the Third Quarter 2006," November 3, 2006, http://www.insolvency .gov.uk/otherinformation/statistics/200611/index.htm; see also Jane Croft, "Sharp Rise in Use of IVA's to Clear Debt," *Financial Times*, November 4, 2006.

21. Thomas A. Garrett and Lesli S. Ott, "Up, Up and Away: Personal Bankruptcies Soar!" *The Regional Economist*, Federal Reserve Bank of Saint Louis, October 2005, http://stlouisfed.org/publications/re/.

22. See http://www.creditcards.com/credit-card-debt-collection-problems.php.

23. In 2007, the Colorado attorney general, for example, was investigating the "confusing" advertising of a group of mortgage brokers who may have lured people into loans they could not afford to repay.

24. Pickard, Knight, and McNulty, "A Nation Starts to Shiver."

25. Warren and Tyagi, *The Two Income Trap.*

26. Ibid.

27. Tomkins, "Profits of Doom"; see also http://www.solutionsforourfuture.org/site/ PageServer?pagename=rising_increases_r&s_oo=iCIwYBh9_ns7PJIr4hsrDA.

28. Alec Klein, "A Tenous Hold on the Middle Class," *Washington Post*, December 18, 2004.

29. Ibid.

30. Randall S. Hansen, "Moonlighting in America: Strategies for Managing Working Multiple Jobs," http://www.quintcareers.com/moonlighting_jobs.html.

31. Paul A. Cantor, "Hyperinflation and Hyperreality: Thomas Mann in Light of Austrian Economics," *Review of Austrian Economics*, 1993.
32. Cantor, "Hyperinflation."
33. Klein, "Tenuous Hold."
34. Ian Dew-Becker and Robert Gordon, "Where Did the Productivity Growth Go?" (National Bureau of Economic Research, Working Paper 11842, December 2005), http://papers.ssrn.com/sol3/papers.cfm?abstract_id=870604.
35. Cantor, "Hyperinflation."
36. Eric Hobsbawm, *In the Global Village, Interesting Times* (New York: Pantheon Books, 2002), 298–313.
37. Jan Pen, *Income Distribution* (London: Penguin, 1971).
38. Data about income distribution compiled by Thomas Piketty, economist at Paris Jourdan Sciences Economiques, and Emmanuel Saez, economist at the University of California at Berkeley. See http://elsa.berkeley.edu/~saez/TabFig2004prel .xls; see also Aviva Aron-Dine and Isaac Shapiro, "New Data Show Extraordinary Jump in Income Concentration in 2004," Center on Budget and Policy Priorities, October 13, 2006, http://www.cbpp.org/7-10-06inc.htm.
39. Krisha Guha, Edward Luce, and Andrew Ward, "Anxious Middle: Why Ordinary Americans Have Missed Out on the Benefits of Growth," *Financial Times*, November 2, 2006.
40. "The Gilded Age: How a Corporate Elite is Leaving Middle America Behind," *Financial Times*, December 21, 2006.
41. Ibid.
42. Thorstein Veblen, *Theory of the Leisure Class: An Economic Study in the Evolution of Institutions* (London: MacMillan & Co., 1899).
43. F. Scott Fitzgerald, *The Great Gatsby*, (Wordsworth, 1999).
44. A. B. Atkinson, "Bringing Income Distribution in from the Cold," *Economic Journal*, Royal Economic Society, 107 (441), 297–321, March 1997. For more information about professor Atkinson, see http://ideas.repec.org/ e/pat36.html.
45. Elisabetta Povoledo, "A Filmaker's Grim Italian Morality Tale," *International Herald Tribune*, November 14, 2006.
46. Peter Woodifield, "Bonus Season Inflates London Home Prices," *International Herald Tribune*, November 9, 2006.
47. Interview with Grant Woods, September 2006. All subsequent quotes from Grant Woods are taken from this interview.
48. George Magnus points to a tepid climate for global capital investment, at the beginning of the 2000s, which left the world awash in dollarized cash. This cash is gathered within hedge funds to produce staggering profits, thanks to its sheer volume.
49. Although packaged as "investments," futures contracts are inherently different from stocks and bonds. Whereas the latter are financial assets, futures are risk transfer instruments that were meant to aid those businesses that are engaged in the production, storage, processing, and consumption of commodities to manage their price risk. As purchase and sales agreements, they can be best viewed as proxies: much like a coin, they are something to hold until their owner is ready to buy or sell the real thing. An oil refiner, for example, might buy crude oil futures contracts to "hedge" against the price going up in advance of securing the real inventory. Once it buys the physical product, the refiner sells the contracts back into the futures market, canceling out its original purchase. Whether the market

goes up or down, the refiner will have "locked in" the price by buying oil futures contracts.

50. The clearinghouse of a futures exchange is the guarantor of all open transactions. It maintains a guaranty fund and collects initial and daily margins to guard against default of any of its members.

51. When investors buy a stock, they lend a corporation capital, on the theory that the capital loan will yield dividends or share-price appreciation in return. That rule was one of the fundamentals of "old economy." But capital allocation doesn't work this way when hedge funds are involved, especially in the derivatives markets.

CHAPTER THREE—THE END OF POLITICS

1. Interview with an Italian undercover agent, October 2005.
2. Author's investigation into the *n'drangheta*. Interviews with members of the Guardia di Finanzia of Catanzaro, October–November 2005.
3. Commissione parlamentare d'inchiesta sul fenomeno Mafia, 1997, "Relazione conclusive," IV legislatura, doc XXIII, n.2, Rome: Camera dei Deputati.
4. "In the 'Ndrangheta, security concerns have led to the creation of a secret society within the secret society: the Santa. Membership in the Santa is only known to other members. Contrary to the code of 'Ndrangheta, it allowed Mafia leaders to establish close connections with state representatives, even to the extent that some were affiliated with the Santa. These connections were often established through the Freemasonry, which the santisti—breaking another rule of the traditional code—were allowed to join." Letizia Paoli, *Mafia Brotherhoods: Organized Crime, Italian Style* (New York: Oxford University Press, 2003), 116.
5. Julie Tingwall, "Move Over Cosa Nostra," *Guardian* (London), June 8, 2006.
6. Dave Clifford, "Original Gangsters, Thug Life Calabrian Style," *Seattle Weekly*, October 2, 2002.
7. Durkheim defines mechanical solidarity as social cohesion based upon the likeness and similarities among individuals in a society and largely dependent on common rituals and routines. Common among prehistoric and preagricultural societies, it lessens in predominance as modernity increases. Emile Durkheim, *The Division of Labor in Society*, translated by George Simpson (New York: Free Press, 1997).
8. Paoli, *Mafia Brotherhoods*, 52.
9. Commissione parlamentare d'inchiesta sul fenomeno Mafia, 2000, "Relazione sullo stato della lotta alla criminalitá organizzata in Calabria," XIII legislatura, doc. XXIII, n. 42, Rome: Camera dei Deputati.
10. Commissione Parlamentare , 2000, "Relazione sullo stato della lotta."
11. Interview with Vincenzo Spagnolo, an Italian investigative journalist, October 2006. All subsequent quotes from Spagnolo are taken from this interview.
12. Federico Varese, "How Mafia Migrate: the case of the *n'drangheta* in Northern Italy," *Law and Society Review* no. 2 (2006), 412.
13. Loretta Napoleoni, *Terror Incorporated* (New York: Seven Stories Press, 2005), chapter 18.
14. The best outlets were in Rome, near the Spanish Steps, because they were frequented by wealthy tourists.

15. This matter will be regulated by the European Commission in a decision that is foreseen to impose the obligation to declare all cash or monetary instruments over 10.000 euros coming into or going out of European Union territory.

16. Salvatore Mancuso's appearance before the Colombian parliament is a milestone in the control of the state by organized crime, July 31, 2004, radio Nizkor.

17. Interview with an officer at Europol, October 2006.

18. Interview with Spagnolo.

19. Hannah Arendt, *Antologia* (Milan: Feltrinelli, 2006), 18. Truls Lie, *Politics and Cosmopolitics*, eurozine, March 9, 2006, http://hannaharendt.net/index/politicsII.html.

20. A German Jewish victim of the Nazi regime who emigrated to the United States, Hannah Arendt always refused to associate her inherited religion with politics.

21. Arendt, *Antologia.* 1–25

22. Lie Truls, *Politics and Cosmopolitics.*

23. Hannah Arendt, *Taking Politics Seriously: The Promise of Politics* (New York: Schocken Books, 2005), 70–80.

24. Jerome Kohn, review of *The Promise of Politics, Harvard Law Review* 119 (2005): 639–645.

25. The essence of the nation-state rests on a few postulates: "Government is trustworthy or legitimate because it promises to a particular coherent nation—both a piece of territory and a fairly homogeneous community—effective defense against outside attack and a high degree of internal stability. The internal stability [is] based on a firm directive hand in the economy and a safety net of public welfare provision. The job of those who ran the state [is] seen as guaranteeing the general good of the community; and its success in managing this [is] the obvious foundation of its claim to be obeyed." Rowan Williams, Archbishop of Canterbury, "The Richard Dimbleby lecture," *Guardian* (London), December 19, 2002.

26. Interview with Cesare Nota Cerasi, Colonel of Guardia di Finanza, fall 2005.

27. Federico Varese, "How Mafia Migrate: The Case of the *N'drangheta* in Northern Italy," *Law and Society Review* 40, no. 2 (2006), 441.

28. Ibid.

29. Interview with a former member of the Bulgarian Mafia, November 2006.

30. Interview with Jivko Georgiev, a sociologist with the Balkan British Social Survey, October 2006.

31. Ibid.

32. Interview with Zoya Dimitrova, a Bulgarian investigative journalist, October 2006.

33. Zoya Dimitrova, "The Business with Death and the Yugo Embargo," Global Investigative Journalism Conference, Bulgaria, December 22, 2003.

34. Interview with Tihomir Beslov, an expert on crime with the Center for the Study of Democracy of Sofia, October 2006.

35. Interview with Vasil "Vasko" Ivanov, an investigative reporter with Nova TV, November 2006.

36. "Transportation, Smuggling, and Organized Crime," report by the Center for the Study of Democracy, 2004.

37. Ibid, 50.

38. Interview with Vladimir, a former police officer who served in the Bulgarian police from 1993 to 1998 and now drives a taxi in Sofia, October 2006.

39. Interview with Beslov.
40. Interview with Kolyo Paramov, chief auditor of the Bulgarian National Bank, October 2006.
41. Dimitrova, "The Business with Death."
42. Truls Lie, *Politics and Cosmopolitics*, eurozine, March 9, 2006, http://hannaharendt.net/index/politicsII.html.
43. None of these policies achieved their desired objective; on the contrary, they ended up damaging the countries that implemented them, and they even boosted criminal activity. Politicians as well as citizens were taken aback by the changing new world. This state of confusion still permeates the relationship between nations and their leaders.
44. Market-states deregulate vast areas of enterprises by abandoning industrial statutes. Thatcher and Reagan privatization programs could be regarded as the embryos of market-states. In sharp contrast to the welfare state of the post-World War II area, market-states are nothing more than minimal providers or redistributors of wealth. As we shall see, the fading away of the role of the state as protector of citizens' rights puts the market-state in an ideal position to exploit the benefits of rogue economics.

CHAPTER FOUR—LAND OF OPPORTUNITY

1. François Jullien, *Pensare l'efficacia in Cina e in Occidente* (Bari, Italy: Editori Laterza, 2006), 83.
2. Carl von Clausewitz, *On War* (Hertfordshire, England: Wordsworth Editions Limited, 1997).
3. Tim Clissold, *Mr. China* (London: Constable and Robinson, 2002), 252.
4. James Kynge, "Shock and Ore," *Financial Times Magazine*, March 18–19, 2006.
5. Jullien, *Pensare l'efficacia*.
6. "The New Titans," *The Economist*, September 2006.
7. According to Arif Dirlik, the Cultural Revolution was part and parcel of the overall project of inventing an alternative modernity for China and the World. See Arif Dirlik, "The Politics of the Cultural Revolution in Historical Perspective," *Law*, edited by Kam-yee (2003), 158–183; see also Susanne Weigelin-Schwiedrzik, "Coping with the Trauma: Writing the History of the Cultural Revolution in the People's Republic of China," *Outline*, http://www.mh.sinica.edu.tw/eng/download/abstract/abstract6-1.pdf.
8. J. L. Gaddis, *The Cold War* (London: Penguin, 2005), 214–215.
9. The Gang of Four was a group of Chinese Communist Party leaders, consisting of Mao's wife, Jiang Qing, and three of her close associates, Zhang Chunquiao, Yao Wenyan, and Wang Hogwen. After Mao's death, all four were held responsible for the Cultural Revolution and removed from their positions.
10. Gaddis, *Cold War*.
11. Interview with Chi Fing Kuong, October 2006. All subsequent statements by Kuong are taken from this interview.
12. Interview with Burley Wang, researcher in Guandong Province, October 2006. All subsequent statements by Burley are taken from this interview.
13. See http://en.wikipedia.org/wiki/Cultural_Revolution.

14. Jonathan D. Spence, *The Search for Modern China* (New York and London: W.W. Norton, 1991), 606. Spence's brief analysis of the Cultural Revolution is a very useful introduction to the subject.

15. Interview with Chi Fing Kuong, October 2006.

16. Spence, *Search for Modern China*, 606.

17. Ibid., 606–607.

18. "Chinese Researcher Criticizes Beijing For Burying Cultural Revolution History," Asia Africa Intelligence Wire, *Financial Times*, May 16, 2006.

19. Spence, *Search for Modern China*, 606–607.

20. Howard W. French, "Chinese Protesters Report a Massacre, Deadly Show of Force Since 1989," *International Herald Tribune*, December 10–11, 2005.

21. E. L. Wheelwright and Bruce McFarlane, *The Chinese Road to Socialism: Economics of the Cultural Revolution* (New York: Monthly Review Press, 1970).

22. Interview with Angie Junglu Lai, a Chinese student in London, October 2006. All subsequent interviews with Junglu Lai are taken from this interview.

23. For a full report on the Henan blood business, see Pierre Haski, *Il Sangue della China* (Milan: Sperling and Kupfer, 2006).

24. Gaddis, *Cold War*, 214–215.

25. Ibid.

26. Ilaria Maria Sala, *Il Dio dell'Asia* (Milan: il Saggiatore, 2006), 134–135.

27. "Secrets, Lies and Sweatshops," *Business Week* Online, November 27, 2006.

28. Interview with Pierre Haski, deputy editor of *Liberation*, December 2006.

29. This sentence represents a dictum as summarized by Angie Junglu Lai.

30. Jeffrey K. Olick and Daniel Levy, "Collective Memory and Cultural Constraint: Holocaust Myth and Rationality in German Politics," *American Sociological Review* 62, no. 6 (December 1997), 921–936.

31. West Germany continued to receive Marshall Plan Aid, while Britain's wartime Lend-Lease arrangement ended in 1945. In addition, the terms of the Washington Loan agreement of December1945, negotiated by Keynes, were not favorable to the British; it may be that the United States wanted to kill any idea of continued global economic predominance for the United Kingdom. Two superpowers were enough for the United States.

32. Gaddis, *Cold War*, 214–215.

33. See "The People's Republic Of China: IV, The Post-Mao Period, 1976–78," http://www-chaos.umd.edu/history/prc4.html.

34. Ma Bo, *Blood Red Sunset* (London: Penguin, 1995), 1.

35. Wheelwright and McFarlane.

36. Sarah Radcliffe, "Imagining the State as a Space," Thomas B. Hansen and Finn Stepputat (eds.), *States of Imagination*, Duke University Press, 2001.

37. Joseph B. R., Whitney *China: Area, Administration and Nation Building*, University of Chicago (Department of Geography): Chicago, 1970.

38. E. L. Wheelwright and B. McFarlane, *Chinese Road to Socialism*, (New York, London: Monthly Review Press, 1971), 24.

39. Henri Lefebvre explains his views on the Chinese "road to socialism" in *The Production of Space* (London: Blackwell, 1991), 421.

40. C. M. Andrew and V. Mitrokhin, *The Mitrokhin Archive II: The KGB and The World* (London: Penguin, 2005), 275–276.

41. Durkheim, *Division of Labor in Society*.

42. Andrew and Mitrokhin, The *Mitrokhin Archive*.

43. Neal Stephenson, *The Diamond Age* (Bantam Spectra Book, 2000).

44. For this concept see also Tim Oakes, "China's Provincial Identities: Reviving Regionalism and Reinventing 'Chineseness'" *Journal of Asian Studies* 50, no. 3 (August 2000).

45. John Tomlinson, "Globalization and Cultural Identity," in David & McGrew ed., *The Global Tranformations Reader: An Introduction to the Globalization Debate* (Cambridge: Polity Press, Blackwell publishing, 2003), 269–277, http://www.polity.co.uk/global/pdf/GTReader2eTomlinson.pdf.

46. Jung Chang, *Wild Swans* (New York: Simon & Schuster, 1991).

CHAPTER FIVE—FAKE IT

1. See http://thinkexist.com/quotation/if_you_haven-t_got_it-fake_it-too_short-wear_big/345211.html.

2. Riccardo Staglianò, *L'Impero dei falsi* (Rome: Editori Laterza, 2006), 47.

3. Adam Sage, "Perfume Cartel Fined 32 Million," *Times*, March 15, 2006.

4. Interview with Valéry, a Parisian shop assistant, February 2007.

5. Walter Benjamin, "The Work of Art in the Age of Mechanical Reproduction," http://design.wishiewashie.com/HT5/WalterBenjaminTheWorkofArt.pdf.

6. Ibid.

7. Sang Ye, *China Candid: The People on the People's Republic* (Berkeley, CA: University of California Press, 2006); Italian translation: *China Candid: per la prima volta I cinesi raccontano i cinesi* (Turin: Einaudi, 2006), 161.

8. "For twenty-seven years we Futurists have rebelled against the branding of war as antiaesthetic . . . Accordingly we state: . . . War is beautiful because it establishes man's dominion over the subjugated machinery by means of gas masks, terrifying megaphones, flame throwers, and small tanks. War is beautiful because it initiates the dreamt-of metallization of the human body. War is beautiful because it enriches a flowering meadow with the fiery orchids of machine guns. War is beautiful because it combines the gunfire, the cannonades, the cease-fire, the scents, and the stench of putrefaction into a symphony. War is beautiful because it creates new architecture, like that of the big tanks, the geometrical formation flights, the smoke spirals from burning villages, and many others. . . . Poets and artists of Futurism! . . . . remember these principles of an aesthetics of war so that your struggle for a new literature and a new graphic art . . . may be illumined by them!" F. T. Marinetti. *The Futurist Manifesto*, http://www.cscs.umich.edu/~crshalizi/T4PM/futurist-manifesto.html

9. Sang Ye, *China Candid*, Chapter 12, 185.

10. Ilaria Maria Sala, *Il Dio dell'Asia, religione e politica in oriente, un reportage* (Milan: Il Saggiatore, 2006).

11. Nigel Andrew, "A Prize Would Be a Catastrophe,"*Financial Times*, March 5, 2007.

12. Benjamin, "Work of Art."

13. "Chinese Immigrants Victims of Labor Exploitation in Paris," International Labor Organisation report, June 21, 2006.

14. Governance, International Law and Corporate Social Responsibility, Seminar organised by the International Institute for Labour Studies, July 3–4, 2006, http://www.ilo.org/public/english/bureau/inst/papers/confrnce/gover2006/gaoyun.pdf.

15. Jay McGown, "Out of Africa: Mysteries of Access and Benefit Sharing," African Center for Biosafety, February 2006.
16. Sheridan Cormac, "Kenyan Dispute Illuminates Bioprospecting Difficulties," *Nature Biotechnology* 22 (2004), http://www.nature.com/cgi-taf/DynaPage.taf?file=/nbt/journal/v22/n11/full/nbt1104-1337.html, 1104–1337.
17. Michael Crichton, "Patenting Life," *International Herald Tribune*, February 14, 2007.
18. Madelene Acey, "Ethiopian Coffee Trademark Dispute May Leave Starbucks with Nasty Taste," *Times*, November 27, 2006.
19. Interview with a Boeing engineer in Seattle, July 2006.
20. Vittorio Florida, Renato Perinu, and Arturo Radini, *La Sicurezza del volo* (Bari: Palomar di Alternative, 2005); see also Riccardo Stagliano, *L'Impero dei falsi* (Rome: Editori Laterza), 2006.
21. Interview with an American aviation consultant, July 2006.
22. *Privatization in Mexico*, Telmex fact sheet, http://www.50years.org/factsheets/telmex.html; see also Pankaj Tandon, *World Bank Conference on the Welfare Consequences of Selling Public Enterprises: Case Studies from Chile, Malaysia, Mexico and the U.K.*, vol. 1, World Bank Country Economics Department, June 7, 1992.

CHAPTER SIX—THE MARKET MATRIX

1. Robert Cockburn, "Death by Dilution," *American Prospect*, December 20, 2005.
2. WHO, *Substandard and Counterfeit Medicine*, Fact Sheet no. 275, November 2003, www.who.int.
3. Presentation of Mike Chan, director for North Asia for product protection of Eli Lilly, in Stagliano, *L'Impero*, 72.
4. Walt Bogdanich and Jake Hooker, "From China to Panama, a Trail of Poisoned Drugs," *International Herald Tribune*, May 7, 2007.
5. Dora Akunyili, the head of Nafdac, Nigeria's medicine agency, says that most of the fake drugs in her country are made abroad, notably in India and China. She wants an international convention enforced by United Nations sanctions to impose heavy criminal penalties on counterfeiters who today often face only modest fines. Andrew Jack, "Bitter Pills: the Fast-Growing, Deadly Industry in Fake Drugs, *Financial Times*, May 14, 2007.
6. Jack, "Bitter Pills."
7. "Counterfeit medicines—what are the problems?" PHARMA-BRIEF *Special*, BUKO Pharma-Kampagne of Health Action International, 2007, http://209.85.135.104/search?q=cache:DSdYG5APjCUJ:www.bukopharma.de/Service/Archiv/E2007_01_special.pdf+%22Buko+Pharma%22+%2B+price+cuts+and+public+health&hl=en&ct=clnk&cd=2&gl=uk; see also http://www.bukopharma .de/english/.
8. Jill Leyland, "A Touch of Gold: Gold Mining's Importance to Lower-Income Countries," World Gold Council, May 2005, www.gold.org.
9. Report of the Group of Experts on the Democratic Republic of the Congo, United Nations Resolution S/2005/436, Security Council, August 26, 2004.
10. Interview with Rico Carish, member of the UN Group of Experts, July 2006. All subsequent statements from Carish are taken from this interview.

11. Interview with Coalition of Immokalee workers, March 2006; see also Kevin Bates, "Of Human Bondage," *Financial Times Magazine*, March 17–18, 2007.

12. Bates, "Of Human Bondage."

13. Ibid.

14. Banana Link coordinated, GMB London/TGWU/ MANDATE, trade union delegation to Costa Rica, March 24–April 1, 2004, http://www.bananalink.org.uk/joomla/images/costa%20rica%20delegation%20report%20march%202004.pdf.

15. See http://www.actionaid.org/index.aspx.

16. Interview with a London public-relations agent for the tobacco industry, March 2006. All subsequent statements are taken from this interview.

17. Joe Nocera, "Is It Just Smoke and Mirrors?" *International Herald Tribune*, June 17–18, 2006.

18. Interview with Dr. James J. Kenney, January 2007. All subsequent statements from Kenney are taken from this interview.

19. PBS, "Diet Wars," *Frontline*, http://www.pbs.org/wgbh/pages/frontline/shows/diet/themes/lowfat.html.

20. Ibid.

21. Interview with Dr. Valerio Nobili, pathologist at Bambin Gesú, November 2006. All subsequent statements from Nobili are taken from this interview.

22. Interview with an American cardiologist, June 2006.

23. The Salt Institute states,"Several systematic reviews have reported that restricting sodium intake in people with hypertension reduces their blood pressure. However, most of the trials in these systematic reviews were short term and did not allow for complete adjustment of blood pressure to altered sodium intake or reduced motivation for following dietary restrictions over time. Also, some trials increased sodium intake in one arm and compared this with reduced sodium intake in the other arm and so did not estimate likely effects of cutting down on sodium in a normal diet" (www.saltinstitute.org). However, another study concludes, "Lower salt intake may help people on antihypertensive drugs to stop their medication while maintaining good control of blood pressure, but there are doubts about effects of sodium reduction on overall health," (Lee Hopper, Christopher Bartlett, Gorge Davey Smith, and Shah Embrahim, "Systematic Review of Long-Term Effects of Advice to Reduce Dietary Salt in Adults," *BMJ*, September 21, 2002, http://www.bmj.com/cgi/content/abstract/325/7365/628).

CHAPTER SEVEN—HIGH TECH: A MIXED BLESSING

1. XXX is the dealer's nickname, taken from the American cult movie by Rob Cohen, *xXx*. XXX communicates via QQ, the Chinese instant messaging system, with my interpreter, who then translates for me.

2. These two are by far the biggest games, with over 5.5 million subscribers.

3. James Less, "Outwit, Outplay, Outsource," *Harper's*, November 2005, 21.

4. Mike Smith, "Massively Addictive," February 15, 2007, http://us.i1.yimg.com/videogames.yahoo.com/ongoingfeature?eid=505289&page=0.

5. See http://www.dfcint.com/news/prjune62006.html.

6. James Lee, "Wage Slaves," *Computer Gaming Monthly*, July 5, 2005, http://www.1up.com/do/featuresIndex?pager.offset=30&ct=FEATURE.

7. David Barboza, "Boring Game? Hire a Player, " *International Herald Tribune*, September 12, 2005.

8. Less, "Outwit, Outplay."
9. Heather Newman, "Gamers are Paying Big Bucks for Virtual Goodies," *Detroit Free Press,* May 12, 2005.
10. Barboza, "Boring Game?"
11. David Carter, "Torturing This Child is a Game Too Far, Says Appalled EU Boss," *London Times,* November 17, 2006, http://www.mediawatchuk.org/newssnippets/November2006.htm.
12. Ibid.
13. Interview with a Chinese programmer, October 2005; see also Sang Ye, *China Candid.*
14. In the 1990s, the Russian Mafia cornered the market in fake credit cards, but today China is leading the way. The Smooth Criminal cartel has access to hundreds of false IPs, credit cards, and computer serial numbers, which are used only for the time required to launder the gold coins.
15. Players can also access legitimate specialized websites, such as www.ige.com and www.mysupersales.com, where gold coins and online game equipment can be bought for real money. These sites are meant to host the secondary market of online game products earned by amateur players.
16. Edward Castronova, *Synthetic Worlds: The Business and Culture of Online Games* (Chicago: University of Chicago Press, 2005), 174.
17. The PayPal service enables anyone with an e-mail address to make and receive online payments quickly and securely, using the existing payment infrastructure with the benefit of the latest fraud-prevention technology. See http://www.Internetstory.com/paypal.htm.
18. See http://www.paypal.com/cgi-bin/webscr?cmd=p/gen/about-outside.
19. See www.e-gold.com.
20. Interview with Ivan, an e-gold currency dealer, November 2006. All subsequent statements from Ivan are taken from this interview.
21. Geneviève Roberts, "£1.7bn Fortune Propels Online Poker Tycoon on to Asian Rich List," *The Independent* (London), April 17, 2006, Business section, 9.
22. Escape Artist, see www.escapeartist.com.
23. Interview with an Italian e-currency dealer, November 2006.
24. Lev Jameson, "Worldwide Pornography Industry 260 Million and Growing," September 26, 2003, http://www.asiansexgazette.com/asg/south_asia/southasia02news77.
25. Interview with Corrado Fumagalli, presenter of a porn show, October 2006.
26. Interview with Oliver Buzz, a porn director, October 2006.
27. Interview with Silvio Bandinelli, a porn director, October 2006.
28. Interview with Luciano Mantelli, a pornography historian, October 2006.
29. See http://www.mpaa.org/researchStatistics.asp.
30. Smith, "Massively Addictive."
31. Joel Stein, "My So-Called Second Life, "*Time,* December 25, 2006.
32. "It is so Real, It's Unreal, Claim Cyber Engineers," *London Times,* January 25, 2007.
33. See the *Second Life* travel book at www.secondlife.com.
34. James Fontanella, "A Make-Believe Money Maker," *Financial Times,* November 23, 2006.
35. *Second Life* manual, 22.
36. Edward Castronova, *Synthetic Worlds,* 48.
37. *Second Life* manual, 223.

38. James Harking, "Get a (Second) Life," *Financial Times*, November 18–19, 2006.
39. James Harking, "Get a (Second) Life."
40. Fontanella, "Make-Believe Money Maker."
41. Ibid.
42. Castronova, *Synthetic Worlds*, 207.
43. Ibid.
44. Philip Bobbitt, *The Shield of Achilles: War, Peace, and the Course of History* (New York: Knopf, 2002).
45. Williams, 2002 Dimberly Lecture.

CHAPTER EIGHT—ANARCHY AT SEA

1. Lewis Smith and Valerie Elliott, "How the Fish on Your Plate Makes You an Accessory to Crime at Sea," *Times Online* (London), June 21, 2006, http://www.timesonline.co.uk/tol/news/uk/crime/article677154.ece.
2. Today the Northern Sea Route handles only 1.5 million tons.
3. One common way in which fishers can circumvent management and conservation measures and avoid penalties for illegal fishing is by registering under a flag of convenience (FOC). Although international law specifies that the country whose flag a vessel flies is responsible for controlling its activities, certain countries allow vessels to fly their flags for a few hundred or thousand dollars, and then ignore any offenses committed. These so-called FOC, or open-registry, countries are often developing states, which lack the resources (or the will) to monitor and control vessels flying their flags, especially when the fisheries being plundered do not belong to them. Belize, Panama, Honduras, and St. Vincent and the Grenadines are the worst offenders among FOC countries
4. "The shell companies owning illegal, unregulated, and unreported (IUU) vessels strongly benefit from the confidentiality of banking systems that are in place in some territories (that is, tax havens). This situation is clearly illustrated by the correlation between the countries declared FOC by the International Transport Workers' Federation (ITF) in July 2003 and the list of tax havens issued by the OECD in 2001. Twelve of the FOC countries (43 percent) appear on the OECD's list: Antigua and Barbuda, Bahamas, Barbados, Belize, Gibraltar, Liberia, Marshall Islands, Netherlands Antilles, Panama, St. Vincent and the Grenadines, Tonga, and Vanuatu. In addition, of the twenty-eight jurisdictions declared FOC by the ITF, 54 percent are members of the Commonwealth: Antigua and Barbuda, Bahamas, Barbados, Belize, Bermuda, Cayman Islands, Cyprus, Gibraltar, Jamaica, Malta, Mauritius, Sri Lanka, St. Vincent and the Grenadines, Tonga, and Vanuatu. This means that almost 25 percent of the Commonwealth countries are listed as FOC. If the governments of the United Kingdom and other Commonwealth countries seriously wish to eradicate IUU fishing, they will surely have to exert pressure on the fifteen Commonwealth members who are failing to control vessels flying their flag, making them behave as responsible Flag States. ("Pirates and Profiteers: How Pirate Fishing Fleets Are Robbing People and Oceans," Environment and Justice Foundation, 2005, http://www.ejfoundation.org/pdf/pirates_and_profiteers.pdf.)
5. Ibid.
6. Smith and Eliott, "How the Fish on Your Plate."
7. "Headed and Gutted: Exposing the Role of European States, Big Business and the Russian Mafia in Illegal Cod Fishing in the Barents Sea," Greenpeace, March 15,

2006, http://oceans.greenpeace.org/raw/content/en/documents-reports/headed-and-gutted-illegal-cod.pdf.

8. "A Third of Cod From the Baltic Sea Stolen by Pirates," Greenpeace, http://oceans.greenpeace.org/en/the-expedition/news/baltic-sea#, September 6, 2006. The Danish company Espersen has a key role in processing and distributing frozen fillets sold under various brands, such as Euroshopper, and even in fast-food restaurants. With a turnover of over 130 million euros, Espersen is regarded as the largest cod-processing company in the world. Its Danish factory supplies fish fingers to Euroshopper, Coop Xtra, Lidl, and McDonalds (at least in Norway, Finland, and Germany). See "Headed and Gutted."

9. "Pirates and Profiteers."

10. Interview with David Agnew, Fisheries Director of Marine Resources Assessment Group Ltd. (MRAG), a consultancy dedicated to promoting sustainable utilization of natural resources through sound integrated management policies and practices. All subsequent statements from Agnew are taken from this interview.

11. Interview with an FAO expert on illegal fishing, March 2007.

12. Interview with Hélène Bours, consultant on illegal fishing, March 2007. All subsequent statements from Ms. Bours are taken from this interview.

13. Marine Resources Assessment Group Ltd., "Review of Impact of Illegal, Unreported and Unregulated Fishing on Developing Countries, Final Report, July 2005, http://www.dfid.gov.uk/pubs/files/illegal-fishing-mrag-report.pdf.

14. "A Third of Cod From the Baltic Sea Stolen by Pirates."

15. Interview with Sebastian Losada, of Greenpeace, March 2007. All subsequent statements from Losada are taken from this interview.

16. "The 22 countries that border the Med face a battle over resources that raises a stark question: To what extent can traditional lifestyles and economic activities coexist with a global appetite for the produce of the Mediterranean region?" Vivienne Walt, "The Mediterranean's Tuna Wars," *London Times*, July 16, 2006.

17. Both countries regularly exceed their fishing quota. France, for example, has reported to Eurostat (the statistical agency of the European Union) that its catches were twice the assigned quota.

18. "Pirates and Profiteers."

19. Most of the ships engaged in illegal fishing or in fishing without a license off Guinea were Chinese (fifty-eight out of ninety-two).

20. Hélène Bours and Sebastian Losada, "Witnessing the Plunder 2006: How Illegal Fish from West African Waters Finds its Way to the EU Ports and Markets," Greenpeace, http://oceans.greenpeace.org/raw/content/en/documents-reports/plunder2006.pdf.

21. Ibid.

22. Ibid.

23. "Pirates and Profiteers."

24. Taiwanese and Korean vessels are also very active in illegal fishing.

25. "Police investigations revealed that the illicit trade in abalone constituted a major component of the business of Chinese organized criminal groups. According to detectives who were monitoring their activities, at least 30 to 40 tons of dried abalone had been exported illegally from South Africa by 1993." Peter Gastrow, "Triad Societies and Chinese Organized Crime in South Africa,"Organized

Crime and Corruption Program, Institute for Security Studies, Occasional Paper No. 48, http://www.iss.co.za/Pubs/Papers/48/48.html, 2001.

26. Ibid.

27. "Hong Kong Mafia Could Wipe Out Australia's Pot-Bellied Seahorse," Cyber Diver News Network, January 11, 2004, http://www.cdnn.info/eco/e040111/e040111.html.

28. Gal Luft and Anne Korin, "Terrorism Goes to Sea," *Foreign Affairs*, November–December 2004.

29. "In the first half of 2006, 127 attacks were reported around the world, eighty-eight of which were concentrated in the following areas: Indonesia (thirty-three), Malaysia (nine), Bangladesh (twenty-two), Gulf of Aden/Red Sea (nine), Somalia (eight), Nigeria (seven)," in "Piracy and Armed Robbery against Ships, Report for the Period, January 1 to June 30, 2006," ICC International Maritime Bureau.

30. Kevin Sullivan and Mary Jordan, "High-Tech Pirates Ravage Asian Seas," *Washington Post*, July 5, 1999.

31. Ibid.

32. Seth Faison, "Pirates, With Speedboats, Reign in China Sea Port," *New York Times*, April 20, 1997.

33. Ibid.

34. In the 1990s, radioactive meat from the former Soviet Union was buried in Zambia after the population had eaten part of it. Starving people will dig up contaminated meat. A second instance is especially depressing. Last year Zambia received cans of contaminated meat as a "gift." After being found to be contaminated, the 2,880 cans were buried 3.5 meters underground and covered with concrete in the village of Chongwe, east of the capital Lusaka. Since then, hungry villagers have been making desperate efforts to get to the meat. A Belgian paper reported in February of this year that they finally succeeded in digging it up and consuming it. See *Gazet van Antwerpen* (Belgium), http://www10.antenna.nl/wise/index.html?http://www10.antenna.nl/wise/351/brief.html.

35. "Sex-Changing Chemicals Found in US Potomac River," *Washington Post*, January 18, 2007.

36. Interview with a worker at the London morgue, March 2007.

37. Such payments are often partly offset by tax breaks. While ExxonMobil continues paying roughly $5 billion to fishing communities and Native Alaskans in punitive damages assessed for the impact of the *Exxon Valdez* spill, in July 2005, the United States Congress passed legislation that gave oil companies a $4 billion tax break.

38. See http://terresacree.org/rechauf.htm; http://terresacree.org/gangsters.htm.

39. See http://www.mcsuk.org/downloads/fisheries/MCS_Fish_Farming_Policy_Aug06.doc.

40. The displacement of wild eggs increases competition for wild resources in specific places. More generally, there is a potential adverse impact on the ecology of sea inlets where environmental carrying capacity has been reached or exceeded. Other activities, such as shellfish culture and shellfisheries sometimes suffer from fish farming. See "Marine Conservation Society Fish Farming Policy Statement," http://www.mcsuk.org/downloads/fisheries/MCS_Fish_Farming_Policy_Aug06.doc; Greenpeace, http://oceans.greenpeace.org/en/our-oceans/fish-farming; Living Oceans Society, http://livingoceans.org/fishfarms/index.shtml.

41. The United Nations Intergovernmental Panel on Climate Change (IPCC) has quite clearly laid out the causes of global warming as the increase of greenhouse gases, and particularly CO_2 in the atmosphere. The measurements of CO_2 increase parallel the slight increase in temperature that, in turn, has seen the melting of glaciers. The resulting rise in sea levels to date is a matter of debate, but it cannot be more than few centimeters. All industrialized countries generate greenhouse gases; the United States and the European Union rank first and second respectively and are followed by China and India.

42. The Intergovernmental Panel on Climate Change was established in 1988 by UNEP and the World Meteorological Association. The report this organization releases every six or seven years represents the scientific consensus on climate change. The panel is composed of about 1,600 scientists from 113 different countries. Part 1 of the report published on February 2, 2007, deals with the scientific basis for climate change.

43. Clifford Krauss, Steven Lee Myers, Andrew C. Revkin, and Simon Romero, "As Polar Ice Turns to Water, Dreams of Treasure Abound," *New York Times*, October 10, 2005; http://www.nytimes.com/2005/10/10/science/10arctic .html?ex=1286596800&en=1f4059714b781260&ei=5088&partner=rssnyt&e mc=rss.

44. See http://www.quakestar.org/Global%20Warming.htm.

45. Krauss et al., "As Polar Ice Turns to Water."

CHAPTER NINE—TWENTIETH-CENTURY GREAT ILLUSIONISTS

1. David Chater, "The Most Important Man in Washington (You Never Heard Of)," *New York Times Magazine*, February 25, 2006.

2. Michael Fullilove, "Celebrities Should Concentrate on Their Day Jobs," *Financial Times*, February 1, 2007.

3. Understandably, celebrities cannot fly economy class—they would be harassed by fans—but they could easily purchase the entire first-class of a jumbo jet. It would pollute the planet much less and cost a fraction of the price of a private jet.

4. Tony Allen-Mills, "Stars in Greem Cars Hit Prvate Jet Turbulence, *Sunday Times* (London), October 29, 2006; see also www.TMZ.com.

5. Lynnley Browning, "'Gimme Shelter' From the Taxman," *International Herald Tribune*, February 5, 2007.

6. Sandro Cappelletto, "La Cooperazione Malata," *Specchio, La Stampa*, March 31, 2007.

7. Edward B. Driscoll, Jr., "We Are The '80's! Live Aid Then, and Now," *Daily Standard*, December 17, 2004, http://www.weeklystandard.com/Content/Public/Articles/000/000/005/031arivi.asp; see also "Live Aid, the End Result," http://www.digitaljournal.com/article/203957/Op_Ed_Live_Aid_The_End_Result.

8. Cappelletto, "La Cooperazione."

9. Interview with various World Bank employees, June 2006.

10. Thomas P. Sheehy, "Beyond Dependence and Poverty: Rethinking U.S. Aid to Africa, The Heritage Foundation," June 25, 1993, http://www.heritage.org/ Research/MiddleEast/bg947.cfm.

11. Profits never exceeded $5.5 billion per year. See Roger D. Congleton, "Terrorism, Interest-Group Politics, and Public Policy," *Independent Review*, Summer 2002, 62.

12. MIPT-RAND database.
13. Interview with Joe Sulmona, aviation consultant, January 2007. All subsequent statements from Sulmona are taken from this interview.
14. This attitude is changing; in the United States and Canada, governments are moving quickly to secure passenger and freight rail systems, and of course, in Europe, where transit bombings have occurred, these security measures are quickly developed.
15. The US State Department defines international terrorism as "premeditated, politically motivated violence perpetrated against non-combatant targets by sub-national groups or clandestine agents, usually intended to influence an audience." An international attack must, therefore, involve the citizens or territory of more than one country. "So when a group of Russian nationals bombed a plane carrying 46 other Russian travellers in August 2004, it was considered purely domestic. A near simultaneous attack on another plane, also perpetrated by Russians, happened to carry one Israeli citizen and was called international." Attacks statistically reported must also be significant; "an incident is judged to be *significant* if it caused death or serious injury to non-combatants or amounted to more than $10,000 in property damage." See http://www.cdi.org/program/document.cfm?DocumentID=3391.
16. MIPT-RAND database.
17. Data refer to the end of 2006. MIPT-RAND database.
18. Laqueur, *Terrorism*.
19. Ibid.
20. Ibid.
21. Thus, we should not be surprised that the United States has just abandoned its ambitious US-VISIT program because of high costs and difficulties in implementing it at all borders.
22. What is shocking is the degree of abuse and waste of taxpayers' money that has taken place since 9/11. A confidential audit performed in 2005 by the Defense Contract Audit Agency at the Transportation Security Administration (TSA) in the United States and obtained by the *Washington Post* shows the following items among expenses: "$526.95 for one phone call from the Hyatt Regency O'Hare in Chicago to Iowa City; $1,180 for 20 gallons of Starbucks Coffee—$3.69 a cup—at the Santa Clara Marriott in California; $1,540 to rent 14 extension cords at $5 each per day for three weeks at the Wyndham Peaks Resort and Golden Door Spa in Telluride, Colorado; $8,100 for elevator operators at the Marriott Marquis in Manhattan; $5.4 million claimed for nine months' salary for the chief executive of an 'event logistics' firm that received a contract before it was incorporated and went out of business after the contract ended; $20-an-hour temporary workers billed to the government at $48 per hour, subcontractors who signed out $5,000 in cash at a time with no supporting documents, $377,273.75 in unsubstantiated long-distance phone calls, $514,201 to rent tents that flooded in a rainstorm, $4.4 million in 'no show' fees for job candidates who did not appear for tests." Overall, the audit questioned $303 million of the $741 million spent to select and employ additional security for TSA since 9/11. The lesson to be learned from this fiasco can be summarized as follows: "If terrorists force us to redirect resources away from sensible programs and future growth, in order to pursue unachievable but politically popular levels of domestic security, then they have won an important victory that mortgages

our future." David L. Banks, "Statistics for Homeland Defense," *Chance* 15, no.1 (2002), 10.

23. Sara Kehaulani Goo, "Going the Extra Mile: L.A.'s Airport Safety Plan Puts Pickups, Drops Far From Curb," *Washington Post*, April 9, 2004.

24. Airport employees have also been mistakenly labeled terrorists. "In Western North Carolina, one group of 66 terrorists was actually 66 illegal immigrants working at Charlotte/Douglas International Airport, who pled guilty to misusing visas, permits, and social security numbers. For their crimes, the workers got about a month in jail, a small fine, and were then released to immigration officers." Alexander Gourevitch, "Body Count: How John Ashcroft's Inflated Terrorism Statistics Undermine the War on Terrorism," *Washington Monthly*, June 2003.

25. Ibid.

26. Siobhan Gorman, "Fear Factor," *National Journal*, May 10, 2003.

27. Francis X. Clines, "Karl Rove's Campaign Strategy Seems Evident: It's the Terror, Stupid," *New York Times*, May 10, 2003.

28. Bruce Hoffman, "Rethinking Terrorism and Counterterrorism Since 9/11," *Studies in Conflict and Terrorism*, 25 (2002): 311–312; see also John Mueller, "Why Isn't There More Violence?" *Security Studies* 13 (2004): 191–203.

29. John McCain and Mark Salter, *Why Courage Matters: The Way to a Braver Life* (New York: Random House, 2004), 35–36.

30. Michael Sivak and Michael J. Flannagan, "Flying and Driving After the September 11 Attacks," *American Scientist* 91, no.1 (2003), 6–9.

CHAPTER TEN—THE MYTHOLOGY OF THE MARKET-STATE

1. Ernst Cassirer, *The Myth of the State* (New York: Oxford University Press, 1946).

2. M. Neocleous, "Radical conservatism, or, the conservatism of radicals: Giddens, Blair and the politics of reaction," *Radical Philosophy*, 93 (1999), 24–34. See also the following works by Mark Neocleous, *The Monstrous and the Dead: Burke, Marx, Fascism* (University of Wales Press, 2005); *Imagining the State* (Philadelphia: Open University Press, 2003); *The Fabrication of Social Order: A Critical Theory of Police Power* (Sterling, VA: Pluto Press, 2000); *Fascism* (Philadelphia: Open University Press, 1997); *Administering Civil Society: Towards a Theory of State Power* (London: Macmillan, 1996).

3. Despite Fukuyama's later retractions about his end-of-history theory, it is unquestionable that the political debate that had characterized the period since the end of World War II has ended; the erosion of the nation-state started when the Berlin Wall came down. In the vacuum created by the disappearance of the ideological distinction between left and right, traditional Communist parties, such as the Italian PCI, had to reinvent themselves, embracing issues that today are very close to those of their old opponents. Equally, the historical right has moved toward less radical positions.

4. Susan Strange, *States and Markets* (London: Pinter Publishers, 1988), 213.

5. CSEU submission to the Ministry of Defense consultation on the Defence Industrial Strategy, October 2005.

6. Strategic Export Controls: annual report for 2004, quarterly reports for 2005, licensing policy and parliamentary scrutiny, first joint report of session 2005–06,

twelfth report from the Defence Committee of session 2005–06, fifth report from the Foreign Affairs Committe of session 2005–06, fifth report from the International Development Committee, seventh report from the Trade and Industry Committee of session 2005–06, together with formal minutes, oral and written evidence.

7. Anthony Giddens, "The Left Must Open up More Clear Water Between Itself and its Opponents," *The New Statesman,* November 1, 2004.
8. Jurgen Habermans, *Legitimation Crisis* (Boston: Beacon Press, 1975), 46.
9. Giddens, "The Left Must Open Up."
10. Thomas Frank, *What's the Matter with Kansas?* (New York: Metropolitan Books, 2004).
11. "Metamorphosis of Power: The Meaning of Popular Role Playing for Berlusconi on His Way to the Top," paper presented at the Annual Meeting of the International Society of Political Psychology, http://viadrina.euv-frankfurt-o.de/~sk/Berlusconi/amsterdam.html.
12. Vincent Cable, "What Future for the State?" *Daedalus,* March 22, 1995.
13. See both Lipset & Rokkan's study of Western party systems, *Cleavage Structures, Party Systems, and Voter Alignments* (New York: Free Press, 1967) and Ronald Inglehart, *The Silent Revolution* (Princeton, NJ: Princeton University Press, 1977), in which he demonstrates his theory of post-materialism, an account of the growing political importance of "quality-of-life" issues in advanced industrialized countries at the expense of left/right materialist issues.
14. Football was invented in Britain in 1863 and imported to Italy by British expatriates in the 1890s.
15. Franklin Foer, *How Soccer Explains the World* (New York: HarperCollins, 2004), 185.
16. Angela Nocioni, "Presidente hip hop," *La Repubblica,* July 22, 2006.
17. Ibid.
18. Ibid.
19. *Petroleum Supply Annual,* vol. 1, Table 21, http://www.eia.doe.gov/neic/rankings/crudebycountry.htm, 21004.
20. Dennis MacShane, "Chaves is a Populist, Not a socialist," *Guardian,* May 15, 2006, http://commentisfree.guardian.co.uk/denis_macshane/2006/05/chavez_is_populist_not_a_socia.html.

CHAPTER ELEVEN—THE EXTRAVAGANT FORCE OF GLOBALIZATION

1. Stephen Johnson and David B. Muhlhausen, "North American Transnational Youth Gangs: Breaking the Chain of Violence," an Executive Summary Backgrounder, Heritage Foundation, March 21, 2005.
2. State-sponsored terrorism often took advantage of such ideals; sponsors exploited the nationalist goals of terror groups to their own benefit. In the aftermath of World War II, the Soviet Union bankrolled both Arab and Jewish armed groups who were fighting against the British protectorate in Palestine. The aim of both groups was to carve out a state of their own; Moscow, instead, was solely interested in undermining British authority in the Middle East; it was irrelevant which of the two armed groups achieved the right of self determination. See Loretta Napoleoni, *Terror Incorporated* (New York: Seven Stories Press, 2005), chapter 2.

3. Interestingly, over the same period, al Qaeda, an armed organization with a strong tribal identity, also began shaping itself along the lines of transnationalism.

4. Interview with Flor de Maria, member of Maras Salvatrucha, June 2005. All subsequent statements from Flor de Maria are taken from this interview.

5. Interview by Pablo Trincia, an Italian investigative journalist, with Okada driver in Lagos, Summer 2005.

6. Global Illicit Drug Trends 2003, United Nations, 2003,110, http://www.dronet .org/biblioteca/bib_zip/Global%20Illicit%20Drug%20Trends%202003.pdf.

7. World Drug Report 2006, UNODC, vol. 1, 2006, 103, http://www.unodc .org/pdf/WDR_2006/wdr2006_volume1.pdf.

8. "Through The Eyes of Children," www.children-express.org, May 1, 2003.

9. See http://news.bbc.co.uk/1/hi/programs/newsnight/4766458.stm.

10. "Through The Eyes of Children."

11. In the 1980s, the Financial Service Act allowed American and foreign banks to operate at the core of British finance, the City of London; the privatization of utilities in developing countries has been masterminded by American merchant banks. Behind such events there was a state, in transition towards the market-state, willing to facilitate such opportunities for business. However, globalization also closes other avenues, spatially very close to the new state, as is the case with the inner enclaves of Western cities.

12. See http://www.brookings.edu/metro/pubs/20060718_PovOp.htm.

13. 4.5 million low-income drivers (households earning less than $30,000 a year) paid on overage 2 percentage points more for their car loans than did middle-class buyers. Home insurance can be $300 per year higher than in wealthy neighborhoods, and auto insurance in urban areas can cost from $50 to $1,000 more in poor than wealthy areas. In 2006, car insurance in low-income neighborhoods in New York, Hartford, and Baltimore was $400 per year higher than in middle-class neighborhoods. Interest rates on car loans can be up to 25 percent greater than in high-income areas. Poor people also shop in "rent to own" stores, where interest rates are exceptionally high and absorb up to 60 percent of their earnings per year. A $200 television set can end up costing $700.

14. Matt Fellowes, "The High Price of Being Poor." Los Angeles Times, July 23, 2006.

15. See http://news.bbc.co.uk/1/hi/entertainment/4527502.stm or http://arts.guardian .co.uk/features/story/0,1666835,00.html.

16. "Through The Eyes of Children."

17. Interview by Pablo Trincia with an Area Boy, Summer 2005.

18. Interview with a member of a South London gang, March 2006.

19. See http://news.bbc.co.uk/1/hi/entertainment/4527502.stm or http://arts.guardian .co.uk/features/story/0,,1666835,00.html).

20. Khalid Howladar, "Shari'ah and Sukuk: A Moody's Primer," March 31, 2006. http://www.zawya.com/Story.cfm?id=ZAWYA20060601070918&pagename=Su kukMonitor.

21. See http://news.bbc.co.uk/1/hi/entertainment/4527502.stm or http://arts.guardian .co.uk/features/story/0,1666835,00.html.

22. Anthony Giddens, Beyond Left and Right (Cambridge, UK: Polity, 1994).

23. Ibid.

24. Dinesh D'Souza, "What is so great about America: A Funeral Oration: Pericles's Dilemma and ours," http://www.dineshdsouza.com/books/america-intro.html.

25. Henry Bergson, *The Two Sources of Morality and Religion* (New York: Doubleday, 1956).
26. David Berreby, *Us and Them: Understanding Your Tribal Mind* (London: Hutchinson, 2006).
27. Decca Aitkenhead, "In With the Crowd: Why Do Humans Need to Stereotype Each Other," *Guardian*, February 4, 2004.
28. Neil McInnes, "Popper's return engagement: The open society in an era of globalization" *Critical Essay*, http://findarticles.com/p/articles/mi_m2751/is_2002 _Spring/ai_85132085/pg_2.
29. Ibid.
30. Ibid.
31. Bergson, *Two Sources*, 31.
32. Foer, *How Soccer Explains the World*.
33. Simon Kuper, *Football Against the Enemy* (London: Phoenix, 1996), 102.
34. Anthony King, *The European Ritual: Football in the New Europe* (Aldershot, England: Ashgate, 2003), 32.
35. Giddens, *Beyond Left and Right*.
36. Foer, *How Soccer Explains the World*, 36.

CHAPTER TWELVE—ECONOMIC TRIBALISM

1. Ann Berg, "Want to buy a sukuk? Islamic financing is growing rapidly and Western institutions are jumping in. What does this mean for the power of the U.S. dollar?" *Antiwar*. http://www.antiwar.com/orig/browne.php?articleid=8627
2. Gillian Tett, "Islamic Banking Confounds Sceptics," *Financial Times*, June 2, 2006.
3. The first Islamic bank was the Faisal Islamic Bank of Egypt, established in 1976. The bank was the first to have a formal sharia board, consisting of selected ulama from Egypt. This tradition continued with the establishment of the Jordan Islamic Bank (1978), the Sudanese Faisal Islamic Bank (1978), and the Kuwaiti House of Finance (1979), and it went on, with other Islamic banks throughout the Arab countries, Turkey, Bangladesh, and more recently, the private sectors in Pakistan, Albania, and Bosnia.
4. Berg, "Want to buy a sukuk?"
5. "Every individual . . . generally, indeed, neither intends to promote the public interest, nor knows how much he is promoting it. By preferring the support of domestic to that of foreign industry he intends only his own security; and by directing that industry in such a manner as its produce may be of the greatest value, he intends only his own gain, and he is in this, as in many other cases, led by an invisible hand to promote an end which was no part of his intention." Adam Smith, *The Wealth of Nations*, Book IV, http://www.econlib.org/ LIBRARY/Smith/smWN.html.
6. Adam Smith, *An Inquiry into the Nature and Causes of the Wealth of Nations*, 1776.
7. Alan Greenspan, Remarks at the Adam Smith Memorial Lecture, Kirkcaldy, Scotland, February 6, 2005, http://www.federalreserve.gov/boarddocs/Speeches/ 2005/20050206/default.htm.

8. Thomas Crampton, "A Strong China May Give Boost to Its Neighbors," *International Herald Tribune*, January 23, 2003, http://www.iht.com/articles/2003/01/23/rchina_ed3_.php.

9. "The Asia Crisis, Capital Flows and the International Financial Architecture," Reserve Bank of Australia Bulletin, June 1998, http://www.rba.gov.au/PublicationsAndResearch/Bulletin/bu_jun98/bu_0698.pdf

10. J. D. Sachs, "The Wrong Medicine for Asia," *New York Times*, November 3, 1997.

11. "The Great Emerging Markets Rip-Off," *Fortune*, May 11. 1998, 68-74

12. Ronald D. Palmer, "Southeast Asia Crisis: Background and Current Assessment," http://www.unc.edu/depts/diplomat/AD_Issues/amdipl_9/palmer_seasia.html.

13. Neil Dias, Karunaratne, "The Asian Financial Melt-Down and the IMF Rescue Package," *Economic Issues,* 10, Department of Economics, The University of Queensland, http://eprint.uq.edu.au/archive/00001096/, 1999.

14. *Straits Times*, Singapore, February 1998.

15. Mahathir Mohamad, Islamic Cultural Center, Northbrook, Illinois, September 1, 2000, http://www.lariba.com/knowledge-center/articles/pdf/Mahathir%20Mohammad%20-%20The%20speech%20of%20Dr%20at%20LARIBA.pdf.

16. Patricia Martinez, "Thumbs Up to Living in Malaysian Diversity," August 10, 2006, http://www.nst.com.my/Current_News/nst/Thursday/Columns/20060810071927/Article/index_html.

17. Mahmoud Amin El-Gamal, "Daily Briefing: The Race to Rule Islamic Finance; Despite the Constraints of Shariah on Interest-Bearing Instruments, a Fierce Banking Rivalry is Developing Among Muslim Nations," *Business Week Online*, October 27, 2003.

18. Zulkifli Othman, "Come up with Innovative Islamic-Style Financial Tools," *Business Times*, December 17, 1996.

19. Gillian Tett, "Islamic Banking Confounds Sceptics," *Financial Times*, June 2, 2006.

20. *Shari'ah and Sukuk: A Moody's Primer,* May 31, 2006.

21. The sole limitation is the restricted number of scholars who command both the necessary religious credentials to issue a fatwa and a good knowledge of global capital markets. People like Sheik Hassan, a well-known scholar, are in great demand and can command fees of $300.

22. International Islamic Finance Forum, March 22, 2006.

23. Berg, "Want to buy a sukuk?"

24. Berg, "The Golden Caliphate," http://www.antiwar.com/orig/berga.php?articleid=8627, March 3, 2006.

25. Alexander Hamilton, the secretary of treasury, was largely responsible for the 1792 Coinage Act that introduced the bimetallic monetary system. The dollar was defined by weight, 371.25 grains of silver and 24.75 grains of gold. The ratio between gold and silver was fixed at 15 grains of silver per one grain of gold. Alvin Rabushka, from *Adam Smith to the Wealth of America*, (New Brunswick: Transaction Books, 1985), 201.

26. Ann Berg, "The Golden Caliphate."

27. Ibid.

28. Jude Wanniski, "Where is the Gold Dinar?" al Jazeera, November 24, 2004, http://www.rumormillnews.com/cgi-bin/archive.cgi?noframes;read=60191.

29. Lawrence Wright, "The Master Plan for the New Theorists of Jihad, Al Qaeda is Just the Beginning," *New Yorker,* September 11, 2006.

30. Karl Polanyi, *The Great Transformation: The Political and Economic Origins of Our Time* (Boston: Beacon Press, 1957), chapter 1.

31. A. G. Hopkins, ed., *Globalization in World History* (London: Pimlico, 2002), 9.

32. Thomas A. Bisson, "Japan Home Front," *Foreign Policy Reports* 14, no. 12 (September 1938).

33. Benito Mussolini, a speech given at the Piazza Venezia, Rome, October 2, 1935, http://www.homolaicus.com/storia/contemporanea/novecento/par36.htm.

34. "Benito Mussolini, What is Fascism, 1932." *Modern History Sourcebook,*www.fordham .edu/halsall/mod/modsbook.html.

35. Polanyi, *Great Transformation,* 246.

36. "Mussolini," *Modern History Sourcebook.*

37. Polanyi, *Great Transformation,* 245.

38. Vera Michaels Dean, "The Economic Situation in Italy: Italy in the World Crisis," *Foreign Policy Reports* 10, no. 24 (January 10, 1935).

39. Jude Wanniski, *The Way the World Works,* (Washington, DC: Regnery Publishing, 1978) 149.

40. L. Mossa, *L'Impresa nell'ordine corporativo* (Florence: 1935), 130.

41. Dean, "The economic situation in Italy."

INDEX

girls: Russia, 20
Glacier Bank, 39
Glasgow: football (soccer) and, 233, 235
Glasgow Airport attack (2007), 203
global warming, 183–187, 285n41, 285n42
gold currency, 148, 251, 255, 256, 266
    gold-dinar standard, 250–253, 266
    Italy, 257
"gold farming" (online gaming), 141–143
gold industry, 126–129
gold smuggling, 127, 128
Goldman Sachs, 47, 147
Google, 151
Gorbachev, Mikhail, 21, 22, 23, 98
Gordon, Robert, 44
Gore, Al, 189
government repression. See repression
government spending: abuse and waste,
    286n22
Graef, Ailin, 159–160
Gramsci, Antonio, 57
Great Britain, 66
    banana-price war, 131
    drug abuse, 221–222
    fishing industry and, 165, 166, 169
    football hooliganism, 233–236
    income inequality, 47, 50
    trade unions, 209
    United States and, 277n32
    World War I debt, 255
    See also British Empire; England
Great Depression, 50
Great Game, 88
Great Gatsby, The (Fitzgerald), 49–56 passim
Great Leap Forward, 99
Greece (ancient), 228–229, 232
Greenpeace, 167, 170, 172, 175
Greenspan, Alan, 32, 242, 272n16
Guardia di Finanza, 57, 58, 65, 70
Guinea Bissau, 174
guns: Great Britain, 222

HIV: Russia, 20
haj, 238, 239
handbag industry, 106
haptic interfaces, 157
Harrison, Tim, 250
Harrods, 245
Haski, Pierre, 97
Hassan, Hussein Hamid, 239
heart disease, 138
hedge funds, 53–55 passim, 273n49
    Islam and, 238
Hepatitis C, 115
heroin sales, 122

high-fructose corn syrup, 135
higher education: labor supply and, 34
Highway E-55, 10, 14
hijacking, 200–201
hijacking of ships, 178
hip-hop culture
    English language and, 230
    gangs and, 227
    Venezuela, 215
    See also rap music
historical fiction, 103, 107
history, 84
    end of (theory), 208
    revisionism and denial, 88–89, 92, 97–98,
        100, 103
Hitler, Adolf, 69
Hobbes, Thomas, 160, 161, 265
Hoffman, Bruce, 205
Holland, 19, 66, 70
Hong Kong: illegal fishing and, 176
hooliganism, 233–236
hope, 78
Hopkins, A. G., 254
housing costs, 37–39
housing foreclosure, 38–39
How Soccer Explains the World (Foer), 235
human smuggling, 111
Hungary, 12
    post–World War I inflation, 255
Hurricane Katrina, 41

IBM, 159
I Ching, 84
IMF, 25, 27, 54, 244–247 passim, 252
Ibrahim, Anwar, 247, 248
idealism: Western culture and, 81–84 passim
identification cards, 111
illegal copying of films, 154
illegal fishing, 165–176 passim, 282n3, 282n4
illegal immigrants
    Chinese, 110–113
    mistakenly labeled terrorists, 287n24
    smuggling of, 111
Illiantzi, 75
immigrants, undocumented. See illegal
    immigrants
immorality. See ethics; morality
IMPACT, 124
impatiens, 114
imperialism
    British, 52, 88
    Chinese, 87–88, 93, 100, 103
    Italian, 261
    income, 42
    China, 98

Mediterranean Sea
  fishing industry, 168, 170, 171
  pollution, 180
Mela di Eva, La, 153
Meluzzi, Alessandro, 207
Memoir of a Geisha (film), 14
meningitis vaccines, 121
men's magazines, 153
Mexican fruit pickers, 129
Mexican gangs, 218
Mexico
  China and, 242
  phone company privatization, 117–118
  middle class, 31–33, 36–45, 50–51, 56
  impoverishment of, 31–33 passim
  work hours of, 48
Middle East: Soviet Union and, 288n2
Milan, 52, 53, 212
military coups: Africa, 193
Milla, Roger, 234
Mr. China (Clissold), 83
modeling, 81–83 passim, 85, 86, 91
Mogilevich, Semion, 21, 270n32
money laundering, 21, 58, 63–67 passim, 76, 79
  illegal fishing and, 166
  play currency and, 145–146
Mongolia, 99
Mongols, 210
Montana, 39
Montreal: disappearance of manhole covers, 83
moonlighting, 42
Morabito, Giuseppe, 63
Morales-Ferrand, Jacky, 39
morality, 51
  China and, 83–84
mortgage loans, 37–39, 41, 272n16, 272n23
Moscow
  human smuggling and, 112
  prostitution in, 12
movie piracy, 154
Mukundan, Pottengal, 178
Murmansk, 165–166, 169
Murmansk Shipping Company, 185
music and politics, 213–215. *See also* benefit concerts
Musk, Elon, 147
Mussolini, Benito, 256–262 passim
Mutras, 73
mythology, 207–215 passim, 227

NAFLD, 137
nanotechnology, 267
Naples, 63

Napoleon I, 81–83 passim
"Natashas," 15–18
nation-state, 69, 78–80 passim, 263, 275n25
National Bureau of Economic Research, 49
national interest, 69
nationalism, 218–219
  China, 86
  Fascism and, 256
  gangs and, 218, 220
  Malaysia, 246–247
Nazism, 45, 69, 78, 97, 98
  technology and, 109
n'dragheta, 57–77 passim
  China and, 102
neoconservatives, 232, 262
neoliberals, 208
Nestle, Marion, 136
Netherlands, 19, 66, 70
Nevis, 148
New Deal, 261
New Orleans, 41, 42
New York Yankees, 48
Niger, 196
Nigeria
  counterfeit drugs and, 121, 125, 279n5
  e-waste and, 179
  gangs, 220–221, 224
  illegal fishing and, 168
  rap music, 227
Nike, 96
Nobili, Valerio, 137
Nokia Ventures, 147
nomenklatura: Bulgaria, 71–77
non-alcoholic fatty liver diseases (NAFLD), 137
North Atlantic Fisheries Organization, 167
North Polar region: global change and, 184–185
North Sea: fishing, 165, 166
Northern Ireland, 235
Northwest Passage, 184
Norway
  fishing industry and, 165, 166
  global change and, 184
Nota Cerasi, Cesare, 65, 70
nouveau riche, 53
OS (magazine), 153
obesity, 4–5, 135–137
offshoring, 34, 35, 53, 71, 148
  Internet pornography and, 151
  to China, 242
oil industry, 10, 36, 132–133
  Arab states, 239
  profits, 181
  Russia, 26

sea pollution and, 181–182
taxation, 284n37
Venezuela, 214–215
See also petrodollars
oil smuggling, 75–76, 77
Olson, Mancur, 27, 29
online gambling, 141, 146, 149
laws, 150
online payment services, 146–149
online pornography, 19, 141, 149, 151–155
online sweatshops, 143
online video games, 141–146, 155
Operation Decollo, 58, 66, 70
opinion polls, 189
Ora Veritá, 153
Oreo cookies, 136
Organization of the Islamic Conference, 239, 251
organized crime, 16–17, 56
China, 91, 110–113, 175–176, 283n25
fishing industry and, 165–166, 171, 283n25
See also Camorra; Chinese Triads; Mafia; n'dragheta
Orthodox Jews: prostitution and, 15–16
outsourcing, 35
overweight, 4–5, 135–137
Oxfam, 115–116

PKK, 16
Palestinians, 17
Panama, 122, 123, 175
pandillas (gangs), 218
Paramov, Kolyo, 76
Parasol, Ruth, 149
Paris: Chinese immigrants, 112–113
PartyGaming, 149–150
patents, 108, 113–114, 266
genes and, 115
Patriot Act, 64–67 passim, 77, 78, 79, 249
"Patterns of Global Terrorism" (State Department report), 204
PayPal, 147, 158, 281n17
peasants: China, 93, 97
Peloponnesian War, 230
Pen, Jan, 46
Penn, Mark, 189, 190
perestroika, 21–22
perfume industry, 105
petrodollars, 10, 36
Pfizer, 121, 125
pharmaceuticals industry, 121–125
Philip Morris, 133
Philippines, 244
philosophy

Chinese, 83
Western, 81
phone company privatization, 117–118
pimps and pimping, 12–14 passim
piracy, Internet. *See* e-piracy
piracy (maritime), 176–179
piracy of biological organisms. *See* biopiracy
piracy of consumer products. *See* counterfeit products
piracy of fish. *See* illegal fishing
piracy of movies. *See* movie piracy
piracy of software. *See* software piracy
Pirates of the Caribbean, 176
Pitt, Brad, 191
placebos, 122
Plan B (rapper), 223, 225, 227
plasma: sale of, 94
Plato, 81, 232
play currency, 141–146 passim, 281n15
Play TV, 152
Polanyi, Karl, 257, 259
police
Bulgaria, 75
contraband seizures, 57–58, 105, 153
police corruption, 75
police states: Italy, 257, 258
political polling, 189
political purges: China, 87, 89
politicians, 189
as performers, 190
polls, 189
pollution, 179–183
poor people
China, 97
income gap and, 46–47
insurance and loan costs, 289n13
United States, 211
pop-up ads, 151
Popper, Karl, 228, 231, 232, 235
populism, 210
Italy, 211–213, 257, 258
Venezuela, 213–215
pornography
film, 152
Internet, 19, 141, 146, 149, 151–155
magazines, 153–154
See also child pornography
PornoTube, 19
Port of Churchill (Manitoba), 185
Portugal, 35
Potomac River: pollution, 180
pounds, 53
poverty, 56, 197, 222–223
Africa, 190–198 passim
China, 97

salmon farming, 182
Scruton, Roger, 18
sea pollution, 179–183
  global warming and, 183
seahorses: illegal harvesting of, 176
Second Life (virtual world), 155–160, 161
Senegal: fishing industry, 172
September 11, 2001, terrorist attacks, 201,
  202, 205, 231
  influence, 237, 248–249
Serbia, 11, 76
Serbian Mafia, 76
sewer covers: theft of, 83–84
sex industry, 18
  Germany, 13
  Israel, 15–17
  See also pornography; prostitution
sex slavery, 1
sex slaves, 11, 17, 270n13
sex, virtual: *See* virtual sex
sexually transmitted diseases, 20. *See also*
  syphilis
Sexy Bar (television show), 152
sharia and finance, 237–253 passim
Sheehy, Thomas, 197
shellfish culture, 284n40
Shield of Achilles (Bobbit), 162
ship hijacking, 178
ship nationality. *See* Flags of Convenience
ship piracy, 176–179
shoe industry: China, 96
Sicilian Mafia. *See* Cosa Nostra
Sierra Leone, 126, 172–174 passim
Siew, Ong Eian, 245
Singapore, 244
single-issue politics, 208, 211
single-parent families: Russia, 12
skilled labor, 34
skin whitening creams, 115
slavery, 1, 127, 129–131
  democracy and, 1–2
  statistics, 130
  See also sex slavery
slaves, 129
  value, 2, 131
  See also sex slaves
Smith, Adam, 28–29, 238, 241–243 passim,
  290n5
Smooth Criminal, 143, 145, 281n14
smuggling, 62, 63, 66, 74–75
  arms, 70, 75–76, 77
  automobiles, 73–74
  cigarettes, 122
  cocaine, 57–58, 62, 66–67
  gold, 127, 128

humans, 111
  oil, 75–76, 77
Snackwell cookies, 136
snakebite fatalities, 206
Snow Crash (Stephenson), 157
soccer: Italy, 212–213
soccer hooliganism, 233–236
social mobility, 46, 49
Sofia, Bulgaria, 73, 75
software piracy, 122, 144–145
Soil & Crop Improvements, 114
Somalia, 175, 193, 239
  e-waste and, 179
Sony, 143
soup: canned, 137
South Africa
  fishing industry, 175–176, 283n25
  gold industry, 127
South Korea
  fish market, 174
  piracy, 177
Spagnolo, Vincenzo, 63, 66
Spain, 66
  illegal fishing and, 170, 171
Sparta, 230
Soviet Bloc. See former Communist countries
Soviet Union, 1, 71
  bankrolls both Arab and Jewish armed
    groups, 288n2
  economy, 22–24, 29, 98
  radioactive meat and, 284n34
sports: organized crime and, 72
Stalin, Josef, 29
Star Wars Galaxies, 143
Starbucks, 115–116
steel, 83–84
Stephenson, Neal, 103, 157
stereotyping, 231
Stevens, Bart, 25
Stiglitz, Joseph, 27, 37, 244
stock market, 54
  Asia, 244
stolen goods trade, 177
subsidies (agriculture), 195
Sudan, 193–194
sugar, 138
suicide
  Eastern Europe, 271n37
  suicide bombers, 226, 232
sukuks, 238
Sulmona, Joe, 200–201, 205
Sun Tzu, 82–83, 85, 87
supermarkets, 131, 132
  club cards, 189–190
superrich. *See* rich people